Date Due

THE NONPROFIT BOARD BOOK

STRATEGIES FOR ORGANIZATIONAL SUCCESS

Revised Edition

Edited by
Earl Anthes, Jerry Cronin and Michael Jackson

West Memphis and Hampton, Arkansas

INDEPENDENT COMMUNITY CONSULTANTS

1985

ISBN 0-916721-04-3

INDEPENDENT COMMUNITY CONSULTANTS

Planning and Training Office
P.O. Box 141
Hampton, Arkansas 71744

Research and Evaluation Office
P.O. Box 1673
West Memphis, AR 72301

To Freeman McKindra and Mike Watts, long time friends,
teachers, cajolers and ICC, Inc. board members, who
together taught us valuable lessons about corporate
stewardship, integrity and timeliness.

Table of Contents

Contributing Authors

Earl W. Anthes

Earl Anthes has been Research and Evaluation Director for Independent Community Consultants, Inc. since 1972. Prior to coming to ICC, Inc., he was editor of Many Voices and executive director of RESPECT, Inc. Earl has published more than two dozens books, articles and monographs and divides his time between helping organizations improve their management structures and systems and conducting research and evaluation projects for nonprofits. He currently serves on several community and regional nonprofit boards.

Bonnie Bernholz

Bonnie Bernholz is Senior Vice-President at the Bean Public Relations Firm, Anchorage Alaska. Bonnie is a graduate of the University of Texas and has more than ten years experience in marketing and public relations. She has worked with a variety of businesses and nonprofit organizations and has substantial experience as a director of nonprofit arts and cultural organizations.

Christopher T. Callaghan

Christopher T. Callaghan, a CPA, is with the international firm of Deloitte, Haskins and Sells. Previously, Chris was a private management consultant and a founder of the Technical Assistance Center, a Colorado management support organization. He is a frequent writer on nonprofit accounting, financial management, marketing and strategic planning.

Jerry Cronin

Having helped found Independent Community Consultants, Inc. in 1972, Jerry Cronin continues work with the organization as Project Manager and chief of staff. He consults with a wide range of organizations on a number of topics and manages the ICC, Inc. Planning and Training Office in Hampton, Arkansas. He has written or edited more than fifteen publications on management in the nonprofit sector. Jerry is currently a board member of the Nonprofit Management Association.

Louise Eberhardt

Louise Eberhardt is a consultant headquartered in New York City. Louise provides management development, human relations and organization consultation to nonprofit organizations, public agencies and private businesses. She is the author of the two volume book, A Woman's Journey: Experiences for Women with Women and has served on local and national nonprofit corporation boards.

Richard J. First, Ph.D.

Richard J. First is Associate Professor at the Indiana University School of Social Work, Indianapolis, where he has been Chairperson of the graduate program in Planning and Management. He has taught at the University of Arkansas, Graduate School of Social Work and been on the staff of statewide nonprofits in Michigan and North Carolina. Dick also does management consulting and serves on the Technical Advisory Committee for Indepenent Community Consultants, Inc. He holds an M.S.W. degree from Michigan State University and Ph.D. from Case Western Reserve University, School of Applied Social Science.

William E. Glenn

Bill Glenn, co-author with Bill Conrad of The Effective Voluntary Board, has spent more than thirty years working as a consultant, teacher and staff member of nonprofit organizations. Bill lives in Glen Ellyn, Illinois and currently is with the National Council of the YMCA of the USA working with Campaign Associates, their fund raising division.

Eileen (Guthrie) Collard

Eileen Collard does community and organization development within neighborhoods and community nonprofits to help them increase their effectiveness. She specializes in issues related to human services and social change. She is co-author of Making Change: A Guide for Effectiveness in Groups (1978) and Process Politics: A Guide for Group Leaders (1981). Eileen received an M.A. in Urban and Regional Studies from Mankato State University in Minnesota.

Sandra M. Haff

Sandra M. Haff has done community organizing for eight years, including efforts to organize tenants, start a food cooperative for senior citizens, and institute self-help programs related to neighborhood rehabilitation, housing, and crime prevention. She is author of The Adventures of Urban Organizer and Her Little Dog U.D., a manual for organizing apartment residents.

Stephen Hitchcock

Stephen Hitchcock is the former president of Public Management Institute. While with this San Francisco based research and publishing firm, he worked with hundreds of nonprofit organizations across the country. He served as executive editor of the second edition of The Corporate 500: The Directory of Corporate Philanthropy and The Effective Nonprofit Executive

<u>Handbook</u>. With Susan Fox, he is the author of <u>The Nonprofit Secretary Handbook</u>. Stephen is currently drawing on his 15 years of work with nonprofit organizations to pursue a number of writing and market research projects for Public Management Institute and other groups.

Terry W. McAdam

Terry McAdam has been the Program Director/Vice President of the Conrad Hilton Foundation in Los Angeles since mid-1983. For the previous ten years he was Assistant Director and Senior Vice-President of the New York Community Trust. He has written widely about improving nonprofit management and has more than sixteen publications to his credit. Terry did post graduate work at the Graduate School of Public Administration of New York University.

Sharon Carden Streett

Now practicing law in Little Rock, Sharon devotes a substantial part of her practice to working with nonprofit organizations. Prior to practicing law, she was on the staff of the Arkansas Legislative Council and conducted research on education-related legislation for the Arkansas General Assembly. Sharon also teaches in the Department of Political Science at the University of Arkansas at Little Rock.

Acknowledgements

Our deepest appreciation is extended to a number of individuals and organizations who helped bring this book from an idea to a finished product. The contributors, Bill Glenn, Eileen Collard, Chris Callaghan, Louise Eberhardt, Terry McAdam, Dick First, Bonnie Bernholz, Steve Hitchcock and Sharon Streett, approached their task with dedication and insight. Vashti Vanardo and Julian Streett, attorneys and ICC, Inc. board members, prepared the contracts for the contributors and gave their time and talent to the project in many other ways as well.

The editorial board helped us find contributing authors, identify topics based on problems facing nonprofit organizations, and was available to discuss the project at any time. The members of this board were Rev. Leo Rippy, Nashville, Tennessee; Dr Barbara Mink, Austin, Texas; Joe Rubio, Texas City, Texas; Joy Beaton, Chicago; Preston Wilcox, New York City; Rusty Davenport, Boston; and Lee Gordon of Little Rock.

Lee Gordon of the Winthrop Rockefeller Foundation deserves special thanks. Not only was he responsible for monitoring the $5,700 publication development grant the foundation awarded to us in 1979, but Lee also suffered though early drafts and endured both production delays and our explanations of those delays. With his commitment, and that of the entire board and staff of WRF, the foundation continues its tradition of supporting training, consultation, and research designed to strengthen the nonprofit sector.

The Nonprofit Board Book is the first publication in our Nonprofit Management Series. The printing of this revised edition has been made made possible by a contribution from Brownie Ledbetter of Little Rock. Her support for our efforts is deeply appreciated. Joining our corporate supporters is David Wells of the South Arkansas Telephone Co., Inc. and Langco, Inc. His continued involvement with our publication program is most welcome.

A final acknowledgement is in order. Cal Ledbetter, Dean of the College of Liberal Arts at the University of Arkansas at Little Rock and a former member of our board of directors was the first member of our board of directors to strongly advocate for the development of a publications program. Cal's position was that publishing would reduce the cost of getting advice to nonprofit groups and would bring new perspective to the staff. He was right on both counts.

Earl, Michael, Jerry
Hampton and West Memphis
January, 1985

Overview of Board Role

Chapter 1

The Board and the Life of the Organization: An Overview

Earl W. Anthes

The duties and responsibilities of the nonprofit board are examined in the following chapters of this book. These chapters include lengthy and detailed discussions of the board's financial management, planning, funding, public relations, oversight and board development responsibilities. This short chapter, in contrast, has a more limited objective: To find a way to tie the diverse board duties together into an overriding concept that can serve as guidance for the board in its pursuit of success.

The thoughts that immediately come to mind are stewardship and the Biblical injunction to "give an account of thy stewardship for thou mayest be no longer steward" (Luke 16:2). While the idea of stewardship accurately denotes the care and prudence required of a board and its individual members, it does not tell us what the board member must do to be a careful and conscientious steward.

To help apply this concept of stewardship to the nonprofit board, we need to look at the organization as it passes through the various stages in its organizational development cycle. This cycle is shown in Exhibit 1-1.

It is my premise that every healthy and effective organization moves through this cycle. It is also my belief that the careful and prudent steward's primary, fundamental responsibility is to lead the organization through this process

Unhealthy and ineffective organizations get off "cycle" and bypass one or more of the stages. All of us are familiar, for instance, with organizations that:

- continue, more out of habit than conviction, doing the same old programs in the same old ways without ever bothering to evaluate whether the programs are producing any results;

- do anything for which funds are available regardless of the amount of prior planning done or the need for such a program;

- is torn apart by recurring internal dissension and disputes because it has no core of shared purpose and values.

EXHIBIT 1-1: The Organizational Development Cycle

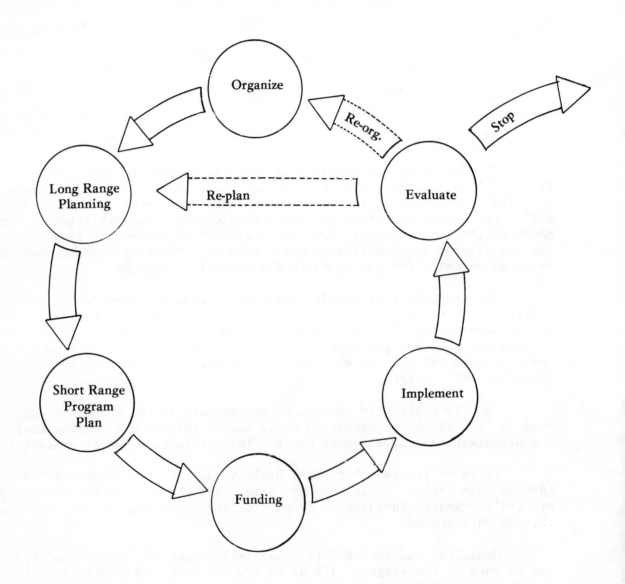

In a very real sense, the avoidance of these and similar problems and the achievement of nonprofit health and effectiveness depends upon the skill and commitment of the stewards, the board. In the long run, this happens only if the board carefully and prudently leads the organization through the developmental steps in the organizational cycle. This, then, is the fundamental duty of the board: It must ensure that the organization has:

- a clear and agreed upon mission statement and set of essential corporate values;

- a congruent and comprehensive corporate plan for its external service as well as internal development;

- a resource development system capable of supporting both program service and internal development;

- a sharply defined and plausible short range plan;

- a timely, efficient, and competent program implementation system; and

- a consistent and valid method for reviewing its own performance so that it can reorganize, replan, or discontinue its operations.

Chapter 2

Ten Questions for the Thinking Board Member

Terry W. McAdam

1. Are the objectives of your organization specifically stated in writing?

    • Were they discussed and approved by the board?

    • Are they measurable?

    • Are they reviewed annually?

2. Is the management information provided to board members timely and useful?

    • Do you ever see reports of agency progress vs. objectives?

    • Do you understand the basic sources and uses of the agency's financial and human resources? (Exhibit 2-1 is a list of reports you may wish to request or discuss with senior staff executives.)

3. Are there written policies regarding board member responsibilities and accountability? Do the policies cover the following areas:

    • Attendance requirements for board meetings?

    • Committee and subcommittee structure and membership?

    • Legal liabilities for board members?

    • Fund raising responsibilities?

- Terms of directors?

- Number of terms before retirement or temporary separation from the board?

- Nomination procedures?

EXHIBIT 2-1: Summary of Board Reports

Report	Suggested Frequency
1. Trial balance sheet	1. Semi-annually
2. Statement of income and expense	2. Quarterly
3. Budget variance report	3. Quarterly
4. Formal performance review of executive director	4. Annually
5. Fund raising progress report	5. Quarterly
6. Programmatic performance vs. objectives	6. Annually
7. Minutes of board meetings	7. After meeting
8. Follow-up reports on topics raised at board meetings	8. Periodically
9. Investment reports	9. Annually

---

4. Do the agency's public financial statements accurately and completely state the agency's financial status? How do you know?

   - Is the FICA account really paid up?

   - Is there an audit committee?

   - Are staff and board bonded? At sufficient levels?

   - If the agency operated at a deficit last year, how was the deficit financed? Was it worth it?

5. Is there an adequate human resource development program for the agency staff?

   - Is there an annual performance review for the executive director?

Are performance expectations spelled out in advance?

Is the director's performance reviewed in writing by the chair?

- Has the executive director implemented sound personnel practices? Are there:

Written performance reviews at least annually?

Specific personnel training plans?

Written job descriptions?

Compensation and expense guidelines?

Written explanations of fringe benefits?

Clear termination procedures?

6. Is there a long term financial resource plan?

- What are the program and financial plans for the medium and long term? Are they approved by the board?

- Has the board initiated any specific longer range development programs?

- If such programs exist, how is progress toward them reviewed?

7. Do the budgetary and actual expenditure procedures reflect fairly the financial capacity of the agency to conduct its affairs? What will prevent the agency from "running away" financially?

8. Is there a periodic board review of the key financial control mechanisms by the finance or audit committee of the board? This review can be as simple as ensuring that two parties handle checks to reviewing the adequacy of your accounting and/or auditing firm.

9. Is there a vigorous administrative improvement effort underway that addresses:

- Cost control?

- Cost reduction?

- Adequate reimbursement from outside sources?

- Aggressive programs to secure new sources of income?

- Cost/program sharing with similar agencies?

10. Does the board periodically reassess the agency's overall performance and its continued need to exist?

- Do board members ever meet clients of the agency?

- Is there a program to ensure that board members visit the field periodically?

Chapter 3

Board Powers, Responsibilities and Liabilities

Sharon Carden Streett

As the nonprofit sector has grown to accommodate a wide range of voluntary endeavors, millions of people have been given an opportunity to serve on the boards of nonprofit corporations. The initial reaction of most newly elected board members has little to do with the legal aspects of board service. Board members think about the purpose of the organization, their role as a board member and the contribution which can be made by the nonprofit corporation. The legal consequences of board service, however, must be considered by the prudent voluntary leader.

Like business corporations, nonprofit organizations are created by state law. The powers, responsibilities and liabilities of board members are generally established by state statutes. Legislative bodies and the courts have imposed substantial responsibility on directors of business corporations and have held directors accountable for both inactivity and improper activity. While courts only recently have extended this liability to nonprofit directors, any director would be well advised to assume that the standard which may be applied to a review of his or her conduct, will be basically the same as those standards applied to "for profit" directors.

Prior to election to a board of a nonprofit corporation everyone needs to consider the extent of the board's powers, responsibilities and liabilities. This chapter is not written for attorneys, nor is it intended as an authoritative statement on the current status of the law dealing with nonprofits. Individuals who are serving as officers or directors of such corporations would do well to become familiar with the laws applicable to nonprofits.

All board members and potential board members need to be familiar with three major standards that should guide their service on nonprofit boards: The business judgment, reasonable care, and the fiduciary relationship standards.

The Business Judgment Standard

The business judgment rule resulted from judicial consideration of the potential liability of directors of business corporations. The standard which the courts applied required directors or officers to exercise their honest, unbiased judgment in the conduct of the affairs of the corporation. Those who met this standard were allowed wide latitude. When they acted in good faith and without improper motive, they were not held liable for their honest mistakes, even if such mistakes were serious enough to have the director's ability to manage corporate affairs called into question. Directors were assumed to be acting in good faith if there was no proven fraud, breach of trust or actions outside the power and authority of the corporation.

Having given the nonprofit corporation a legal life of its own, state statutes empowered nonprofits to exercise many of the powers given to individuals. If agreed to by the board, the corporation can buy, sell, lease, hire, fire, borrow, lend, grant, trade and do other things reasonably necessary to achieve the lawful purposes for which the corporation was organized. It is the board's exercise of these powers that is subject to the business judgment rule.

The business judgment rule provides a guide to the courts in determining whether they should intervene in the affairs of the nonprofit. Courts have been reluctant to substitute their judgment in the review of complex business decisions for that of the shareholders who have, by virtue of their financial interests, an incentive to pay close attention to the businesses. Nonprofit board service can be treated as "honorary" only at great risk to the board members, the corporation and the constituents of the organization.

The Reasonable Care Standard

Recent decisions by courts and changes in state laws apply the standard of "ordinary and reasonable care." A seemingly simple concept, the reasonably prudent person standard has been the subject of many lawsuits. The standard is broad enough to allow every case to be decided on its own facts and in each instance the court will determine whether the skill, diligence and care given by the board member to the affairs of the corporation is sufficient to enable the court to decide that the directors are not liable. In deciding questions of board member liability, the courts are likely to consider such factors as the qualifications of the individual board member, the amount of time devoted to board service, the remuneration provided to the director, and the nature of the affairs of the corporation.

The Fiduciary Rule

As a basis for applying the ordinary person rule, the courts have recognized that an individual elected to a nonprofit board serves as a fiduciary of the corporation. As a fiduciary, the director undertakes to act primarily for another's benefit in matters connnected with the corporation. The concept of being a fiduciary is not a recent development, having originated in English common law, and is now embedded in the case law of this country. As state legislatures have sought to strengthened their regulation of nonprofits and have codified court decisions into statutory law, the fiduciary concept has appeared in state statutes.

In determining what duties and responsibilities are imposed due to the fiduciary nature of the relationship, it is helpful to consider that they are much the same as that of a trustee. In general, the fiduciary relationship is not imposed by statute, but is a requirement of the courts. As in most areas of law applying to nonprofit corporations, the bulk of the case law deals with business corporations so it is helpful to review the areas in which the courts have found that a director has breached the fiduciary or trustee relationship.

A major area in which courts have imposed liability upon directors of business corporations is applicable, to some degree, to nonprofit corporations. This is in the area of the sale of control of the corporation. Obviously, nonprofit corporate directors cannot be held accountable for the sale of a controlling share of the stock of the corporation, but they may be held accountable under some circumstances for corporate decisions to either transfer control of assets or to terminate the existence of the corporation. In such areas as competing with the corporation, either by using inside information to act in a manner detrimental to the corporation, or having some interest which conflicts with the corporation, the standard is clear. The same prohibitions that prevent directors of a business corporation from using their position for personal economic gain apply to nonprofit directors.

A useful rule of thumb for deciding if the fiduciary rule applies to any situation arising out of **service** on a nonprofit board is this: "If you have to ask, you probably shouldn't do it." Service as a director requires the individual to be loyal to the corporation, obedient to the requirements of the charter of the corporation, diligent in making decisions, and always prepared to act in a responsible manner.

It is important for directors to realize that service on a board of directors is not largely "Thou shall not." Perhaps the most important responsibility of a director is to act, not to avoid acting. The responsibility for the management of the corporation rests on the shoulders of the directors. The duty to manage the affairs of the corporation includes both overseeing and controlling the operations of the corporation. Generally, the statutes provide that all corporate powers are controlled by the board. The daily administrative operation are normally delegated to the officers who are hired by the directors, but the basic responsibility for their actions remains with the board.

Powers and Responsibilities

As stated above, the board has the basic responsibility for the operation of the corporation. In addition to having the power to select the officers who will manage the affairs of the corporation, the board is responsible for setting the policies for the board, staff and officers to follow. The accompanying responsibility of directors is to oversee the operation of the corporation, both to aid in setting policy and to ensure that the policies of the corporation are carried out.

In order to fulfill their board duties, individuals must know about the operation of the corporation, both fiscally and in policy matters. This responsibility requires directors to regularly attend board meetings, and the failure to do so will not relieve the director of potential liability. Directors have the responsibility to see that the corporation obeys the law, and in order to do so, they must be well enough acquainted with the laws of the state in which their corporation operates to be aware of whether the corporation is in compliance with the law.

The director also has the duty to see that the operation of the corporation is within the limits set in its charter and that it is properly pursuing the goals articulated for it in that charter. Directors may be held accountable for the unauthorized acts of the corporation to third parties, and where the corporation suffers a loss due to the directors failing to carry out their responsibilities, they may be held liable to the corporation itself. Such actions may be brought in the name of the corporation itself, or may be brought by the attorney general or other state officials, or by the persons who were supposed to benefit from the activities of the corporation.

Standard of Care Required in Performance of Duties

We have previously described the ordinary person or the prudent person rule. This is a relative concept, and the courts treat it as such. The duty of care required will depend on the kind of corporation, the circumstances involved and the role of the individual director, both as to her role in the corporation and her particular background and knowledge. In requiring all individual directors to be accountable to the extent of their knowledge, the law generally will require more from a doctor in overseeing the role of a medical corporation, from an attorney as to legal matters, an accountant as to fiscal matters, and so on. In the same way, a director who is involved in the day to day affairs of the corporation, such as co-signing checks, may be held to a higher standard than other directors.

At this point an individual may be understandably confused about the real or potential liability arising from service as a director of a nonprofit corporation. In order to carry out the functions of a director, and avoid liability for the actions of the position, an individual should recognize that independence may be the most important character trait to bring to the job.

The notion of independence does not require the director to assume an adversarial stance with the corporation's staff, or to come to meetings with the proverbial chip on the shoulder. Nor is it necessary to frequently dissent, or to assume that the officers or other directors are not acting in good faith. What is required is vigilance and a healthy skepticism. A sense of fairness, coupled with sufficient knowledge of the fiscal condition will serve well to avoid possible liability for wrongdoing by corporate directors.

It is important to avoid the pitfall of over reliance on the chief executive officer. The temptation to do so is real, often due to the executive's knowledge of the affairs of the corporation, and frequently due to a feeling that the director may owe his or her position on the board to the executive. Further, some directors assume that "I'm just a volunteer" is a legitimate reason for deference to the "paid, professional staff."

Orientation

No director can function properly without access to information about the corporation's purposes, activities and goals. To become acquainted with the corporation, a new director should demand an orientation. Indeed, a potential director would do well to inquire about the type of orientation which the corporation will provide for new directors.

This is an important place to exercise the independence mentioned above, and considerable thought should be given to serving as a director of a corporation which does not have an appropriate orientation program. If the decision is made to serve without the benefit of the orientation being offered by the corporation, a top priority should be to see that this shortcoming is redressed.

Subsequent to orientation, or following the decision to serve in spite of the lack of a sufficient orientation program, the new director should seek assurance that proper information about the affairs of the corporation will be provided. The first requirement should be for a copy of the articles of incorporation which are required by the state before the charter is issued. Since the articles may have been changed or amended subsequent to the original filing, an inquiry should be directed to the staff for any such changes. The articles may be specific, or they may contain generalities which provide little or no assistance to the new director in evaluating the corporation and becoming familiar with its ambitions and goals. The director also should be provided with copies of the adopted bylaws. If properly prepared, they will provide considerable insight into the behavior of the corporation.

Corporate Policies

The new director should also ask for important policy statements which have been adopted by the corporation. Such items as personnel policies may seem pedestrian or mundane to one who has looked forward to an opportunity to be of service to humanity, but the fact remains that such things as reasonable compensation for staff is an important part of a director's role. Indeed, the new directors may find that either the corporation or the individual directors may be held accountable to the corporation, or to the state or federal government, if they neglect to ascertain that the "nonprofit" corporation is in fact nonprofit, and that neither officers nor directors are receiving unreasonable compensation for their services to the corporation.

A recent review of state statutes indicates that many states now have statutory provisions that prohibit board members from being compensated for their services on the board. A more delicate question that requires policy, however, is the compensation of board members for service above and beyond that required by normal standards of care (e.g. paying the carpenter on the board to remodel the corporation's office).

Ideally, every new director will be provided with a corporate director's book which contains all of the items mentioned above in addition to other materials which would be of assistance in serving as a director. In the real world, many nonprofit corporations are small, and not perfectly managed, and it is unlikely that the new director will be given all of the necessary information in a handy package. For the intrepid soul willing to forge ahead, the absence of the materials should be dealt with in the same fashion as the lack of an orientation program. The fact that the informaton has not been proffered does not mean that it does not exist. If it does not, then perhaps it is time for even the intrepid soul to exercise a little caution, and retire. In the era of the ubiquitous copy machine, all of these materials can be assembled at little cost, and the benefits to the directors, the constituents and to the corporation will far exceed such costs. The inquisitive and independent new director may also feel the need to ask if the other directors have been furnished such materials, and if not, why not.

Another important source of information for the new director is the minute book. Depending on the age and size of the corporation, previous minutes may be quite voluminous. The new director should be furnished with copies of minutes for a sufficient period of time to become acquainted with the corporation. There is no definite period which is applicable to all cases, but for lack of a better recommendation, ask for the minutes of the previous year's meetings. Frequently much valuable information can be obtained from this source, and in situations where there has been considerable turnover in officers and directors, they may be the only source of information to explain past decisions.

Information

Once the new director has had the benefit of an orientation and become acquainted with the policies of the corporation, attention should be given to the appropriate amount of data needed prior to board action.

Depending on the importance of the matter, information may be presented verbally or it may consist of many pages of supporting documents. Of critical importance is the agenda itself. A well run nonprofit board will provide its members with a detailed agenda far enough in advance of each meeting so that the directors will have an opportunity to become familiar with each issue on the agenda. Since each director has the responsibility to make an informed decision, adequate notice should be provided. In addition to the agenda, information should be provided about each important item on which the directors will be called upon to review, act or advise the staff. There is perhaps no better reason for putting a matter off until the next meeting than the failure of the staff to provide sufficiently detailed data to make wise decisions. If the directors feel that they do not have sufficient information provided prior to the meeting to make an informed decision, there should be no reluctance in calling for further information or requesting that the matter be delayed until an opportunity is afforded to carefully study the issue that has been brought before the board.

Financial Reports

The flow of information should include, in addition to the agenda and supporting materials, sufficient financial information to provide a meaningful understanding of the fiscal affairs of the corporation. Depending on the size of the corporation, the financial data may be a monthly or quarterly report of the activities of the corporation. In any event, the materials should provide the director with sufficient understanding of the fiscal status of the entity, and should enable the director to analyze the operation of the corporation and give proper consideration to all areas of finance. (More detailed information on the type of financial information the board needs to prudently monitor the corporation is described in Chapter 11.)

Operations Reports

Board meetings should be viewed by both officers and directors as an opportunity for directors to be briefed on the current status of the corporation. This report may be provided verbally by the chief executive officer, or it may be distributed in memorandum form prior to the meeting. If the report is important enough to be presented in writing, it should be placed on the agenda, and the memorandum should have been provided ahead of the meeting to allow sufficient time for directors to become familiar with it. These reports should cover both current events since the last board meeting and plans for the future. Careful attention should be given to issues which may represent critical decisions for the corporation. The information should be presented in such fashion that the director is able to make judgments as to whether the decision or policy is properly within the area in which the corporation may legally act, whether it is within the goals established for the corporation, and how it fits into the short and long range financial plans of the corporation.

Plans and Planning

Given the board member's powers, responsibilities and liabilities, consideration of appropriate corporate planning activities is critical. The board will be forced to slow down long enough to ensure that the directors understand the operations sufficiently to enable them to prudently plan. If the directors give sufficient consideration to the question of whether to have a plan, the end result of the deliberation will benefit the corporation, whatever the plan may be. The importance which the officers and directors attach to the issue of planning may indicate more about the operation of the corporation than a ream of financial statements.

A lack of a long range plan may or may not be indicative of bad management, but a lack of systematic planning will certainly result in bad management. Insist on planning, don't allow the corporation to operate without it. If a plan is to be adopted, insist that it be the result of a planning process involving the board. If the proposed plan arrives in the mail with the agenda and a note that the plan will be discussed at the next meeting, regain your inquisitiveness and independence. Remember, it is the board of directors' function to set policy, and the staff's responsibility to carry it out. A planning process which allows the original document to be drafted without input from the directors is unlikely to provide an opportunity for meaningful decision making and oversight by the board.

Put plans and planning in perspective: If the directors and officers participate in the planning, the process may be more substantial proof of careful stewardship than the resulting plan. Once a plan is adopted it should not be regarded as permanent, but should be used as a guide to making decisions during the period covered by the plan. Active involvement in the planning process and reference to the plan once it is adopted may be one of the better forms of insurance against liability arising out of the failure to carry out one's responsibilities and duties as a director.

Expert or Professional Advice

We have discussed earlier the standard of care required of a director and mentioned that the standard may vary depending on the background of the individual director. How does the director deal with reports or statements which may be presented to the board by an attorney or accountant, or other professional? If the director reads the report, or is present at the time an oral statement is made by one who is a professional in a recognized field, she is entitled to rely in good faith on the opinions and conclusions expressed therein, unless she has knowledge which would lead an ordinary person to question the report or statement. If a director has knowledge of facts other than those relied on by the expert, knows that the expert is incompetent, has a conflict of interest, or that the conclusions expressed are contrary to the law, she is not entitled to rely on the information presented.

If the director has doubts about the legal aspects of the question or has information which causes doubts to arise about materials presented, she should act in a prudent manner and seek professional advice outside the corporation. To fail to do so may be construed as a violation of the fiduciary position in which the director serves. Once the director has sought outside advice from a professional, the same standards apply in determining her right to rely in good faith on such opinions. The director must exercise reasonable care in the selection of the outside expert, and should exercise the same reasonable care in determining that the expert has access to the necessary facts and has made such investigation as may be indicated by the situation.

Generally, when the directors have acted properly in delegating responsibilities to appropriate officers of the corporation, they are entitled to rely on the information provided by such officers in good faith in performing their duties and carrying out their responsibilities. The right to rely on such materials extends to financial matters, including financial statements and yearly reports. It should be emphasized that the director has the responsibility to determine that the officers to whom the delegation of authority is made are honest, reliable and competent. The right to rely on reports or statements also extends to the corporate records and books, subject to the same restrictions mentioned above.

Conflict of Interest

The classic case in which a conflict of interest may arise is for a director to contract with the corporation. There is no absolute prohibition in most states against a director contracting with the board but such contracts should be carefully examined and should be approved by a disinterested majority of the board after full disclosure has been made of of the director's interest. Such an inside contract will be subject to careful scrutiny by the courts and may be voided if it is not in the best interest of the corporation. In the same vein, if a director acquires information by virtue of service on the board, he should be careful to avoid acting in such a fashion as to benefit personally from such information. If the question of a director benefitting from his service as a director arises, he may have the burden of establishing good faith and that the transaction was handled in a manner fair to the corporation. By serving on the board, a director has assumed the role of fiduciary or trustee; therefore, if a transaction is questionable, it should be avoided.

Recent changes in the statutes of many states that govern the behavior of nonprofit corporations have included explicit descriptions of those conflicts of interest that must be avoided. The careful board will review the state law prior to entering into contracts with members of the board. Given the frequency with which this matter arises in the normal workings of nonprofits, boards might be well served by including a discussion of the appropriate state statutes in the orientation program that either now operates, or will operate after the intrepid soul encourages its development. Should a formal board policy not exist that describes "conflicts of interest," immediate attention should be given to developing such a policy that both complies with state law and reasonable judgment.

Tax Exempt Status

Exempt organizations range from the familiar 501(c)(3) charitable organizations to 501(c)(14) groups operating cooperative telephone companies to 521 (a) farmer cooperative associations. The information that follows pertains to those 850,000 groups exempt under Section 501(c)(3) because they are organized and operated exclusively for religious, charitable, scientific, testing for public safety, literary, or educational purposes, or for the prevention of cruelty to children or animals and the promotion of international amateur athletics.

Generally, all corporations which are granted such status are not required to pay federal income tax. Many states have also adopted laws which exempt 501(c)(3) corporations from the payment of state income taxes. These state exemptions generally have similar requirements to those of the federal government. Income from sources that are related to the purposes that enabled the corporation to obtain the tax exempt status is not subject to taxation. This exempt status also allows people who make donations to the corporation to qualify for a personal tax deduction. The exemption does not apply to income which is not related to the corporation's purpose. Such "unrelated business income" is taxed as though it were income of any other business.

The exempt status may be in danger if the corporation becomes involved to a substantial degree in activities which are not related to its exempt purpose. The director should be familiar with the tax exempt status of the corporation, and should be careful to ascertain that the necessary reports are filed to maintain status. In considering the activities of the corporation, the director should ask if income from a project is subject to taxation and whether that income may have a negative effect on the corporation's tax exempt status.

As a side note, it is important to remind directors and organizers of nonprofit corporations that the assertion, "We're tax exempt because we have a charter from the state" can only lead to trouble. The prudent director will take the time to inquire if a Form 1023 has been filed and if a copy of the advanced or definitive ruling has been received from the IRS. Nonprofit corporations failing to file a request for exempt status (Form 1023 for "charitable, educational", etc. groups) run the risk of being presumed by the IRS to be operating as a "for profit" corporation and, thus, be liable for payment of corporate income tax. Some precedent exist to help the board rectify this situation, but the time and energy required are avoided by the prudent exercise of asking for proof of exempt status. Failing to receive this from the staff should cause the conscientious board member to immediately move to have the organization apply for such status.

The funding sources for nonprofit corporations are varied, but for the purposes of this section we are concerned with the need of the corporation to seek donations or contributions from the private sector. The ability to obtain a tax deduction for a contribution to the corporation plays a large part in successful fund raising. From the prospective donor's point of view, a corporation that is tax exempt is much more likely to receive favorable consideration.

In an era in which less money is available from state and federal governments to support activities within the traditional role of the nonprofit corporation, the need to acquire and retain tax exempt status may be the difference between survival and failure. The director should be familiar, in general terms, with the requirements to obtain tax exempt status. In monitoring the activities of the corporation, the director should keep in mind the requirements for retaining its tax exempt status.

One final point in seeking to preserve tax exempt status: Organizations which have acquired tax exempt status are closely regulated as to their lobbying or political activities. The actual restrictions vary depending on the type of lobbying and the annual budget of the corporation. The prudent board member will determine the restrictions applicable to the board on which he or she serves and closely monitor the corporation's activities to ensure that the lobbying regulations are adhered to. The penalty for noncompliance may be the loss of tax exempt status.

Insurance

Each director should be aware of the areas in which either the corporation or the individual directors may be held liable. One of the primary responsibilities of the director is to ensure the continued existence of the corporation. In today's litigious society, a lost lawsuit can destroy the work of many years. The failure to provide adequate insurance coverage can result in a judgment against the corporation which could exhaust corporate resources. The directors should exercise the same diligence as would be exercised in the conduct of their business affairs to provide adequate insurance coverage. In addition to such coverages as unemployment and worker's compensation, which are generally required by state or federal law, the corporation should be insured against negligent acts of its employees. Depending on the role and scope of the corporate activities, the corporation may need errors and omissions coverage to protect it against potential loss. Insurance providing coverage for the corporation's property should be reviewed regularly.

The director may also wish to inquire whether the corporation carries insurance providing coverage for directors and officers which will provide a defense for the director in the event that litigation is filed against individual directors. Coverage is also available which will protect directors against judgments which may be obtained against them in their role as members of the corporate board.

Restrictions

Every board member should understand that state law has granted the charter which creates the nonprofit corporation they serve. The same state law will define the powers of the corporation and govern the manner in which they will be exercised by a board of directors. These powers are accompanied by corresponding duties and legal liabilities if the board (and, in some instances, individual board members) fails to fulfill those duties.

There are four general restrictions on the powers of the board of directors. First, directors must, as a part of the fiduciary role, be loyal to the corporation and seek its best interest. Second, directors must not cause or allow the corporation to exceed its powers and act _ultra vires_ or outside its stated purpose. Third, the board must insure that the corporation complies with its own charter, bylaws, and policies. Fourth, directors must operate with diligence and due care in prudently carrying out their duties.

Guidelines: A Summary

1. Board members must understand the primary corporate documents: The articles of incorporation or charter, the bylaws, corporate policies, financial statements, and management reports. Board members should have an opportunity to understand these documents in an initial orientation session and by having regular board training sessions.

2. The board should establish clear position descriptions for the officers and assignments for committees so that all critical management areas get detailed continuous review by directors. These areas include program operations, planning, personnel, tax and legal compliance issues, and financial reporting.

3. The board should meet regularly and frequently. Board members must be serious about their attendance at board and committee meetings and must do their homework between meetings. Being absent from meetings and ignorant of what is going on in the corporation are virtual admissions that you have failed the "prudent person" test. Boards should remove directors who do not attend meetings.

4. Clear board policies on conflict of interest should be adopted and enforced strictly.

5. Board members should diligently seek information from staff and others in the community about the operation of the organization. The board, as a whole, must be responsible for determining what information it wants and needs from management. Individual directors should be encouraged to seek additional information from management. (If this is abused and becomes a form of harassment of the staff, it should be brought to the attention of the full board. Corrective action should be taken by the full board.)

6. Clear policies should be adopted to describe and control political campaign and lobbying activities.

7. Board members should raise issues and concerns, register their dissents, and insist that their views be recorded in the minutes. A prudent person does not let the building burn without yelling "fire".

8. Be cautious and protective of the assets of the corporation and ensure that they are utilized in the pursuit of the mission or purpose of the corporation.

9. Ensure that the corporation has adequate access to legal counsel and maintains proper accounting practices. The corporation should have an annual audit by an outside accountant.

10. If directors have reasonable doubts about a course of action, they should seek outside independent advice and counsel from an attorney,

certified public accountant, or other expert in the matter.

11. Routinely verify that all state, federal and local tax payments, registrations, and reports have been filed in a timely and accurate manner.

The invitation to serve as a director of a nonprofit corporation should be regarded as an opportunity to be of service to one's community. An awareness of the liabilities which may ensue from inattention or from failing to exercise due care in carrying out one's duties as a director will enable you to be a better director. A more thoughtful and careful exercise of the powers vested in a director of a nonprofit corporation will result in a pleasant experience for you and greater benefit to the community and corporation you serve.

Further Readings

S. Becker and D. Glenn, OFF YOUR DUFFS AND UP THE ASSETS: COMMON
SENSE FOR NONPROFIT MANAGERS. New York: Farnswarth Publishing
Company. 1984

Tracy Connors, THE NONPROFIT ORGANIZATION HANDBOOK. New York: McGraw-
Hill. 1980

R. Dimieri and S. Weiner, "The Public Interest and governing Board
of Nonprofit Health Care Institutions," VANDERBILT LAW REVIEW.
Vol. 34, No. 4, May 1981. p.1029-1066

K. Eye et al., EFFECTIVE PARTICIPATION OF CONSUMER BOARD MEMBERS:
INVOLVING ELDERLY AND LOW INCOME PERSONS. Denver: Colorado
Congress of Senior Organizations. 1982

P. L. Hanson and C. T. Marmaduke, THE BOARD MEMBER: DECISION MAKER.
Sacramento, CA: Han/Mar Publications. 1972

Bruce R. Hopkins, CHARITY UNDER SIEGE: Government Regulation of
Fundraising. New York: Ronald Press, 1980

Bruce R. Hopkins, THE LAW OF TAX EXEMPT ORGANIZATIONS, 4th edition.
New York: John Wiley & Sons, 1983

M. J. Lane, LEGAL HANDBOOK FOR NONPROFIT ORGANIZATIONS. New York:
American Management Association, 1981

Howard L. Oleck, NONPROFIT CORPORATIONS, ORGANIZATIONS AND
ASSOCIATIONS, Englewood Cliffs, NJ: Prentice Hall, 1974

K.G. Provan, "Board Power and Organizational Effectiveness Among
Human Service Agencies," ACADEMY OF MANAGEMENT JOURNAL. Vol. 23,
No. 2. p. 221-236

A. Swanson. THE DETERMINATIVE TEAM: A HANDBOOK FOR BOARD MEMBERS OF
VOLUNTARY ORGANIZATIONS. Hicksville, NY: Exposition Press. 1978

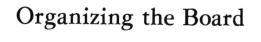

Organizing the Board

Chapter 4

Organizational Mission and Values

Jerry Cronin

Developing Mission Statements

For all the importance placed by consultants on mission statements, the average nonprofit board has rarely given any attention to the matter of developing and agreeing upon one. This is unfortunate because the well developed mission statement will have, at least, the following benefits:

1. enable the board to define the "business of the organization" so that all of its energy can be spent in pursuit of compatible results,

2. enable the board to decide how to spend resources so that budgets can be tied to the most critical results the organization wants to achieve,

3. enable the board to clearly and concisely state to funding sources, cooperating organizations, prospective board members and the public its reason for existing,

4. suggests to the board the kinds of skills that it must have or recruit to be effective in daily operations,

5. enable the board to make decisions about which programs and projects to undertake and which to avoid, and

6. enable the organization to begin its planning with a shared assumption about the nature of the organization.

A side benefit of a well developed mission statement is that the process of development will cause the board members to begin to form closer bonds, share expectations about the future of the organization, and understand the differences between among board members.

In the life of a nonprofit organization there are few steps more important than those taken to develop a mission. Other than filing the articles of incorporation and developing bylaws, the mission is the most fundamental item for consideration by the board of directors. It far overshadows annual budgets, executive reports, reviewing new publicity materials and discussing salaries even though such matters seem to occupy much of the time of the average board.

The mission is the fundamental statement of why the corporation exists, the style in which it will operate, the constituency it will serve and the variety of people who are its members. It becomes the common or core element that gives life, meaning and basis of unity to the corporation. In times of tension, conflict and dispute, the wise board can refer back to its mission for guidance.

This, of course, assumes that the corporation has a mission. For many, if it exists, the mission is something the staff remembers when it is time to respond to funding applications that ask for the mission of the corporation. And then each staff member seems to remember it differently.

The conscientious board will take it upon itself to develop, in conjunction with staff, volunteers and membership (or whatever combination of such groups exists), a mission statement. To be as useful as possible, the statement should:

1. avoid technical language,

2. stress the results the organization will achieve,

3. avoid becoming a simple listing of organizational activities,

4. be broad in scope,

5. provide a challenge to everyone in the organization,

6. indicate the style in which the corporation will operate,

7. provide a key to understanding what is distinctive about the organization,

8. concentrate on services offered or goods produced rather than on the internal operations of the corporation,

9. be sufficiently detailed to avoid confusion of interpretation,

10. indicate who could be a member of the group, if appropriate, and

11. define the constituency of the organization.

Review the following mission statements, taken from existing nonprofit organizations, and compare them to the eleven guidelines.

GROUP A

"ABC, a nonprofit, multi-purpose human service corporation, consisting of representatives of the low-income
population, public officials and private interest groups
of ABC County, will develop and provide, or encourage
others to provide support, services, and opportunities
in the areas of basic human needs with the objective of
assisting those with limited opportunities or means to
help themselves and to encourage society and individuals
to assess their own needs in order that they may be enabled
to remove barriers which perpetuate poverty. This mission
will be accomplished through the mobilization and direction
of public, private and human resources to combating the
causes and effects of poverty."

GROUP B

"The purpose of BCD is to provide a ministry to Illinois
teenagers in need of reconciliation with families and society.
Our purpose is to further reconciliation through a program
of preventive care, residential treatment and aftercare."

GROUP C

"Our purpose is to provide the planning, research,
training, evaluation, and information services needed by a
broad range of organizations so that there might be full and
equal civic, social and economic participation by all people
in the life of their communities.

Some of the mission statements do a better job of meeting the eleven
guidelines than others, but each statement helps the board, staff, volunteers, and members and general public understand why the organization is
"in business." Certainly, some of the statements raise as many questions
as they answer, but the point is that the statements are clear enough that
they can serve as reference points for answering day-to-day or broader
questions.

The missions provide guidance to the boards when they try to determine who should be served by their programs, sources of funds that are
compatible with the mission of the organization, strategies followed by
programs or projects and to whom its primary allegiance should be given.

As a decision making tool the mission is only useful when the board
has been primarily responsible for its development and when the board members have internalized the statement.

The formal adoption of a mission statement by the board is best done
by consensus or acclamation. A simple majority vote on a mission can well
mean that 49% of the board does not agree with the statement even though it

is the major statement of the reasons for the existence of the corporation.

The time spent by the board coming to agreement on the mission may reveal that board members have significant differences of opinion about the purpose of the organization. Health clinic boards often discover that some members think the mission should be to "cure illnesses" while others want to "prevent sickness." Still other board members want to serve the poor and elderly while some want to serve the entire community. Such differences may well explain why the board has had bitter fights in the past or why attendance is spotty and board member commitment seems weak. These differences may be resolved as the mission statement is developed.

Now let's look at some procedures for developing the mission.

The Board Retreat

Becoming increasingly popular, the retreat gives the board and staff an opportunity to think through its mission, policies and goals during an extended working period, frequently a weekend. The prudent board will find an objective outsider to facilitate the retreat. The outsider, paid or volunteer, will prevent the staff from dominating the event and will keep the board on track during its deliberations.

When you consider that boards need people with a wide variety of skills to be effective, you realize that a discussion of mission and organizational values among people of diverse backgrounds will take quite a while and will produce real disagreements. The facilitator's job is to help the board members explore the areas of disagreement rather than cover them up. In this way, the board members come to know and appreciate the different views represented by the board. Such knowledge makes the board stronger and better prepared to work through the remainder of the planning process.

A successful schedule, such as Exhibit 4-1, illustrates the board retreat process. All times, however, must be adjusted to the size of the board and the degree to which board members are familiar and comfortable with each other. Boards that have a history of working well together, or newly organized boards that by chance or plan have little disagreement about a mission, can develop and agree to a mission in a few hours. The balance of the board retreat can then be spent in working on policy and planning considerations.

EXHIBIT 4-1: A Design for a Board Retreat

6 - 7:30 P.M.   Dinner and registration.

7:30 - 8 P.M.   Introductions;
clarify objectives of retreat;
ground rules for conducting the retreat are
agreed to.

8 - 8:30 P.M.   Small group discussion and listing of the
strengths and weaknesses of the corporation
This should be done by having the
facilitator divide the board into small
groups of no more than five members.
Members should join those with which they
are least familiar.

8:30 - 9:30 P.M.   In the same small groups, review the history
and accomplishments of the organization (for
existing organizations) or discuss major
problems the organization was created to
address (for new organizations). Each
group gives an oral report to the large
group.

9:30 - 10 P.M.   Facilitator presents a sample mission statement and guidelines for mission development.
Particular emphasis should be placed on the
use of the mission statement to address the
organizational weaknesses and problems
identified by the small groups.

10 P.M.   Adjourn for the evening and encourage members
to socialize informally.

SATURDAY

7:30 - 8:30 A.M.   Breakfast

8:30 - 9 A.M.   The large group reviews the work of the previous evening.

9 - 10 A.M.   Form new small groups of no more than 5
members. Each group is to develop the
components of a mission statement by
reaching consensus on the answers to the
following questions. (If they can't agree,
they should attach minority reports.)
Small groups put work on newsprint and
report to the large group.

Continued

EXHIBIT: Continued

Questions for writing a mission statement:
1. Why do we exist? What is our purpose?

2. Who do we serve or benefit?

3. Who are "we"? Who should belong to the organization?

4. How do we operate? What kinds of things do we do?

10 – 11 A.M.	After each group has presented its work, the entire group identifies areas of agreement and disagreement. Discuss and seek resolution of disagreements.
11 – 12 noon	As a large group, compose a preliminary draft of a mission statement.
LUNCH	
1 – 1:30 P.M.	As a large group, brainstorm a list of areas of disagreement from past board meetings. Check the preliminary mission statement by reviewing these issues.
1:30 – 2:30 P.M.	Facilitator leads large group in modifying the preliminary mission statement.

At this stage, the board needs to decide whether it is comfortable with the mission, or if the mission needs more work by a committee that can submit a draft to the board at its next meeting, or if the board is ready to move on to the consideration of essential policy statements.

Some boards, however, are too large or spread over too much territory to have a cost effective weekend retreat. In this case, the mission can be developed at a regular board meeting. In order to do this, a significant amount of pre-planning is required. One way to do this pre-planning is described below.

1. Send each board member a questionnaire that (a) explains the reasons for developing a mission and (b) gives the guidelines for sound mission statements. (Exhibit 4-2 is a sample questionnaire.)

2. Ask each board member to submit a statement of mission to the chairperson of the board planning committee (Remember: The mission is primarily a board responsibility) within a week.

X   3. The chairperson will prepare a simple list of all responses and return the complete list to the board members prior to the board meeting and ask them to review the list for areas of of agreement and disagreement.

X   4. The board meeting then begins with a discussion of the agreements and disagreements until they are resolved. The board, working as a large group, then drafts a preliminary mission statement.

X   5. At the following board meeting, the mission statement should be reviewed, modified as needed, and adopted.

EXHIBIT 4-2: Mission Development Questionnaire

Every nonprofit corporation needs a clear and agreed upon mission statement. Once developed, the statement will enable us to proceed with our planning, fund raising, program implementation and evaluation with a shared definition of our organization. It is the board's responsibility to develop a mission ... and adhere to it. A mission statement should provide answers to four clear, concise questions.

1. Why does the organization exist? What is our purpose?

2. Who do we seek to serve or benefit? Who is our constituency?

3. Who are "we"? Who should make up the organization? What should be the basis for membership?

4. What should be our style as an organization? What should characterize our operations? Should some actions be "out of bounds" for us?

To help develop a mission statement that we can use for the future, complete the above and submit your answers to these four questions about XYZ Community Center. All the answers will be compiled and sent to each board member for review prior to the board retreat.

Many other alternatives are available to the nonprofit board for developing a mission statement. Whatever method is chosen, however, it should be one that recognizes that it is easy to short-circuit the process of mission development by simply assigning it to the staff, volunteers or a board committee. In this way, you are guaranteeing that the board will not develop the broad understanding of each others views that will occur in the fully participatory processes outline above. You must remember that individual board member's commitment to the mission will be directly proportional to their level of involvement in its development

Obstacles to Mission Development

1. Board members feel that they don't know enough about planning to shoulder the responsibility for developing a statement. The process of developing the mission and sharing what board members have gained through education and experience will prove to be sufficient to the task. The board that attempts to beg out of the task with this excuse is one that probably just doesn't feel comfortable with itself —and that's all the more reason to hold a retreat so that more interpersonal communications can occur among members.

2. Board members are busy and can only volunteer small amounts of time: Let the staff prepare it and submit it for approval by the whole board. It is true that the board members are volunteers and that their time is important. It is also true that this will be the most important time they will spend as board members. Attendance at such retreats or board planning meetings should be 100%. Lesser attendance serves the board and its clients or constituents poorly.

The time spent developing the mission may well be what is needed to show the board members that (a) they, rather than the staff, are in control of the planning of the corporation, (b) the corporation's work is vital and in line with the personal goals of the individual board members, or (c) they have little in common with the organization and ought to resign so that their energy and talents can be used elsewhere.

3. The executive director is a "take charge" person and founder of the organization who sees that he/she should have exclusive control over the development of the mission and submit it only for review by the board. The board must remind the energetic director that the board must control organizational direction and that the board members' motivation for working with the corporation is tied to the members being given an opportunity to take this critical formative step that is given to the board.

4. An aggressive board or staff member dominates the discussions during the retreat and subsequent planning meetings. The facilitator and the other members of the board have a responsibility to help the domineering person realize that her/his comments are best given infrequently and over a longer period of time. Clear rules for conducting the retreat and planning meetings need to be developed and agreed upon so that it is acceptable to remind the domineering person of the effect of his or her behavior.

5. Nit-pickers argue over individual words rather than concentrate on the substance of the mission statement. The facilitator and other board members must resist the temptation to be stopped by this ankle high barrier. Mission statements must first be analyzed for serious concept and content. When that has been settled, choices over individual wording may be made. Keep such discussions in perspective and be aware that they can easily get the meeting off track.

Going Beyond the Mission: Essential Corporate Values

With the mission statement developed and agreed upon, the board is ready to move one step further in organizing or reorganizing the corporation. The next step is reaching agreement on a set of "essential corporate values."

Nonprofits, perhaps more than most kinds of organizations because they are value based organizations, must be anchored by a set of values which are shared by the staff and board. These values and the organization culture will be unconsciously and covertly developed and directed by the staff, unless the organization's board and staff seeks to affirmatively clarify and define their shared values. This is a vital organizing and control responsibility which the board must carefully fulfill.

Corporate decision making is enhanced if the board takes time to identify the implicit values that each member uses when attempting to make decisions about the organization.

For example, boards have to decide how the corporation will be financed. On any given board, there will be some members who will take money from any source and others who prefer that the organiztion be self-supporting. Discussions about corporate financial goals and objectives are made more manageable if the board has defined the values it holds concerning financial status. The process of identifying and agreeing to a consistent and complete set of corporate values provides the board with a set of principles for governing the internal and external behavior of the organization.

The "Corporate Value Statement Worksheet" can be used by boards to identify some of the major values held by individual members. If each board member completes the form (either at a retreat, through the mail, or at a meeting with little on the agenda other than "corporate development"), then the responses can be collated and reviewed by all of the members. Members then discuss critical differences and come to agreement on essential corporate values.

It is important to limit this list of values to those core beliefs that are literally "essential" to the life of the corporation. These are the core values which you are prepared to require everyone in the organization to support.

31

EXHIBIT 4-3: A Corporate Value Statement Worksheet

List below ten (10) value statements which you feel should characterize the internal and external operations of your organization.

I.

II.

III.

IV.

V.

VI.

VII.

VIII.

IX.

X.

Now review your ten value statements and put an "X" in front of
the five statements which you consider essential or most important as core values for your organization.

```
EXHIBIT 4-4: Sample Corporate Values

1. ICC, Inc. will work with any nonprofit organization so long as the
   group is not consciously and deliberately oppressive of others.

2. Clients must be willing to look beyond the symptom to the cause
   of its organizational and community problems.

3. Long term consultative arrangements are discouraged because they
   hinder the development of strong, autonomous groups.

4. Consultations must result from requests from those affected by
   the consultation.

5. Money, whether from grants, contracts, or donations, will result
   from consultations only when the client is satisfied with the
   quality of the consultation.

6. The quality of the work for a client shall not vary according to
   the fee charged.
```

Summary

The board has now put itself in a position to become an effective
decision making body. It has adopted a mission that enables all board,
staff, volunteers and members, funding sources, regulating agencies and the
general public to know the reasons for the corporation's existence. The
value statements provide value guidance for both the board and staff.

Many board members may find the time spent on developing a mission
and agreeing on corporate values to be wasteful. They will talk to their
friends who serve on other nonprofit boards and find out that few, if any,
nonprofit organizations in their area have gone through this process. If
the board member probes further, he/she will find that organizations without explicit mission and value statements are plagued by at least the
following symptoms:

1. Attempting to be all things to all people.

2. Being unable to implement an effective public relations and
   public information program due to the board's inability to agree
   on the way in which the organization will be presented to the
   public.

3. Low or highly variable attendance at board meetings.

4. Inability to tie fund raising and budgeting to corporate goals.

5. Inability to agree on ways to evaluate the quality of the
   organization's programs.

6. Inability to make quick and clear decisions on major issues of survival, growth and development.

7. Inability to identify and resolve tension between competing factions at the board, staff or membership levels.

Some organizations seem to be more comfortable than others with the process of analyzing the values that its board, staff and volunteers bring to the decision making process. It is important for all boards to become comfortable with this process because, once identified, the values need to be reviewed at least annually by the full board. The values, in conjunction with the mission, will also be used by the board on a regular basis to see if the organization is fulfilling its commitments to its members, consumers, funding sources, and regulatory bodies.

Further Readings

Theodore Caplon, HOW TO RUN ANY ORGANIZATION. New York: Holt, Rinehart and Winston, 1976

Tracy D. Connors (Ed.), THE NONPROFIT ORGANIZATION HANDBOOK. New York: McGraw-Hill, 1980

Peter Drucker, MANAGEMENT: TASKS, RESPONSIBILITIES AND PRACTICES. New York: Harper & Row Publishers, 1974

P. L. Hanson and C. T. Marmaduke, THE BOARD MEMBER: DECISION MAKER. Sacramento, CA: Han/Mar Publications, Inc., 1972

James Hardy, CORPORATE PLANNING FOR NONPROFIT ORGANIZATIONS. New York: Association Press, 1972

Dale McConkey, MBO FOR NONPROFIT ORGANIZATIONS. New York: American Management Association, 1975

John Merson and Robert Qualls, STRATEGIC PLANNING FOR COLLEGES AND UNIVERSITIES. San Antonio, TX: Trinity University Press, 1979

Oscar Mink, James Schultz, and Barbara Mink. DEVELOPING AND MANAGING OPEN ORGANIZATIONS. Austin, TX: Learning Concepts, 1979

George Morrissey, MANAGEMENT BY OBJECTIVES AND RESULTS FOR BUSINESS AND INDUSTRY. Reading, MA: Addison-Wesley Publishing Co., 1979

Gerald Zaltman (Ed.), MANAGEMENT PRINCIPLES FOR NONPROFIT AGENCIES AND ORGANIZATIONS. New York: AMACOM, 1979

Chapter 5

Holding Productive and Satisfying Board Meetings

Louise Eberhardt

One of the most frequently identified nonprofit board problems is the time spent in meetings. People often experience board meetings as dull, long, unnecessary and unproductive. Board members who attend these meetings often feel frustration from the sense of not being needed or used during the meetings. Certainly in many meetings very little is accomplished and everyone's time is wasted.

For example, recently I was conducting a retreat for a nonprofit board. Several members had expressed dissatisfaction about the way board members worked together. One man in particular stands out: He had been brought on the board for his political knowledge, skills and connections in the state. In the three meetings he had attended, he had never been asked to contribute anything. As a result, he was feeling useless and was thinking of resigning. The tragedy is that the rest of the board valued his service and wanted him to be active, but many other problems stood in the way. This and similar problems happen more often than people realize. This and similar board meeting problems are dealt with below.

Why have meetings anyway? To answer this question, let's look at some basic functions of meetings. A meeting defines a board, giving it a sense of collective identity. It is a place where information and ideas that members have acquired separately or in small groups since the last meeting can be shared and exchanged. Testing and arguing about these ideas usually produce better ideas, plans and decisions than an individual can determine alone. Meetings can help build commitment to decisions. A meeting helps members see how they fit into the larger organizational picture and reminds them of the board's overall goals and the ways they can contribute to the attainment of the goals.

In addition to the external rewards given to board members when they accomplish a task well, the board can also experience internal, interpersonal rewards: Those good feelings which occur during a board meeting when an idea is accepted, when one is invited to join in, when a member feels that she or he has made a helpful contribution. Meetings also serve to fulfill people's need to belong to and participate in a social group.

Characteristics of Effective Meetings

Before discussing ways to change "bad" meetings, it would be instructive to identify some characteristics of an "ideal" meeting: One that is is both productive and satisfying. The working atmosphere at such meetings tends to be informal, comfortable and relaxed. People are involved and interested. You can spot few signs of boredom such as doodling, looking out the window or sleeping. Participation is high and mainly pertinent to the tasks at hand. Group members listen to each other. Ideas are responded to by others. Disagreement is permitted and even encouraged. Suppression or overriding of others is not found.

Generally, the group at an ideal meeting makes decisions by consensus: Everyone agrees and is willing to go along with the decision even if it is not their top priority. Consensus occurs only after all opinions and ideas have been aired and heard. Formal voting is kept at a minimum (except when prudence requires careful tallying and recording in the minutes). Feelings are brought out in the open and hidden agendas are at a minimum. Group decision making is clear. Task assignments are made easily and are readily accepted by the board members. All group members share leadership functions and the chairperson facilitates rather than dominates the board meeting.

The members are open to examining their way of working together and often put such an examination on their agenda. Feedback is freely given and accepted in a non-judgmental and supportive way. This supportive atmosphere stimulates creative solutions to problems. Tasks are completed on time and at an optimum level of performance.

On the other hand, ineffective meetings will often be characterized by such conditions as:

- domination by the chairperson

- cliques or sub-groups constantly arguing

- unequal participation with high authority members dominating

- uneven use of member's resources

- rigid or dysfunctional group norms and procedures

- only ideas are expressed; feelings are ignored

- a climate of intimidation and defensiveness pervades

- avoidance, denial or suppression of differences

Basic Procedures

Boards of directors can function more effectively if certain techniques and processes are used during meetings. This chapter will address some of these fundamentals, starting with procedural matters and progressing to more complex processes.

Determining Meeting Dates

Never hold a meeting unless there are clearly defined issues that require board action. Hold only the number of meetings a year that are needed to productively accomplish the board tasks. Old ideas about the need for monthly meetings should be rethought, taking into consideration the many demands on the time and talent of your board members.

Setting dates for meetings can be quite a headache as peoples' schedules are so varied and busy. To avoid this constant problem, have fixed dates such as the first Wednesday of every other month. If that's not possible, then set the next meeting date while you are still in session. Sending out notices which include all the information about decisions to be made and telephoning members are excellent ways to remind people of the coming meetings.

Seating Arrangements

Since visibility and physical presence are important factors in clear communication, it is essential to have board members seated so that all can see each other without strain. Consider the appropriateness of sitting around a table. Being seated in a circle allows everyone to be easily seen or heard and encourages participation and involvement in the meeting. Tables, especially long, narrow ones, tend to show status (i.e., the greater the distance from the chairperson, the lower the status) and prevent much member-to-member communication.

Agenda

A productive agenda lets a group use its meeting time effectively by giving clarity to the meeting. An agenda, whether distributed prior to the meeting or posted on an easel or a wall, permits everyone to see what needs to be done. Some boards like to have the agenda sent out prior to the meeting: Others spend five minutes at the start of each meeting building an agenda.

In building an agenda, consider the following points. First, list all the items to be considered at the meeting. Then decide upon a priority for each item by asking, "What must we accomplish at this meeting? What items could we hold over to the next meeting if there is not enough time?" Divide the agenda into clear categories such as "For Information", "For Discussion", and "For Decision", so those at the meeting know what they are expected to with each item.

The early part of a meeting tends to be more lively and creative, so if an item requires high energy and great ideas, it may be better to place it high on the list. Some boards like to assign time limits to agenda items to prevent members from dwelling too long on any one item and to ensure that appropriate time is allocated to the issues at hand.

Productive meetings usually have ending times assigned or agreed to. Hold to such times if at all possible. Openly negotiate for additional time if it is needed. ("It is 10:00, the time at which we agreed to conclude. Could everyone stay until 10:30 in order to complete the last item on the agenda?") To avoid long meetings, do not set an impossibly long agenda. Many meetings just drag on until all the members are frustrated and exhausted. Very few meetings achieve anything of value after two hours.

Flip Charts

Large sheets of newsprint or flip charts, should be a basic tool for all board meetings. Everything significant that occurs in connection with a meeting is posted so that it is visible to everyone during the meeting. Newsprint also can be used to display data that were collected prior to the meeting; build and agree upon an agenda; record significant ideas, issues or feelings that occur during the meeting; present facts or concepts; compile action lists; record quick ideas; and affix individual responsibility for carrying out decisions.

Formulate Operating Guidelines

Guidelines and procedures enable the group to do that which it wants most effectively. If there are too few rules or procedures, the meeting will waste time and energy on routine matters. Too many rules can result in rigid and dull meetings.

In the first meeting of the year establish the way in which the board will work together by setting operating norms and procedures. Some areas to agree upon include:

- the way in which the board will make decisions

- how the board will resolve conflicts

- how the board members will be accountable to each other

- how the meeting will generally operate (i.e., will there be an agenda, facilitator, process observer, etc.)

Set Board Goals and Priorities

Goals are guides for action. Group meetings will be impaired if board goals are vague, or in opposition to each other. Conflicts and differences are more likely to be resolved by rational, analytic processes when the board has agreed upon clear goals. Goals direct and motivate board members' behavior. Participation in setting the goals heightens members' motivation to work toward their accomplishment. Until there is general agreement on goals and objectives for the work of the board, its meetings will not move effectively or in a consistent direction.

At the start of each year, the board should inventory the issues facing the board and organization and then develop board goals and objectives for the year. These might include such things as the need for new policies, board development needs, major funding efforts, or old issues that the board has avoided for years. The board should formulate these issues into a "macro-agenda." Such a macro-agenda helps the board cope with internal and external changes. As the organization matures and conditions in the community change, the need for revising the direction of the board becomes more critical. The setting of board goals is necessarily tentative and must be re-examined at least annually in order to test their adequacy and relevancy. Board members also derive satisfaction from seeing their plans brought to fruition by the dedicated work of the staff and board.

Clarify Member Expectations

People on a board usually have widely differing interests, time and commitments to give toward goal accomplishment. It is helpful to have board members identify their time, interests and commitments. Several ways are available:

- Each person is asked to write down the amount of time he or she would be willing to commit to the work of the board over a period of time (6 months or a year.) This information is shared with the board at the next meeting. The board can then allocate its work rationally, or can decide to recruit additional members.

- In a meeting, all members state their major interests and the amount of time they have available to work on these interests.

After either of the above procedures, the board develops realistic expectations about the amount of time and energy that each member will give. Persons with more time or higher commitment can then accept more time consuming or difficult tasks. Making this decision openly reduces the resentment some have for doing more and the guilt of others for letting them do the work.

With its board goals established and the interests, time and commit-

41

ment of members identified, meetings of both the board and its committees become more productive. The meetings can now be a time for taking action or reviewing actions previously taken to accomplish the goals. In the absence of such work having been done, the board's meetings will never be more than an occasion for giving advice to staff, wrestling for internal power or enduring utter boredom.

Sub-groups

For many tasks at a meeting, it helps to divide into sub-groups. If the board has always worked as a large group, the members may resist this idea at first. (If a group is not willing to work in sub-groups it may indicate a lack of trust, thereby creating a need for "group maintenance" work.) Sub-grouping keeps people more involved in the meeting by giving each person an opportunity for more "air" time and can be a fast way to complete the tasks.

The purpose of sub-groups is not to make major decisions, but to develop proposals for the full board. Before breaking into specific sub-groups, give time for the board to provide guidance or advice on the task. Members of the sub-groups are usually more productive if they choose the group they want to join. To use sub-groups effectively, do this: (1) be sure each sub-group understands what it is expected to do and the amount of time available for completion of the task, (2) appoint or have the sub-group elect a leader or facilitator for the group, (3) request that their report to the total group be presented on flip charts or with other visual aids, (4) schedule time on the agenda to hear each group's report and to discuss any necessary revisions or reactions and then move to decision, if required.

Brainstorming

Meetings are widely noted for being occasions at which the "old" members dominate discussion and "new" members feel intimidated, uninformed and uncomfortable. The chairperson can change such an unproductive and inhumane environment by careful use of "brainstorming." Brainstorming is a technique used when divergent thinking is needed in a meeting in order to generate many ideas. It equalizes participation, encourages creativity and adds excitement and variety to decision making. The rules for brainstorming should be presented before the exercise begins. These rules are:

1. all ideas will be recorded
2. wild, crazy ideas are encouraged, quantity counts
3. no discussion or evaluation of an idea is allowed during the brainstorm
4. building on the ideas of others is encouraged
5. definite time limit is placed on the session
6. repetition is allowed
7. no drifting from the topic until time has expired

The chair has at least two ways of conducting the brainstorming session.

THE FREE FOR ALL. Any board member can contribute ideas at will. This has the advantage of giving free reign to the most imaginative and quick members. The obvious disadvantage is that some members will have a hard time getting their contributions heard and recorded.

THE ROUND-ROBIN. Each board member in turn gives one idea. Members are free to "pass" if they have no ideas, need time to clarify their thoughts or are uncomfortable with the process. This approach has the advantage of controlling participation so that both those anxious and reluctant to talk get to be involved without being either unnecessarily forced or unduly restrained.

Shared or Functional Leadership

There are so many functions to be performed in a meeting that no human being can possibly perform them all well, yet some people still think that the "leader" must do everything. This is the traditional concept of leadership. Shared leadership, on the other hand, implies that all persons in a meeting are responsible for carrying out the necessary leadership functions. Power in a group meeting is shared by everyone present: The power to "chair" a meeting is just one of the ways power may be exercised.

Task and Maintenance Problems

When a board gets together it can expect to encounter both task and interpersonal problems. Task difficulties may take the following forms: An unclear job, lack of information to solve the problem, or an insufficient amount of time in which to complete the task. Interpersonal, or maintenance difficulties involve that which is happening between and with group members while they are working on a task. Maintenance problems include leadership struggles and communications problems. Paying attention to interpersonal issues includes examining such items as morale, meeting atmosphere, participation, styles of influence, conflict, competition and cooperation.

In many meetings, very little attention is paid to the processes of human interaction. Knowing about and being sensitive to group process will enable board members to diagnose problems early and to solve them more effectively.

The ideal situation is one in which a balance is struck between task and maintenance processes. If the board concentrates only on the task, the job may get done, but the group members will not feel "ownership" of the project and will tend to hold negative feelings about the board. ("I'll never volunteer to work on that board again!"). If a group only focuses their attention on maintenance, everyone may have a wonderful time in the short run, but little gets accomplished: Confusion and frustration result as surely as when task is over-attended to.

The nature of the leadership functions which are needed in a meeting varies with different situations and from one moment to another. At one moment someone needs to break the silence. Ten minutes later, as Susan Knowitall goes into the tenth paragraph of her favorite monologue, someone needs to perform the function of limiting the length of her contribution. At another point, the group appears to be blocked because it needs a procedure for moving ahead with its work. The first two examples are maintenance functions; the third is a task function.

In order to know what leadership functions are needed, members must be able to diagnose the meeting difficulties by sensing the group's needs or its missing functions. Shared leadership uses the resources of more members and stimulates creativity, higher group morale, interest and concern. Exhibit 5-1 illustrates some membership-leadership tasks and maintenance functions that can be performed by any member. Behaviors that are not helpful are also noted.

EXHIBIT 5-1: Task and Maintenance Leadership Functions

Task Functions

Functions required in selecting and carrying out a group task:

Initiating. Suggesting ways to proceed, ideas for solving a problem or ways to tackle a task

Seeking Information or Opinions. Asking for facts, ideas, opinions, feelings, feedback on or clarification of suggestions

Giving Information or Opinions. Offering facts or generalizations, giving ideas and suggestions, providing relevant information

Clarifying and Elaborating. Interpreting ideas or suggestions, clearing up confusion, defining terms, indicating alternatives and issues before the group, presenting examples, developing meanings

Summarizing. Attempting to summarize what has been discussed, pulling together related ideas

Consensus Testing. Asking if a group is nearing a decision, offering a decision or conclusion for the group to accept or reject

Continued

Maintenance Functions

Functions required in strengthening and maintaining group life and activities.

Harmonizing. Attempting to reconcile disagreements, reducing tension, getting members to explore differences.

Gate Keeping. Helping others to get into the discussion, suggesting procedures that permit remarks by all.

Encouraging. Being warm, friendly and responsive to others, indicating by facial expression or remarks the acceptance of others' contributions, praising others and their ideas

Compromising. When your own idea or status is involved in a conflict, offering a compromise which yields status, admitting error, modifying position in the interest of group cohesion or growth

Standard Setting and Testing. Testing whether the group is satisfied with its procedures or suggesting procedures; pointing out explicit or implicit norms which have been set

Expressing Group Feelings. Sharing own feelings, expressing perceptions of the feelings of the group

Non-Facilitative Behaviors

Some behaviors are not helpful and detract from the group's work.

Aggressing. Criticizing others, attacking others or the group, insulting colleagues

Blocking. Pursuing tangents, talking about personal experiences unrelated to the problem, arguing "beyond reason" without hearing others

Withdrawing. Acting indifferent or unconcerned; being passive or uninvolved in the group task in an attempt to avoid the source of uncomfortable feelings

Competing. Trying to produce the best ideas, talk the most, and be the most popular

Dependency-Counterdependency. Leaning on or resisting anyone in the group who represents authority

Process as an Agenda Item

Allow fifteen to twenty minutes at the end of the meeting to reflect on how the meeting went and how people worked together. Some questions to raise: "How did the group feel about the meeting today?" "How does each of us feel about the decisions made, their participation and the participation of others?"

One of the board's norms can be that if the work on a task isn't moving smoothly during a meeting, then a board member may stop the task and ask the group to spend a few minutes examining how they have been interacting and feeling. The purpose of this break is to re-establish the working relationships necessary to function effectively. Releasing feelings and clearing the air is appropriate at such times.

A member can suggest that each member, in turn, state his/her feelings and thoughts as they were working on the task. For example, at a recent meeting a group could not get anywhere with the task before it. There was a great deal of disagreement and many members were silent during the interchanges among a few. A board member suggested going around the room and having each person express his or her feelings about the past few minutes of work. Comments would be placed on newspring and hung on the wall. By listening to the feelings of each member, the real issue was identified as a power struggle between two members. Silent members then began to participate and the dominant ones to listen more to others.

"Going around the room" is also an excellent way to start or end a meeting. At the start of the meeting, having each member say something helps members to feel involved and included in the meeting. Dealing with maintenance of the group before the meeting begins helps to avoid later interpersonal difficulties. As a wrap-up to a meeting, this procedure can surface important issues or feelings people did not feel comfortable identifying earlier in the meeting. Valuable information is produced that can help improve future meetings.

Feedback in Meetings

Specific actions, functions, or personal styles and strategies on the part of one or more people may influence meeting effectiveness. Thus, it is legitimate to give people feedback during or after the meeting. The objective of feedback is to share data about behavior so that difficulties can be resolved. Through receiving this information, a person can discover the influence his or her actions and words have upon others in the group. All feedback should reflect a genuine willingness to work cooperatively and be more effective together. The guidelines shown in Exhibit 5-2 should be followed to ensure that feedback is effective.

EXHIBIT 5-2: Guidelines for Feedback

Descriptive
It is descriptive rather than evaluative. By describing one's own reaction to the behavior of the other, the recipient is free to use the feedback or ignore it.

Specific
It is specific rather than general. To be told that one is dominating will probably not be as useful as to be told that "just now when we were deciding the issue, I felt forced to accept your arguments or face rebuttal from you."

Appropriate
It takes into account the needs of both the receiver and the giver of feedback. Feedback can be destructive when it serve only one's needs and fails to consider the needs of the person receiving the feedback.

Useable
It is directed toward behavior which the receiver can do something about. Frustration is only increased when a person is reminded of a perceived shortcoming over which he or she has no control.

Requested
It is solicited rather than imposed. Feedback is most effective when the receiver has formulated the question which the observers can answer.

Timely
It is well timed. In general, feedback that is given at the earliest possible time following the behavior is most useful.

Clear
It is checked for clarity of communication. Asking the receiver of the feedback to rephrase the comments is a simple way to ascertain clarity.

Accurate.
When feedback is given, both the giver and receiver have an opportunity to ascertain the accuracy of the feedback by soliciting observations from other members of the group. It is important to remember that not all the members of the group see and interpret behavior in the same way. We often see that which we are prepared to see. Telling Ralph that "your comment makes me boil" is more accurate and helpful than to say "your comment is inflammatory." It could well be the case that the comments only inflamed you.

Process Observer

Some groups appoint a "process observer" for each meeting or hire a consultant for this purpose. The role of the observer is to improve the effectiveness of the meeting. The observer usually takes little part in the task discussions, but carefully watches what occurs during the entire meeting. The observer may occasionally stop the meeting and ask members to look at what has been happening to them as they work on their tasks. Observers, in reporting to the group, follow the guidelines for feedback described in Exhibit 5-2. A process checklist which might be used by an observer is shown as Exhibit 5-3.

EXHIBIT 5-3: Process Review Checklist

Who did or did not participate in the discussion?

Who participated the most? The least?

How clear were the goals of the meeting?

How well did people listen to each other?

How were decisions made?

Were difficult issues dealt with thoroughly?

Were conflict and differences encouraged?

Were creative ideas suggested? By all? By a few?

What were the most helpful actions?

Was the time well spent?

Were feelings as well as information and opinions discussed?

What was the group atmosphere during the meeting? Did it change?

What leadership functions were exhibited? Absent?

Decision Making at Meetings

Many boards experience difficulty at the point of making decisions. Some members become paralyzed when confronted with a decision; some argue interminably over a minor point; others rush to a vote, only to reverse their decision later (or fail to carry it out); others appoint a committee or look for a savior to deliver them from having to make a decision.

By their very nature, decisions suggest conflict or controversy which many people believe is negative and to be avoided at all costs. There is often social pressure to conform during group meetings. Groups often quickly agree, believing that relationships among its members are so fragile that conflict will be destructive. Some group members will choose to keep their disagreements to themselves or voice them to a few board members after the meeting. This is unfortunate. When managed well, conflict can be highly constructive and essential to effective problem solving during board meetings.

In our competitive world most people conceive of conflict in "win-or-lose" terms. Someone must win and someone must lose. Individuals push the board to choose their ideas rather than work with the whole group to find a mutually acceptable solution to the board's common problem. Common examples of disruptive conflict behaviors include:

- taking a "win-lose" position
- aggressive, personal attacks on board members
- withdrawing or denying that a conflict exists
- smoothing over negative feelings or ideas
- forming cliques simply to push an idea from a "win-lose" position

Making effective decisions when such behaviors are being exhibited is, at best, difficult. Attempts to reach a decision under such conditions will normally result in a conclusion that dissatisfies most members or fails to gain the commitment of many of the board.

Constructive conflict occurs when board members take a "win-win" stance, believing that the best ideas and decisions occur when disagreement is openly encouraged and undertaken with high commitment and spirit.

Choose an appropriate time in the meeting to deal with conflict. To start a discussion that is bound to involve differences of opinion fifteen minutes before the time of adjournment, or when many of those in opposition are absent, is detrimental to the life of the board. Trust and group cohesion are increased when conflict is faced openly in a supportive atmosphere. Board members then reach decisions which they feel are prudent and they also feel good about the processes used.

Boards also experience other difficulties in reaching decisions which center around two factors. First, there may be reservations about the consequence of the decisions. In some boards, the possible outcomes of an impending decision may bring divisions, disagreements and litigation. Frank acknowledgement of these reservations or fears often causes board members to identify effective solutions to the problems. The second factor is conflicting loyalties. Board members often belong to any number of other boards and organizations which frequently can lead to divided loyalties. An atmosphere in which it is possible to bring conflicts out into the open without threat to the individual is a major factor in conflict resolution.

A prime measure of a board's decision making effectiveness is the degree of commitment its members show to their decisions. Decisions are also affected by: (1) the number of group members actively participating in making the decision, and (2) what happens to individual members in the process of making decisions.

People tend to support an action if they feel they have been given an opportunity to participate in making that decision. With high levels of participation, they will be more committed to carrying out any needed actions resulting from the board's decisions.

The following exhibit describes various types of group decisions.

EXHIBIT 5-4: Types of Group Decisions

Self-authorized. A decision made by one member of the board who assumes authority from the group to do so. The board may find it expedient to concur with such a decision rather than become involved in the processes leading to a decision.

Handclasping. A decision made by two members of the board joining forces. Such a decision usually emerges so suddenly that it catches the group unprepared, thus presenting the board with the more complex problem of dealing with a team.

Cliques. Decision made by segments of the group outside of a regular group meeting and acted out at a subsequent meeting. The perceived necessity for a few members to make decisions in this way further divides the board into competing factions.

Baiting. "Does anybody disagree that...?" "We all agree that this is needed, don't we?" When the climate of the board inhibits open discussion of ideas and concerns, decisions made by the implied threat of conflict tend to be short-lived and carried out, if at all, with minimal commitment.

Majority rule. A decision made by some form of voting. Vote tallying tends to solidify opposing forces, lowering the losing factions' commitment to the decision and negatively influencing future decisions by establishing competitive factions within the group.

Unanimity. A decision apparently made by complete

Continued

---

agreement of the board. Pressure to conform may be strong enough to force overt consent, but tends to bury opposition. If pressure to conform is not sufficiently strong and the group feels that unanimous decisions are required, then the board will find itself unable to conclude discussions and move to action.

Consensus. A decision made after all aspects of the issue and all possible solutions are heard and dealt with until all members feel that the board's choice is the most operable under the circumstances. Because of the open participation, boards that make decision by consensus tend to experience deeper commitment.

Effective decision making by a board on the basis of consensus is both realistic and possible. It is not, however, always easy. Six steps should be followed by the board that wishes to use a consensus style in an effective manner. These steps are outlined in Exhibit 5-5, below.

EXHIBIT 5-5: A Decision Making Model

1. Define the problem. The process of defining the problem and sharpening the focus so that the issue(s) is clear and understood by the board members.

   Blocks: the assumption that the problem is clear; over-abstraction of the problem

   Helps: small group discussions to clarify the problem; general discussion; redefinition of the problem

2. Identifying Selection or Decision Criteria. The process of getting agreement among the members on the factors or criteria they will use to choose the solution or make the decision.

   Blocks: feeling of insufficient time; extreme value differences in the board; assumption that "everyone thinks the same"; low trust in the group; dominance by the chairperson

   Helps: group discussions; brainstorming lists; small groups

Continued

3. Suggesting Alternative Solutions. The process of getting members to suggest the various alternative solutions to the problem.

 Block: lack of data; lack of experience; group size; strained formality; inadequate attention to maintenance functions; limiting the search for alternatives

 Helps: brainstorming; gathering data; fostering a climate of freedom; thoughtful and quiet contemplation

4. Testing the Alternatives. The process of examining the alternatives in light of all the available data, past experience, possible consequence, relevance to the problem and members' attitudes

 Blocks: lack of data; premature voting; over-protection of ideas by members; inadequate maintenance functions; dominance by a few members

 Helps: group discussion; reality testing; expression of feelings by all members

5. Choosing Among Alternatives. The process of reaching a decision by choosing one of the alternatives or a combination of alternatives that will solve the problem.

 Blocks: inadequate testing; lack of clarity about the problem; premature voting; no testing the strength of the consensus; avoiding the need for making a decision

 Helps: expression of feelings by all members; maintaining an agenda for future reference; summarizing the discussion; thorough probing to insure the existence of a consensus

6. Planning for Action. The process of making detailed plans for carrying out the decision by examining the implications of the choice and testing the proposed action. It should be noted that the planning step, at times, results in the board rethinking the decision and returning to one of the prior steps in the consensus model.

 Blocks: failure to reach consensus; failure to

—— Continued

EXHIBIT: Continued

> explore adequately the implications
> of the proposed action; assignment of
> total responsibility for implementation
> to an inappropriately sized group
>
> Helps: feedback; observer reports; evaluation;
> post-meeting reaction reports; data
> analysis; climate of freedom

Conclusion

Board decision making is, at times, exhausting, enraging and elusive. At other times, the effective board will find its decisions are easily made and cheerfully carried through.

Unavoidably, however, it is the board that is charged with making major decisions that will determine the quality of the nonprofit corporation's life. Proper attention to task and maintenance functions will insure that meetings will be productive and exciting times for the members.

Further Readings

B. Biagi, WORKING TOGETHER: A MANUAL FOR HELPING GROUPS WORK MORE EFFECTIVELY. Amherst, MA: Citizen Involvement Training Project, 1978

L. Bradford, MAKING MEETINGS WORK: A GUIDE FOR LEADERS AND GROUP MEMBERS. LaJolla, CA: University Associates, 1976

Bills Communications, Inc., MANUAL FOR SMALL MEETINGS. Philadelphia, 1977

M. Doyle and D. Staus, HOW TO MAKE MEETINGS WORK. Chicago: Playboy Press, 1977

Leslie G. Lawson, Franklyn Donant and John Lawson, LEAD ON! THE COMPLETE HANDBOOK FOR GROUP LEADERS. San Luis Obispo, CA: Impact Publishers, 1982

Rensis Likert and Jane Likert, "A Method for Coping with Conflict in Problem Solving Groups," GROUP AND ORGANIZATIONAL STUDIES JOURNAL. Vol. 3, No.4, 1978

Public Management Institute, SUCCESSFUL MEETINGS. San Francisco: Public Management Institute, 1980

Jerry Robinson and Roy A. Clifford, TEAM SKILLS IN COMMUNITY GROUPS. Urbana, IL: University of Illinois at Urbana-Champaign, Cooperative Extension Service, 1977

Jerry Robinson and Roy A. Clifford, LEADERSHIP ROLES IN COMMUNITY GROUPS. Urbana, IL: University of Illinois at Urbana-Champaign, Cooperative Extension Service, 1977

A. Swanson, THE DETERMINATIVE TEAM: A HANDBOOK FOR BOARD MEMBERS OF VOLUNTARY ORGANIZATIONS. Hicksville, NY: Exposition Press, 1978

Joseph Weber, MANAGING THE BOARD OF DIRECTORS. New York: The Greater New York Fund, 1975

Mike Woodcock and Dave Francis, UNBLOCKING YOUR ORGANIZATION. La Jolla, CA: University Associates, 1975

Chapter 6

Relationships: The Key to Effective Committees

Eileen (Guthrie) Collard

in collaboration with

Sandra M. Haff

Sooner or later, most boards of directors find it necessary to form committees. To a large degree, the secrets for developing and maintaining effective committees lie in the realm of art, not science, since there are few fixed rules that can guarantee success. Nonetheless, certain principles that contribute to committee functioning can be identified. This chapter will present some specific examples and models for thinking about committees, with particular emphasis on interpersonal relationships that occur within committee settings.

No committee exists in a vacuum. Rather, it exists in a web of expectations and relationships, all of which are set within a broader context of time, organization, community, and institutional dynamics. The work of a committee is inherently political in that its dynamics revolve around issues of power, influence, expertise, self-interest, and interpersonal effectiveness.

An effective committee, within that context, is one that knows itself, is clear about its responsibilities and relationships to others, and is flexible over time. No committee can expect to operate without conflict nor can it expect to be successful all of the time. No committee can hope to represent everyone, nor can it hope to accomplish anything overnight. Committee members must give themselves permission to disagree, take their time, and fail as they work toward their long range goals. The conscious process of sharing ideas, personalities, and dreams can result in decisions and actions that make sense and help us all strengthen our organizations and, in turn, our communities.

Purpose of Committees

Committees are established for a variety of reasons. Sometimes, they're needed to help spread out the work load of the board. At other times, a committee is needed to develop a special expertise that will enable the board to act more responsibly on an issue. Other committees are formed to save time, to perpetuate tradition, or to handle a continuing responsibility for the organization.

On the negative side, committees sometimes are set up to kill an idea or project. Forming a committee may be a way to avoid an issue, or it may appease dissident members and diffuse their energy. In addition, committees may be formed because no one knows what else to do to address a problem.

Types of Committees

Committees vary a great deal from one another. They vary in the degree of autonomy they have in relation to the board. They vary in their duration and may be set up either as an ongoing body or with a limited life. They vary in their style of operation, ranging from slow moving study groups to fast paced crisis teams.

> A board of directors of a mental health project had five standing committees, as spelled out in its bylaws: Outreach and Public Relations, Finance and Fund Raising, Personnel, Program Development and Evaluation, and Special Events. From time to time, other committees were set up on an ad hoc basis and given a specific task to complete. New members could only join at the annual meeting.
>
> On the other hand, a food cooperative was set up loosely to enable new members to join at any time. A number of project teams were formed as needed, with open-ended membership, each of which disbanded as soon as its particular job was done.

The variations are unlimited and depend on a particular organization's needs, style, and philosophy. Even in the case of formal committees established in bylaws, change and flexibility are possible since bylaws can be amended and temporary task forces can always be set up to meet unanticipated needs.

Basic Needs of Effective Committees

Despite the variations among committees, there are some needs which all effective committees must address.

1. All Committees Need Clear Direction.

Committees need to know what their task is and when it must be completed. This does not limit their scope, but it states a minimum expectation on the part of the board of directors and lets the committee members know when they are done. It is important that the board be realistic in determining the "charge" to the committee, taking into account the resources available, the experience of the members, and the nature of the task.

To be meaningful, a committee's charge should include a statement of required tasks, the staff support and funds available, the scope of authority of the committee, a timetable for completion of the task, and some idea of the reporting mechanism that is desired. The purpose of the charge is not to limit the committee's work; rather it is to provide a clear statement of what the board expects. If it is not possible to be very specific, be clear in letting the potential committee know that "all we have is an idea for now."

Exhibit 6-1 shows the written direction received by a sub-committee on crime prevention from a board of directors.

2. All Committees Need Written Records.

Because of the nature of committee work and since so many different people are likely to be involved during the life of any single committee, the written communication system of any committee is vitally important. Written documentation of committee action serves to provide a sense of continuity and history to a committee as well as to interested others. Meeting minutes are useful to refresh members' memories about the ultimate goals toward which they are working, to minimize confusion for new members, and to settle differences of opinion. For legal purposes and in the event of any dispute, committees should keep accurate records of all formal decisions they make. Minutes also perform an accountability function in case there is ever any question about the committee's activities or intentions. They also provide a means of reporting to the broader community if that is desired.

3. All Committees Need To Succeed.

The key to achieving success is to develop a plan of action that incorporates short term, achievable objectives into an overall long range vision. Committee members who experience a feeling of accomplishment and can see that they are moving toward their goal are more likely to stay involved. Short term objectives are most effective when they can be reached in six to eight weeks: Delaying gratification beyond that does not work. A short term objective of a human services council was to hold a community wide "teach in" on service needs within two months.

Successes, both short and long term, need to be acknowledged and celebrated. It can be great fun, in fact, for committee members to plan to celebrate the achievement of each short term objective in a different way! Going out for a beer, holding a potluck dinner party, or seeking local press coverage are good ways to celebrate accomplishments.

EXHIBIT 6-1: Sample Committee Charge

Crime Prevention Sub-Committee

Goal: To reduce crime and fear of crime in our neighborhood.

When?	What?
December	1. Learn techniques from Minneapolis Community Crime Prevention staff for training crime prevention specialists (neighborhood residents) in the neighborhood.
Jan. - March	2. Sponsor communitywide programs in areas that appear relevant to neighborhood residents such as (a) rape prevention, (b) personal safety, and (c) purse snatching prevention. This must be done in conjunction with the board.
Ongoing	3. Establish ongoing rapport with police to keep lines of communication open.
Ongoing	4. Confront citywide policies which have an impact on crime prevention in our neighborhood, such as: (a) Flame Bar closing and (b) Closing of 6th precinct.
January - ?	5. Serve on 5th Precinct Advisory Board
Ongoing	6. Work with other committees as required.

--Monthly reports to the board of directors are required to be submitted by the committee chair.

--No staff support is available, but up to $200 can be used for events.

--This program is **not** designed to serve as a vigilante group or to
  serve as a vehicle for racism. It is designed to educate people
  with specific crime prevention techniques and to foster self-help
  and self-awareness.

---

4. All Committees Need Healthy Working Relationships Among Their Members
   and With Others.

   Committees which operate in isolation cannot operate effectively.

Members need to maintain both formal and informal contact with other board committees and with others who are likely to be affected by their actions. They also need to maintain positive relationships with organizations or community groups with whom they have similar interests or goals.

This does not mean that they must always agree with everyone. In fact, the healthiest committees regularly air differences of opinion. What makes them healthy is that they are skilled at analyzing the type of conflict that exists, building on their group's diversity, and developing win/win approaches to problem solving.

Healthy working relationships imply trust. Unless members have some personal contact with each other, they cannot be expected to trust each other. Thus, in planning a committee's activities, it is vital that attention be paid to helping members learn about each other. If there is informal contact outside of the meetings among members, then not so much time needs to be spent within the formal meetings for trust building activities. The point is, though, that formal discussions of "trust" do not build it; encouraging opportunities for self-disclosure and personal contact among members does.

Getting off on the Right Foot: Team Building

Of the four basic needs of effective committees, the most difficult to address is the one related to building healthy relationships. In preparation for writing this chapter, Sandra interviewed people to find out what they wanted to learn about having effective committees. Almost all of the responses related to interpersonal relationships involving conflicts, power struggles, motivation and group building.

All groups go through various stages of development as they deal with different issues and individuals. Committee members' needs in relation to these variables change over time, as do external conditions affecting the committee's work.

The key to good working relationships in light of these constantly shifting circumstances is to talk about what's going on. Open communication channels and regular evaluations of how the board, committees, and community are relating can enable the committee to be flexible and adapt appropriately to changes. In contrast, if there are no opportunities for looking at ways for people to work together better, problems are bound to get worse, and it becomes harder and harder to succeed.

> One board requested that each committee's monthly report include comments about how committee meetings were going, in addition to the summary of their work-to-date. Board members were invited to offer suggestions in response to task and process related problems that were mentioned.
>
> At the end of each meeting, the chairperson asks the

members to quickly state what they liked, disliked,
and learned during the meeting. This frequently leads
to discussion of concrete ways to improve meetings and
increases members' satisfaction.

Processing meetings (that is, talking about how they went) may also
include deciding how to decide an issue currently before the committee.
Too often, committees assume that the only way to make a decision is by
Robert's Rules of Order. This is not so. Depending on the issues and
group style, committees can choose among a number of procedures for decision
making, including majority vote, consensus, and minority reporting. They
should also realize that not to decide is, in fact, to decide. The key to
coming to decisions in an effective way, then, is to talk about the decision making process in addition to the discussion of the task at hand.

Several committee members thought meetings lasted
too long. They decided to ask the other members what
they thought about the practice of allowing everyone
to speak and never cutting off discussion. Almost
all the members expressed a preference for open-
ended debates; the two who preferred a time limit
agreed to go along with the rest but serve as
process observers to point out when remarks seemed
to get repetitious. Everyone agreed to try that
for the next two months and then talk about it again.

Relationships can get touchy sometimes, especially if there are
differences in values. If a committee strongly disagrees with board
policy, for instance, it may not be possible for the committee to continue.

The official board policy endorsed the construction
of low-income housing units in the neighborhood.
Difficulties arose when the Housing Committee, with
its open-door membership policy, found that the
majority of its members were in opposition to the
official board position.

This situation might have been avoided by making sure that new
members were aware of the committee's operating policies before they
joined. Nevertheless, there are bound to be struggles from time to time
between the board and its committees, as they deal with turf, power,
recognition, trust, philosophy, and authority questions. These periodic
struggles are not anyone's "fault"; rather, they are an inevitable feature
of human interaction and, as such, need to be acknowledged, dealt with
directly and not swept under the carpet and denied. Also, it's important
to remember that when it comes down to the wire, the board itself is the
legally recognized entity and bears legal responsibility for decisions. The
fact of the matter is that all committees of a board are subordinate to the
board.

The relationship between a committee and the staff also deserves
mention. In some situations, committees are little more than rubber

stamps. Working committees, however, must negotiate these relationships and divide its tasks. In general, it's best to assume that there won't be staff around at all. This mindset helps insure that the committee takes the main role and minimizes the chances of the staff "taking over."

The staff's role can fluctuate between providing support, doing behind the scenes research, taking care of busywork that volunteers shouldn't have to do, lining up materials, or preparing discussion documents. An extremely valuable role for staff is to concentrate on helping the committee develop good decision making and leadership skills, by helping the members to put together agendas, prepare for meetings, and learn from the staff.

> A community mental health center hired a part-time
> "process coordinator" to teach committee members
> how to conduct effective meetings. She was responsible
> for sending out notices and minutes, working with
> committee members to orient new people, and providing
> personal support and encouragement to committee
> people who had never served on a board before.

Again, the key to good committee/staff relationships is to maintain explicit channels for open discussion about how the relationship is going.

Relations between committees also need attention. At least some contact between committee chairpersons is a good idea in order to avoid duplication and assure cooperation. Some of this exchange occurs at board meetings, but some has to be sought through other channels.

A sometimes overlooked relationship is between the committee and its constituency —those people who are potentially affected by decisions. This may include clients, district residents, or the more nebulous body of supporters out in the community who think the committee's work is important.

> An advocacy organization had an Outreach Committee
> to keep the community informed through a variety
> of means. On a monthly basis, articles were
> submitted to neighborhood newspapers in the form
> of "Dear John" letters in response to questions
> raised by residents. Public service announcements
> were used, along with leaflets and doorknocking.
> From the other side, community thoughts were solicited
> by talking with people in the neighborhood, listening
> to street corner conversations, and checking with the
> staff receptionist who frequently picked up informa-
> tion from residents who stopped by.

This job of maintaining two way communication with the constituency may be the job of the board itself, or it may be more within a particular committee's realm. In any case, do not forget the importance of keeping these channels open and active.

Getting down to Business

The creation of a healthy working committee begins early, even before its first meeting. Basically, a clear "charge" must be agreed upon by the board and a convenor should be selected.

> The board of directors of the Community Development Corporation formed a committee to study a new program idea and present a recommendation to the board in six months about whether or not the board should make a change in services. A staff member was assigned to spend up to six hours per week on committee work and a board member was appointed to set up and convene an initial meeting within the next month.

It is imperative of the convenor to carefully consider the purpose and format of the first meeting since this is often the best opportunity to set the tone for things to come. New or potential members can be expected to attend for the purpose of sizing up both what the group will be doing and whether or not they will fit in.

Since it's easier to get people to attend one session than it is to recruit them for a committee, calling the initial meeting an "Information Session" is a good idea. A number of activities are important prior to the information session: Logistics have to be arranged, a tentative agenda and handouts must be prepared, and invitations need to be distributed. Each of these components must be thought through and used as a way to set the over-all tone; shortcuts at this stage simply do not pay off!

Potential committee members can be recruited through a variety of approaches. It is usually best to employ several means of recruiting members, including phone contacts, media announcements, personal invitations, doorknocking, and word-of-mouth. If people with particular expertise are needed, additional efforts may be required with help from other board members or staff. Several reminders about the meeting, including a personal contact a day or two before, let potential members know they're wanted, gives them a chance to ask questions, and gives the convenor the opportunity to "sell" the committee and begin establishing a relationship. Remember, too, that flattery, if it's sincere, can get you far in your recruiting processes!

It also may be useful to do a one page description of the new committee with: a description of the charge, a statement of desired member characteristics, benefits of committee membership, the date/time/place of the information session and the name of the person(s) who can give further information. This can be circulated during recruitment efforts and at the information session.

The convenor's responsibility for setting the tone of the information session cannot be emphasized too much. It includes paying attention to details about the location and the image that the site conjures up for potential committee members.

Since many of the potential members of the new Parent Advisory Committee had not participated in meetings before, the information session was held in someone's home, beginning with light refreshments. A child care worker was available to supervise the children at a nearby playground during the meeting.

The information session for a citywide planning group was held in a public building located near downtown buslines. The convenor arranged the chairs in a square so that people would be able to see each other. Name tags and coffee were provided to encourage people to visit informally before the session began. The proposed agenda was posted within sight of all.

Cues, such as the physical accessibility of a meeting place and the availability of name tags and refreshments, are not insignificant; they let potential committee members know that their presence is truly welcomed and appreciated.

The agenda for the information session might include time for people to introduce themselves and tell how they happen to be there, followed by time to brainstorm and discuss questions they have about the committee. The final step could be a summary of the discussion and a request that people reach decisions within a week about whether or not they would like to make a commitment to join.

The follow-up to the information session also needs attention, as potential members think about whether to commit themselves and what they have to contribute. Personal follow-up contacts are best for finding out individuals' decisions and exploring alternative ways for them to participate. For example, someone who is not able to join the committee might want to contribute informally as a behind the scenes advisor. Once people have agreed to participate, a regular meeting time can be set and the convenor can schedule and plan the first regular committee meeting.

It is no tragedy if only a few people agree to serve on the committee. These few form a core group and can begin work, including an assessment of whether membership needs to be expanded and, if so, how that can happen.

If a staff person convened the information session, the follow-up process must include consideration of how and when a regular committee member will take over that leadership function. It may take some time until members feel ready to accept the responsibility, but the transfer should not be delayed too long. In the meantime, the staff member can work with a committee person to plan meetings and prepare for them.

Bringing in New Members

Formal orientation to a committee usually takes place at the start of each year, or when a number of new members are starting at the same time. Attention is needed to both task related aspects of the committee's work and the maintenance related aspects concerning how the members work together.

> Each year, the Finance Committee schedules an orientation picnic hosted by old members for the benefit of new people. A cheerful invitation, together with some background materials, is mailed out to new members two weeks in advance. Each person is asked to read the information and to bring his or her favorite cheese to the potluck gathering. A new T-shirt is sent as a special bonus.

The orientation builds on the Information Session by giving new members an idea of what will be expected from them, some background information, and a chance to raise questions about the committee.

Individuals join a committee for a number of reasons. An orientation process needs to acknowledge the variety of reasons for joining and give members "permission" to take steps to get what they want in an open manner. A committee that fails to do this only promotes hidden agendas and unmotivated members.

As orientation needs continue, particular attention should be paid to creating opportunities for old and new members to interact informally. This can be accomplished through a variety of means and is the key to building trust among committee members.

> The Education Committee of a child care agency offered new members some options when they joined. They could: (1) participate in a "buddy system" to pair them up with someone who'd been on the committee for a while; (2) attend the pre-meeting training sessions held each month, in order to practice effective communication, lobbying, conflict resolution, and assertiveness skills; or (3) help organize the quarterly potluck dinner for the whole agency board.

> Although the activities were not mandatory, nearly all of the committee members took advantage of at least two of them and felt their ability to contribute had been enhanced.

Other Dimensions of Effective Committees

The ongoing maintenance of a committee requires that some other dimensions and dynamics be kept in mind. Some of these are briefly noted below.

Member Roles: Much has been written about the various roles that are needed within a group for it to function well. (See EXHIBIT 5-1,

Task and Maintenance Leadership Functions.) In summary, these roles relate to both work and interpersonal functions that need to be performed in a group.

Some additional roles that are needed, particularly when a committee is composed of volunteers are:

- <u>Cheerleader</u> who reminds the committee of its successes, keeps energy flowing, and injects humor and fun into the group.

- <u>Handholder/Nurturer</u> who supports the involvement of quiet members, encourages their risk-taking, and coaches those who are hesitant to express themselves.

- <u>Payer</u> who pays attention to the rewards and stroking systems of the committee and makes sure that both personal contributions and committee accomplishments are talked about and recognized.

These vital roles can be taken by committee members or by staff; it is important that the need for them is consistently addressed.

The leadership role can be viewed as a function to share within a committee, according to expertise, time availability, skill, interest, and desire to learn. Anyone who helps the committee move toward its shared goals can be said to be performing a leadership function.

<u>Member Motivation:</u> Committee members are motivated when they see that they will get something from their involvement. Thus, the question of motivation (and its flip side, apathy) is basically a question of self-interest. As mentioned, people join committees for a number of reasons. They hope to meet new friends, gain financially, learn skills, make professional contacts, contribute to a worthy cause, accomplish something, gain experience or information, win a battle, or even be a "star." None of these motives is inherently bad. Unless members receive some personal payoff, they can't be expected to stay around.

Members' motivation changes over time. Members may resign because their priorities shift and they can no longer devote time, because they do not feel important or they do not know how to cope with conflict they are experiencing with another member. Sometimes, they resign out of boredom, lack of interest, or simply because it's time for them to move on to something new.

As a regular part of its routine, a Long Range Planning Committee has its staff person contact members who have missed three meetings to find out whether their absences have been for personal reasons or because of some concern related to the committee and its operation. If appropriate, that

65

concern can then be talked about by the committee
as a way to prevent more dropouts.

Group Development Phases: Another dimension of committee life
relates to its developmental stages (see Exhibit 6-2, "Group Development
Phases: Identifying Them and What to Do"). At first, group members are
dependent on the leader for information about what to do. As they get more
comfortable, they move into a period (counter-dependency) where they challenge the leadership and seek to establish their own spheres of influence,
ownership, and control. Eventually, healthy committees develop interdependent styles that enable them to draw on each other in constructive ways.
Although variations may occur in this sequence of developmental stages,
they are unusual. Awareness of these phases, in relation to individuals,
issues, and the whole committee, can provide insight into the psychology of
committees and help members not take things too personally.

Differences: No two committee members are alike. Successful committees must go through a team building process which leads members to accept
and value the diverse world views of committee members. Such affirmation of
differences requires a high level of trust and respect among the group.

Conflicts are bound to arise in committees, over tactics, goals,
philosophy, or style. Some are irreconcilable, with the only approach
being to acknowledge that differences exist, accept them, and move on to
work on shared issues. The avoidance of conflict, however, leads nowhere
and often results in sabotage, behind the scenes maneuvering, and intense
frustration or anger. Conflict resolution approaches that build on individual differences can be valuable for helping a committee sort out its
issues, identify areas of agreement, and pinpoint those areas where members
will probably never agree. The members can then "agree to disagree" on
some questions and take joint action on points where there is agreement.

Endings: Committees frequently outlive their usefulness. Unfortunately, there are not many graceful ways to terminate a committee and, as a
result, the termination process may get messy.

One committee began suspecting that its demise was
at hand when the board denied its budget request,
tabled its report for three meetings in a row, and
neglected to notify the members about a change
in the meeting date.

On the other hand, boards can adopt norms that recognize the need
for committees to end (similar to "Sunset Laws") or, at least, renegotiate
their task and relationship to the board of directors. Timelines for the
completion of specific tasks imply a renegotiation once the tasks are done,
as an example. Sometimes, a funeral-like ritual may ease the break-up of a
long standing committee and formally acknowledge the start of new
relationships between those members and the board.

Committees can relieve the awkwardness related to individuals'
leaving by talking about endings during the orientation and making explicit

EXHIBIT 6-2: Group Development Phases: Identifying Them and What To Do

Development Phase	Characteristics	Appropriate Actions To Be Taken
Dependence	1. Few members participate. 2. The leader is allowed to be in charge. 3. The leader must push for implementation of decisions. 4. Members appear passive.	1. Actively include members in discussions at a low risk level. 2. Support the skills that the members already possess. 3. Pay attention to maintenance activities.
Counter-dependence	1. The leader is frequently challenged by the members. 2. A great deal of behind the scenes activity goes on. 3. The leader feels puzzled and ineffective. 4. The leader and members feel separated from each other. 5. Decisions are not carried out. 6. The members blame the leader for the groups problems. 7. Cliques are formed. 8. Internal personality clashes are evident.	1. Acknowledge what is happening in the group. 2. Encourage the leader to seek support from friends. 3. Actively include members in discussions and activities. 4. Seek a variety of viewpoints on each issue; encourage members to voice differences of opinion. 5. Rotate the responsibility for facilitation. 6. Clarify issues. 7. Encourage members to accept responsibility and follow through.
Inter-dependence	1. A balance exists between task and maintenance activities. 2. Humor is manifested. 3. Friendships develop outside of meetings. 4. Roles are comfortable and understood.	1. Maintain a regular process for integrating new members. 2. Focus on both task and maintenance concerns. 3. Build in time to celebrate. 4. Have a yearly retreat to cement relations and plan for the future.

From E. Guthrie, W.S. Miller and W. Grimberg, A TRAINER'S MANUAL FOR PROCESS POLITICS. La Jolla, CA: University Associates, 1981. Used with permission.

mention that there are valid reasons for members to leave before their
commitment expires. Explicit endings are more energy efficient than
endings that are uncertain.

Time: This theme recurs throughout the discussion of how to have
effective committees. Time can be regarded as an infinite asset ("Things
resolve themselves in time") or as a non-renewable resource ("There's never
enough time to do things right"). Committee members can feel victimized by
time ("I don't have the time") or in control of it ("I won't make the
time").

The importance of time in relation to effective committees cannot be
overlooked. Building group effectiveness cannot be rushed, nor can thorough work be done without adequate time. Decision making, where decisions
are reached and carried out, is a delicate process that involves being
aware of varied self-interests, levels of expertise, priorities, and
expectations --all in relation to other things that are happening at the
same time. It is critical that committees be sensitive to timing issues
throughout their work.

On the other hand, too much time can decrease effectiveness, as
committees find themselves doing busy work in order to fill the allotted
time. Boards that set appropriate deadlines for committee work are defi-
nitely an asset.

Pro-Acting: Committees can view themselves as reactors to situations or pro-actors who take the initiative. The pro-act mindset is much
less crisis-oriented and tends to help committees feel in control of their
efforts and time, a prerequisite for effective planning and prevention.
Individuals, too, can benefit from pro-acting in relation to the committee,
by asking for what they want and not waiting to be placed in a reactive
position.

Ethics: Committees and their members have a responsibility to
behave ethically and not abuse the power and trust given to them. Above
all, this implies being honest and not acting in conflict with either group
or personal values. Questions of ethics are not usually clearcut, as when
a committee member is told some information "in confidence" that turns out
to be vitally important to matters under discussion. In such a case, it's
usually best for the member to go back to the source and reveal the necessity of disclosing the information, rather than breaching the commitment of
confidence. The bottom line, it seems, is one's conscience, although
responsibility to constituency and co-workers must enter in as well. Similarly, if a committee member feels that an unethical action has occurred,
it is incumbent upon that person to raise the concern as one that could
jeopardize the credibility and effectiveness of the committee in the long
run.

Confidentiality: There are times when committees must act confiden-
tially in regard to such matters as personnel or in certain union negoti-
ation processes. Clarity, before the fact, is important so that people
know what to expect. Confidentiality should be agreed upon before any

specific matter is under discussion.

   Burnout: Even the most effective committees can get burned out, as
can their individual members. Burnout is best dealt with before it happens,
by insisting that staff and committee members take time off regularly and
get some play time as part of their committee involvement. If the work
load is too large or too emotional to handle without burning out, it needs
to be re-examined and reduced. Responsibility for monitoring the committee
for signs of burnout needs to be shared by all. People are not expendable
commodities.

   Humor: The ability to laugh at ourselves and keep our committee's
efforts in perspective is invaluable. Sometimes, the most important function a particular committee member serves is to maintain the ability to
inject a joke into a situation that otherwise seems quite humorless. That
individual needs to be cherished. Taking the work of a committee too
seriously results in a loss of perspective that is bound to lead to unhappy
endings.

Wrap-up

   The purpose of this chapter has been to provide a framework and some
helpful hints about committees. Consider this a starting point to build
on, drawing on your group's knowledge and experience. The "right" answers
are those that work for you --so let your creativity flow!

Further Readings

Leonard Berkowitz, GROUP PROCESS. New York: Academic Press, 1978

B. Biagi, WORKING TOGETHER: A MANUAL FOR HELPING GROUPS WORK MORE EFFECTIVELY. Amherst, MA: Citizen Involvement Training Project, 1978

Leland Bradford, MAKING MEETINGS WORK: A GUIDE FOR LEADERS AND GROUP MEMBERS. LaJolla, CA: University Associates, 1976

Eileen Guthrie and Sam Miller, MAKING CHANGE: A GUIDE TO EFFECTIVE- NESS IN GROUPS. Minneapolis: Interpersonal Communication Programs, 1978 (Can be obtained from Eileen Guthrie, 2412 First Avenue South, Minneapolis, MN 55404 for $ 6.95.)

Eileen Guthrie, Sam Miller, and William Grimberg. MAKING CHANGE TRAINER'S MANUAL. Minneapolis: Interpersonal Communication Programs, 1979

K. Eye et al., EFFECTIVE PARTICIPATION OF CONSUMER BOARD MEMBERS: INVOLVING ELDERLY AND LOW INCOME PERSONS. Denver: Colorado Congress of Senior Organizations, 1982

Leslie Lawson, Franklyn Donant and John Lawson, LEAD ON! THE COMPLETE HANDBOOK FOR GROUP LEADERS. San Luis Obispo, CA: Impact Publishers, 1982

Gordon L. Lippitt, VISUALIZING CHANGE: MODEL BUILDING AND THE CHANGE PROCESS. La Jolla, CA: University Associates, 1973

P. Schoderbek, THE EFFECTIVE USE OF COMMITTEES. Alexandria, VA: The United Way of America, 1979

Chapter 7

Board Recruitment and Orientation

Earl W. Anthes

An active, responsible board of directors is necessary for the long term program success and organizational health of the nonprofit corporation. Such a board does not occur by accident: It must be carefully crafted and maintained by the joint efforts of the board of directors and the executive director. There are, I think, three critical ingredients in the construction of the effective board:

1. An organizational commitment to board excellence,

2. A well thought out, consistently implemented board recruitment program, and

3. A consistent and continuing board orientation and training effort.

If your board is inactive, unfocused, conflict ridden or generally dysfunctional, it is because you or someone else, consciously or unconsciously, constructed it to be inactive, unfocused or dysfunctional.

This chapter focuses on how to prevent, through appropriate recruitment, selection and orientation and training of board members, some of the common problems seen in the life of the many boards.

Recruitment

The development of a planned board member recruitment program must begin with the identification of basic qualifications. There are two aspects of the organization's life that serve as starting points. First, is the recognition that any nonprofit must affirm its need for diversity on the board. This need includes diversity of demographics such as sex, age, and race; linkages to various sectors of the community; and diversity of individual skills and interests which the members bring to the board. Strong boards of directors almost always have a board composition that is in some way representative of the larger external world in which it operates. This helps insure that the policy deliberations of the board remain sensitive to the diverse set of expectations and demands put upon the organization.

The need for board members with diverse linkages to different communities and groups is vital to the board's ambassadorship on behalf of the organization. This becomes a critical feature of the board composition when it seeks to become active in fund raising and public relations for the organization. The need for diverse skills and interests on the board is obvious given the financial, personnel, programming, fund raising and public relations duties of the board.

The second starting point for defining your recruitment program is the recognition of the board and organization's need for commonality in its members. While acknowledging the above need for diversity, the board must also ensure that members have (a) a shared belief in the mission and essential values of the organization and, (b) sufficient commitment to give the time needed by the organization. Without a belief in the organization and sufficient commitment of time to the organization, a person does not belong on the board. It's as simple as that.

This brings us to the obvious protestation of "What about the rich person or the corporate president who only can open all these doors for us by letting us use his or her name on our letterhead? We can't really expect them to actually come to our meetings or do the regular board work." If they are going to hold a position on the board, then they must be willing and able to commit to fulfilling all of a director's responsibilities. To let some members "buy out of their board responsibilities" is to undermine performance expectations for the other members. This frequently leads to a situation where the real work of the board evolves to a smaller and smaller group of directors while other members are satisfied with merely being listed on the letterhead.

If you must formally recognize "name" people, who do not have time to serve as directors, then create a "Friends of _____" fund raising arm of the organization, an advisory committee, or a special "honorary fund raising chairperson" position.

The Recruitment Process

The objective of the recruitment process is to identify and select a collection of persons that can effectively operate as a team in performing the diverse duties of the board. The work of the board --and its need for internal strength-- should be the framework which guides the recruitment process.

The first step in this process is the assessment of the current board. A simple way of assessing the board is to use a chart such as the one shown in Exhibit 7-1. This chart allows you to identify those skills,

EXHIBIT 7-1: Board Member Inventory Form

		Committee Interest																									Total	Number Needed
Skill Areas	--Program area: _____																												
	--Program area: _____																												
	--Program area: _____																												
	--Legal																												
	--Personnel																												
	--Financial management																												
	--Planning																												
	--Publicity																												
	--Fund raising																												
Access to Community Sectors	--Legal																												
	--Low income																												
	--Human service agency																												
	--Education																												
	--Commerce																												
	--Government																												
	--Industry																												
	--Labor																												
Personal Background Factors	--Small town																												
	--Urban																												
	--Rural																												
	--Hispanic																												
	--White																												
	--Black																												
	--Over 65																												
	--46 – 65																												
	--35 – 45																												
	--Under 35																												
	--Male																												
	--Female																												
Name of Members																													

73

backgrounds, and linkages needed to round out the board. This is done by listing the current board members down the right side of the form and identifying the characteristics which need to be present on the board across the top of the chart. The entire board should be involved in identifying the ideal mix of characteristics that should be represented. By checking off the characteristics that apply to each member, you develop a profile of the current board. Comparing the profile of the current board with the description of the ideal board gives you a profile of the kinds of board members which should be recruited.

Once you know the profile of what the board needs from new members, you are ready to begin the active search phase of the recruitment process. This process will be outlined for three kinds of organizations: (a) The self-perpetuating board in which new members are nominated and elected by the current members, (b) The "coalition" organization whose board members are appointed or elected by other organizations to represent them on the coalition's board, and (c) The membership organization where the board members are elected by the membership. The board and staff, in each of these types of organizations, cannot afford to adopt a passive stance and "take whomever they give us." In each of these cases, the recruitment process can be an affirmative effort to get the kind of board member needed by the organization.

The Self-Perpetuating Board

The nominating committee should begin its work by collecting names of potential candidates for board membership. Names can be collected from board members, staff, and active volunteers as well as other supporters in the community. A simple board member identification sheet which asks for the pertinent information about the individual should be completed for each of the potential board members in order to ensure that comparable information is gathered on all persons.

While identifying potential candidates, the nominating committee should be developing a recruitment and selection schedule and a recruitment information kit which can be given to each candidate. This kit should contain the same kinds of information as a press kit (See Exhibit 13-2). The recruitment, under ideal conditions, will provide at least several months of activities before the final selection of new board members. A useful recruitment schedule is shown below.

The Coalition Board

A similar calendar would also be developed by the executive committee of a coalition board, except that the critical initial candidates orientation session would be directed to the board or group which is to elect the representative to the coalition's board. This orientation would brief the selecting group on the type of person needed for the board, the time required for board and committee work, as well as the ground rules and expectations of a board member. This gives the selecting group guidance for their selection of a representative.

EXHIBIT 7-2: Recruitment Schedule

November 15	Begin potential candidate identification by contacting other board members, staff, volunteers and supporters.
November 25	Nominating committee identifies primary candidate pool of approximately 3 persons for each position. This preliminary selection should be based on the inventory of characteristics needed on the board. Begin preliminary contact with each candidate to see if he or she is interested in serving on the board, and is willing to attend a preliminary orientation session.
December 10	Conduct orientation session for candidates. This will be about a 2-hour session covering: -- mission and purpose -- philosophy and history -- time requirements for board work -- other expectations. The information recruitment kit should be distributed and any questions answered. Emphasize that not everyone at the orientation session will be seated on the board.
December 20	Determine if each candidate is still willing to serve.
December 30	Give the full board an opportunity to review the list of candidates to see if any board member has any objections to anyone on the list.
January 10	Make final selection of nominees to the board. Notify, in writing, both the nominees and other candidates of your decision. Schedule orientation session for nominees prior to the meeting at which they will be seated.
January 20	Hold pre-service orientation
January 25	Seat new board members

It may also be possible to have the group identify a number of candidates for the representative position who could then be given a more detailed orientation to the organization's history and philosophy. After being fully briefed at the orientation, the candidates have an opportunity to decline the appointment if they feel they do not fit on the coalition's board.

The Member Elected Board

The board composed of directors elected by the membership have to be especially careful in the recruitment effort so that it does not appear that the board is interfering in and manipulating the members right to elect their representatives on the board. Although this is a danger, the board still must affirmatively seek the right mix of backgrounds, skills and linkages on the board if it is to function as effectively as possible.

The basic strategy of the board recruitment process in a membership organization is two pronged: It must conduct both a nominating process to identify candidates and a continuing membership education program so that the members are informed about the functioning and needs of the board. The membership education program can take the form of newsletter articles about the board's needs, a special flyer about the duties of a board member, a short board orientation program at the annual membership meeting, or all of the above. The point is, that when members vote for directors, they must appreciate that a board position is more than a prize in a popularity contest or a reward for past good deeds. They must know, in short, the duties and qualifications of the position.

Another option, particularly useful when directors are nominated from the floor or declare their own candidacy, is to hold an open board orientation session thirty days or so before the deadline for nominations. Anyone who is considering seeking a board position can then attend the session and be briefed on the board's operations. This orientation would be the same as the candidates orientation shown in Exhibit 7-2. An added advantage of this session is that people who have the skills and time to be good board members, but who lack board experience have an opportunity to gain self-confidence.

The premise of all of the above discussion is that a healthy system of board recruitment is based upon giving information to potential board members so they can make informed decisions about service on the board. Then, if a potential board member discovers that she or he is not sufficiently interested in the purpose of the organization, does not share its values and philosophy, or cannot devote the time that is required for the position, she or he can gracefully decline to be considered for the position. Like lung cancer, many board problems are more easily prevented than cured.

Orientation and Training

Orientation and training of board members have two intertwining objectives: To inform board members about the organization and its programs and to get new members integrated into the board team as quickly as possible so that they can make appropriate decisions and contribute to the organization's success.

The orientation and training process actually begins, if you follow the above recruitment strategies, prior to the person being seated on the board. At this time, the new board member will know the basics of the organization and its history, but will be far from a fully functioning board member.

A half day or a long evening orientation session should be scheduled with the members between their seating and the next meeting. This session, to be lead by more experienced board members with necessary staff support, should cover such topics as the board's committee system, the standard procedures and rules of order used in board meetings, the articles of incorporation and bylaws, as well as descriptions of the programs operated by the organization. The program descriptions should include a discussion of funding, licensing or regulatory requirements, and staffing.

The new board member should also be given a copy of a current board manual as soon as he or she is seated on the board. The board manual is a basic board development and orientation tool. An outline of a board manual is contained in EXHIBIT 7-3. This board manual should be prepared by a board and staff task force or committee. Members of the board should be responsible for maintaining their own manuals after receiving them. The manual serves as a comprehensive reference and briefing book for the members. It is especially helpful to the new board member.

EXHIBIT 7-3: An Outline of a Board Manual

Section 1. Board and Staff Directory

This should be a current listing of all board members' name, address, phone number, who they represent, and committee assignments. All staff members should also be listed by job title, home and office address and phone number.

Section 2. An Overview of the Organization and Board of Directors

This should include the mission statement, a short history of the organization, and a statement of the general role of the board in the life of the organization; and, could include key news articles, annual reports,

Continued

---

and the organization's brochures.

Section 3. Board Activities and Membership Expectation

This third section should include an annual
board schedule (budgeting, planning, etc.)
a brief overview of board committee structure
and activities, and a clear statement of
what is expected of board members.

Section 4. Board Committees

This section of the manual will provide the
new board member with detailed information
about each of the committees of the board.
This will include an annual schedule for
each committee, a specific statement of the
committee's charge, operating procedures,
and committee membership.

Section 5. Program Information

Section 5 should contain a one or two page
synopsis of each program operated by the
organization. This will include: The objectives of the program, major program
guidelines and administrative procedures.
A listing of key staff people in the program
and a description of past program performance
should also be included.

Section 6. Organizational Policy Statements

This section is a collection of all the
board approved policy statements currently
in force. This would include, among
others, personnel policies, equal employment
policy, client grievance procedures, confidentiality policy, and board conflict of
interest policy.

Section 7. Board Minutes

This section of the manual will include
minutes from at least the last 12 months.
An index to all substantive board votes
should be included as a subject index and
should be updated at least quarterly.

Section 8. Staff Reports

Continued

This section should be a collection of the
most recent staff reports. At least the
last 6 monthly reports should be retained
at all times.

Section 9. Organizing Papers, Laws and Regulations

The section should contain the articles of
incorporation, bylaws, a summary of the
state nonprofit statutes and IRS regulations, a summary of the key provisions of
the guidelines imposed on boards by major
funding sources, and a parliamentary
procedures guide.

Section 10. Finances.

This should contain the organization's
current budget and all of the current
year's financial reports.

So far the new board member has received (a) a candidate's orientation, (b) a copy of a board manual, and (c) approximately a half day
detailed orientation to the organization and its programs. All of this
orientation has been under the direction of the board, usually the executive or the nominating committee. There are, however, two other forms of
orientation and training still remaining: Committee orientation and
service area training.

First is an orientation to each of the committees on which the new
member serves. This orientation should cover the purpose of the committee,
the procedures used by the committee, and the policy domain of the committee. The latter item will include a detailed review, for example, of the
personnel policies and practices of the organization for the new personnel
committee member or the financial management policies and budget for the
new budget committee member. Normally, the committee chairperson will be
responsible for orientation of new committee members.

The second remaining orientation and training need for the new board
member is service area training. This is simply a short training session,
usually conducted by the staff, which aims to give the new board member a
solid information base in the program areas of the organization. A service
area training session in a domestic abuse center, for instance, might cover
such topics as why men batter, alcohol and drug use related to battering,
institutional response to domestic violence, demographics of domestic
violence and client statistics from the program. This kind of training
achieves a number of benefits for the new board member and board. It helps
equalize the information level between the new and old board members,
allowing new board members to play a more active role in decision making
during their early months on the board. The subject area training, since

it is directed by a staff team, also gives new board members an opportunity to develop a working relationship with staff of the organization.

The orientation and development process does not end with the completion of the formal orientation plan for new members. Part of the orientation and integration of new members occurs informally and in the natural flow of organization business. During the first few months of a new member's term, the staff and board should be particularly sensitive to the new members' need for background information about the organization, its programs and its jargon.

It is very easy for the board and staff during the course of a busy board meeting to fall into the use of verbal short hand such as referring to the "Jones case" as a precedent for the current decision or referring to the ubiquitous "Title III." These discussions force the new member into silence or force him or her to interrupt the board and request an explanation. The avoidance of this problem is possible if both the board and staff are conscious of the special need for more detailed explanations of issues and background information during the early part of members' terms.

Some organizations have had good results by specifically designating an experienced board member to serve in a "big sister/big brother" role for new members. By formalizing this "gatekeeping" function, it is easier for new board members to feel comfortable in asking for background briefings.

All of these orientation and training efforts are aimed at getting the new board member involved and active in the organization as soon as possible. The true tragedy of board development is when good board members are recruited and then lost because, after three or four months, they feel they have contributed nothing to the organization. Almost all new board members come to the board committed and motivated: Healthy boards grow out of an orientation and training process that allows them to remain so.

Board Member Evaluation

Board member evaluation is generally unmentioned, and perhaps unmentionable, on most boards. Nevertheless, it is a critical part of continuing board training and development.

Your organization's personnel policies probably call for at least annual evaluations for all employees. You do this to insure that (1) minimum performance standards are met, (2) staff training needs are identified, and (3) consistently sub-standard performers are weeded out. Do you do the same for board members?

Board member evaluation can take the form of a simple attendance and participation record with several rating scales which are completed twice a year on each board member. A sample of such a form is provided on pages 82 - 84. The evaluation should be conducted by the nominating committee or a special committee established specifically for board development and training.

The evaluation results are useful in several ways:

1. It clearly tells potential board members what will be expected of them. It will also tell them that the board is very serious about its work.

2. It forms a basis for identifying board development and training needs.

3. It gives feedback to a board member about how other members of the board see his/her performance, attendance and participation.

EXHIBIT 7-4: A Board Member Evaluation Form

Board Member: _____

Term begins: _____   Term ends: _____

Meeting Attendance: Enter the name of all board committees on which this member serves. Enter the date of the meeting or event in the date box provided on each line. (Space can be subdivided if more than one meeting is held in a month.) Put an "x" below the date of the meeting if the board member attended the meeting or event.

		Jan	Feb	Mar	Apr	May	June	July	Aug	Sep	Oct	Nov	Dec
1. Regular & called board meetings	Date Att.												
2. Board committees													
A. _____	Date Att.												
B. _____	Date Att.												
C. _____	Date Att.												
3. Special events													
A. Annual corp. meeting	Date Att.												
B. Board orientation	Date Att.												
C. Board training	Date Att.												

82

Board Member's contributions to the corporation.

	Amt/Item	Date	Amt/Item	Date	Amt/Item	Date
Financial						
Equip/Supplies						
Skill/Time						

Rate the member's performance on the following criteria. (To be completed by nominating committee.)

1. This member's level of preparation for board meetings (eg. reads board packets, staff reports) is...
____ very high ____ somewhat above average ____ average ____ somewhat below average ____ very low

2. This member independently seeks information outside of that routinely provided by staff reports...
____ almost never ____ rarely ____ sometimes ____ frequently ____ almost always

3. This member's level of participation in meetings is...
____ very low ____ somewhat below average ____ average ____ somewhat above average ____ very high

4. This member represents the organization and serves as its ambassador to other organizations...
____ frequently ____ often ____ sometimes ____ rarely ____ almost never

5. This member has demonstrated overall interest in and commitment to the organization and its mission...
____ below average ____ average ____ above average

This board member has voiced or indicated concern about the following aspect(s) of the organization.

Notes

____ The board's process
____ Organizational planning
____ Fund raising
____ Personnel management
____ Program evaluation
____ Financial management
____ Public relations
____ Board/Staff relations

This board member needs improvement or training in the following areas.

As a result of this evaluation, the nominating committee recommends that this board member be ...

____ A. immediately separated from the board.
____ B. scheduled for separation at the end of this term.
____ C. retained on the board.
____ D. encouraged to remain on the board and recognized for excellence in performing the duties of a board member.

Other comments:

Further Readings

William R. Conrad and William E. Glenn, THE EFFECTIVE VOLUNTARY
BOARD OF DIRECTORS: WHAT IS IT AND WHAT IT DOES. Chicago: Swallow
Press, 1976

Edward J. O'Donnel and Otto M. Reid, "Citizen Participation on
Public Welfare Boards and Commissions," SOCIAL ADMINISTRATION,
Simon Slavin (Ed.). New York: The Haworth Press, 1978

Research and Forecasters, Inc., THE TOUCHE ROSS SURVEY OF BUSINESS
EXECUTIVES ON NON-PROFIT BOARDS. New York: Touche Ross and
Company, 1979

The Tasks and Essential Concerns of the Board

Chapter 8

Board and Staff Relations

William E. Glenn

Simply defined, an organization is a group of people brought together for some purpose. One uniqueness of the voluntary organization is that these people are, in most cases, made up of both paid professionals and volunteers. The board volunteers are very special people who operate in a realm of "obedience to the unenforceable."

The phrase "obedience to the unenforceable" is borrowed from an address before the Author's Club of London. Lord Moulton said, "we live under the discipline of three domains: one, the positive law which prescribes rules of conduct and exacts penalties for disobedience; two, the realm of free choice which is covered by no statutes; and three, that domain in which neither positive law nor free choice prevails. In this sphere, the individual imposes obligations upon himself. In this realm, the individual is not wholly free since he has accepted a responsibility. Although he knows that no law or individual can compel him to fulfill this commitment, he also knows that he cannot disobey without betraying himself."

Here is the domain in which the board volunteer lives and as Lord Moulton concluded, "the real greatness of a nation, its true civilization, is measured by the extent of this land of obedience to the unenforceable."

Such an organization of special people requires excellence of definition and planning. Clear purpose, goals and objectives are required for organizing people and developing understandings from which action and achievement may come. The first concerns for a new board of directors will be: (1) Who are we as an organization? (2) What goals establish our direction and validate who we say we are? (3) What are our program objectives to achieve these goals? The next concern is how will these people relate to each other.

EXHIBIT 8-1: Role of the Staff Member in the Voluntary Organization

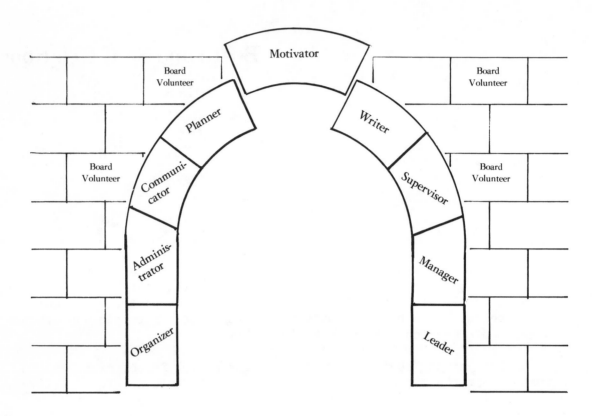

If we envision the above wall as representing a voluntary organization, the bricks being the board members, and the supporting arch being the staff members, it is clear that the staff may be seen as the wearer of many hats. Please note, however, that the keystone of the arch is the "MOTIVATOR" role.

A rather harsh observation is that a board is rarely any more effective than the staff wants and helps it to be. It is very unusual for board volunteers to take over and actually "lead" the voluntary organization. Let us take a closer look at that keystone "MOTIVATOR" role.

In this context, the staff enables board volunteers by:

1. Providing a cause to believe in. Every board volunteer, to be effective, must be proud of the voluntary organization he/she serves. Members must be able to identify with the purpose of the organization in order to represent it with confidence.

EXHIBIT 8-2: The Motivator Role

PROVIDES

-A CAUSE TO BELIEVE IN
-A FRAMEWORK WITHIN WHICH TO WORK
-SPECIFIC TASKS TO BE ACCOMPLISHED
-DEADLINES FOR TASKS TO BE ACCOMPLISHED
-AN OPPORTUNITY TO PARTICIPATE IN THE
DECISIONS THAT AFFECT THE FIRST FOUR

SUPPORTED BY
PROMPT, ACCURATE AND SUSTAINED ASSISTANCE

2. Providing a framework within which to work. During the recruitment process, a board volunteer usually asks: "Where do I fit?" In other words: "What is the framework within which I must work?" Prospective members want to know precisely where they stand.

3. Providing specific tasks to be accomplished. The next question asked is: "What do you want me to do?" It is important, therefore, that staff identify those tasks which need to be accomplished.

4. Providing deadlines for tasks to be accomplished. The next question is: "When do you want this done?" Staff must have a definite calendar in mind for the tasks which are to be accomplished by board volunteers.

5. Providing an opportunity to participate in the decisions that affect the first four points. This is the key. The first four points imply that staff literally "provides" all these items for board volunteers. If this happens in fact, then a board or committee will merely follow the lead of the staff, giving only superficial attention to the issues of the organization. In order to avoid this superficial "rubber stamping," it is extremely important that board volunteers have an opportunity to discuss and decide those issues raised by the first four items.

All these items must be supported by prompt, accurate, and sustained assistance on the part of the staff. Board volunteers are successful only to the extent that they are supported by the staff. Let a staff member fail to return a telephone call, provide inaccurate information, or embarrass a board volunteer, and all the knowledge and degrees in the world will not support him or her.

Board volunteers expect competence and personal integrity from their staff; they expect performance to keep pace with promises; they expect satisfaction with both direction and pace. Staff must remember, too, that board volunteers expect reasoned responses, not "I guess." Most of all, board volunteers should be able to predict the behavior of the staff. Constancy is the key. In Exhibit 8-3 we will examine the four fundamental roles of board volunteers.

EXHIBIT 8-3: Roles of the Board Member

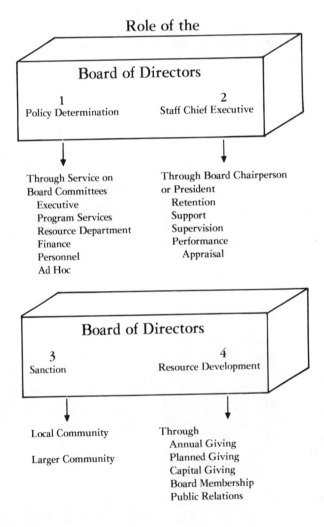

Role of the

Policy Determination

For our purpose, a rather simple guideline statement should suffice. What the organization is to do is policy. How the organization does it is procedure. Determination of policy is board role, whereas developing procedure falls within staff responsibility. Board volunteers set policy for a voluntary organization as they serve on board committees and bring resolutions back from committee to the board for action.

In structuring itself, the board identifies management divisions requiring attention if the organization is to be well managed. Exhibit 8-4 is one way to look at management divisions. We would suggest that these provide the basis for committee development.

EXHIBIT 8-4: Management Divisions for a Voluntary Organization

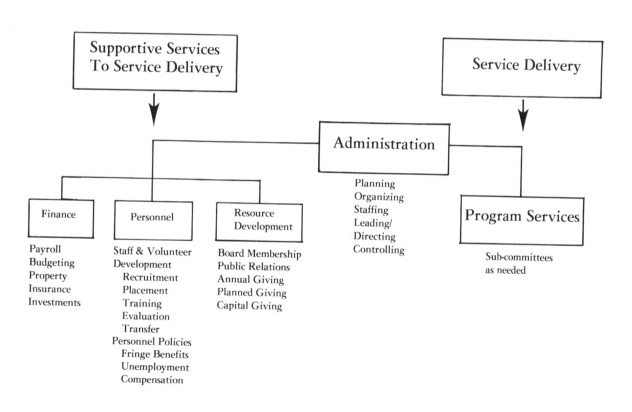

For daily operations, staff is also organized into management division. How this fits together becomes quite logical as is seen in Exhibit 8-5.

EXHIBIT 8-5: Staff/Board Accountability

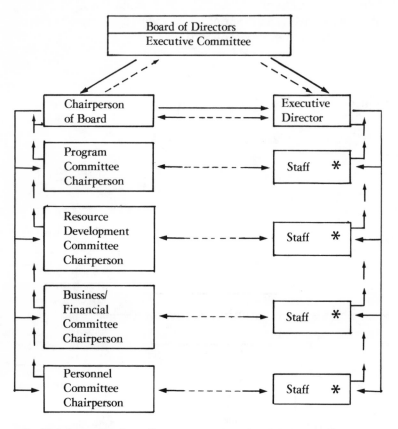

*   This is usually the staff person most directly related to the function of the committee opposite her/him.

– – – – – – ► Feedback, Communication, Consultation, Advice
——————► Line of Authority

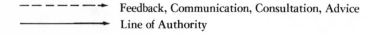

Realism dictates that any voluntary group, including a committee of the board, should be supported by staff if it is to function well. The above Exhibit 8-5 demonstrates a staff to staff line of accountability on the right and a board volunteer to volunteer accountability line on the left. Please note the dotted lines linking the staff to the committee chairpersons. The staff is accountable only to the executive director who is, in turn, accountable to the board of directors. The staff person must be able to relate to the committee chairperson through professional com-

petence as there is no power going either way. The committee assignment of
a staff person usually corresponds to his or her professional duties. The
board member recruited as a committee chairperson also is usually placed in
an area of his or her special competence.

Shall we look at Exhibit 8-6, below, and track an issue through the
policy making process?

EXHIBIT 8-6: The Policy Formulation Process

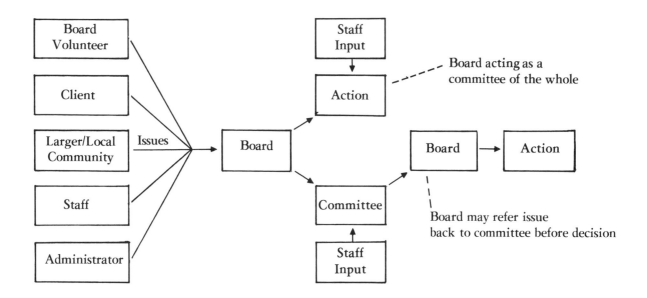

Issues may come from anywhere: From board members, clients, the
public, funders, staff or whomever. Orderly management requires that the
board deal with all issues brought before it. This board attention may
range from policy creation to a determination that no action is indicated.

Under certain conditions, the board may take direct action by
acting as a committee of the whole. This is usually undesirable since
it bypasses the committee structure and may lead to decisions being made
with too little deliberation. In addition, bypassed committees tend to be
less enthusiastic about future assignments.

More desirable is for the board chairperson to assign the issue
directly to committee where it receives committee and staff attention and
returns to the board for action on an agreed upon schedule. The premise is
that any issue falls naturally into one of the established committees. Once
it is assigned to a committee it remains on the flow chart until it is
resolved.

As staff provides support to committees, it has professional input into the study of policy options. Policy determination, however, is strictly a board function. Policy implementation is usually a staff function (with full board support). Policy monitoring is a function of board and staff together on the committee level.

EXHIBIT 8-7: Board and Staff Roles in the Policy Process

Consideration of policy options	board and staff
Policy determination	board
Policy implementation	staff
Policy monitoring	board and staff

Staff Chief Executive

The second role on Exhibit 8-5 relates to the board responsibility for providing the agency with a competent chief executive and providing that executive with the support and feedback necessary to succeed.

It has been said, and only partially in humor, that most boards of directors have only two important agenda items. The first is "Should we fire the chief executive?" If the answer is yes, then the second item is "Who should serve on the search committee?" If the answer to the first question is no, then the second agenda item should be , "How can we most effectively support this administration?"

Please turn to Exhibit 8-5 again and examine closely the staff/staff, board/board and staff/board relationships. Note that the solid line is the authority line and the dotted line denotes communication, consultative and advisory relationships. You will observe that the chief executive is the only staff person who is directly accountable to the board or voluntary side of the organization. The chief executive is accountable to the board of directors through the chair of the board. Therefore, authority passes from the board to the board chair and to the chief executive. The dotted line from the executive director to the board would indicate that the chief executive must give staff support to the board through his/her professional competence rather than through power going the other way. Any supervisory attention that a chief executive may require may take place only by or through the board chairperson. This avoids multiple accountability. All other staff are accountable to the chief executive directly or through an orderly staff chain of command.

There is simple truth in the present climate of nonprofit voluntary organizations: The staff executive must have a harmonious, trustful and respectful relationship with the board of directors in order to be successful.

EXHIBIT 8-8: A Balance Between Board and Staff

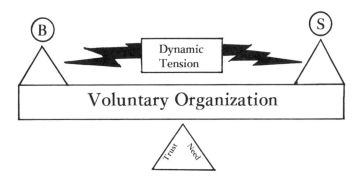

This does not mean elimination of conflict, but it certainly would imply management of conflict. Many otherwise competent chief executives have been dismissed for being unable to find and maintain the delicate balance of power, influence and control in the relationships between board and staff within their organizations. Balance exists when both staff and board understand, accept and fulfill their respective roles. A certain tension or push-pull is natural between board and staff, but it need not be harmful. It can be a creative, dynamic tension, where the fulcrum of the balance is a mutual trust and need.

The key to the development and maintenance of this delicate balance is the relationship between the chairperson of the board and the chief executive of the organization. These two individuals must build a relationship firmly based on trust, goal agreement and shared values. They must be able to "level" with each other, to discuss honestly and straightforwardly the issues before their organization. They must spend enough time together so that they are in agreement as to how the board and chief executive are to work together. When problems arise with individual board members, the board chairperson and chief executive should be able to plan the strategy for resolution.

Agenda building for meetings should also be an important part of their lives together, and there should be agreement between them on all recommendations. If they cannot arrive at such agreement, the issue can still go before the board, but with the clear understanding that the chairperson and the chief executive will be on opposite sides. The condition of delicate balance in a voluntary organization is directly related to the quality of the relationship between the chair of the board and the staff chief executive.

This same type of high quality relationship must be maintained between the committee chairpersons and staff support persons. Staff people are assigned to give support to a committee, usually in the functional area most closely related to the staff person's professional duties. Note that there is a dotted line relationship between the committee chair and the staff support person. This is the main point of difference between the board chair/chief executive relationship and the committee chair/staff support person relationship. The staff person is accountable through the staff accountability chain, whereas the committee chairperson is accountable to the chair of the board. We have here a relationship based on staff competence and a shared commitment to the work of the committee and the organization.

It would seem important to remember that most people join boards and committees to help, not to take over or interfere with the operation. Board volunteers and staff both want to be successful in their roles. Relevant, clear, complete and accurate communication is the vehicle which moves staff and board volunteers from understanding, through confidence, to trust, thereby allowing a productive personal relationship to develop. Board volunteers need to be able to predict the behavior of their staff, calling for such things as staff performance which keeps pace with promises, professional competence, personal integrity and reasoned responses.

Board committee work is just group work. The same dynamics may be observed as in any other group. (See Chapter 6 for a detailed discussion of the role of task and maintenance functions in group work.)

The Sanction and Linkage Role

Board volunteers give us the right to exist as an organization. The board is the corporation and is the front line of credibility. The local community refers to the immediate locale of the organization. The larger community refers to those community segments outside the local community. Sanction of the larger community, such as the "downtown" or business community, has been a necessity for financial survival. Until the sixties, sanction of the local community was rather ignored as not too important. We found that the absence of clients could close us down as surely as the absence of funds. It is a responsibility of the board of directors to know the various power bases and assure that they have linkages with those which are relevant to achieving the goals and objectives of the organization.

Resource Development Role

Each board volunteer has a role to play in the area of resource development. Resource development is a broader concept than just fund raising as can be seen in Exhibit 8-9. Resource development rests on program services, the organization's reason for being. If the three pillars necessary for resource development are in place, we have financial stability and the capacity to provide program services.

EXHIBIT 8-9: The Pillars of Development

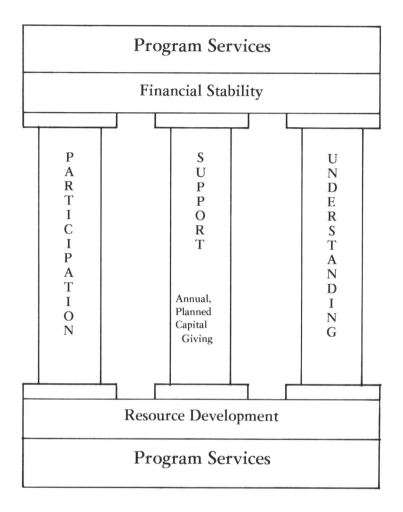

As can be seen from Exhibit 8-9, resource development depends upon:

Understanding. We must determine how the organization must be
    perceived if it is to achieve its goals and objectives. That
    perception, or image, must then be designed and made real. This
    includes our public relations and publicity work.

Participation. It is a board role to keep its own group strong in
    numbers and motivated to produce.

Support. With help from the staff, it is the responsibility of the board to assure that the required contributed dollars are raised.

In order for a staff person to fulfill her or his role and artfully support the board side of the organization, serious thought must be given to the reasons people join boards.

EXHIBIT 8-10: A Balance Between Demands and Need Satisfaction

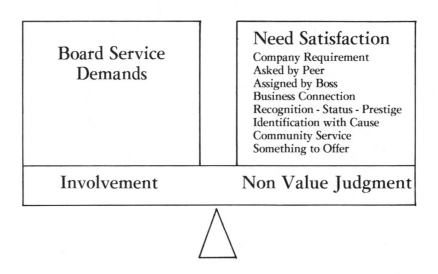

On the right side of Exhibit 8-10 is a representative list of the reasons people join boards. They range from the highly altruistic to the self serving. A sharp, concerned chief executive will know the board members well and will have a pretty good idea of what attracted each of them to the board. It is important that this be knowledge without value. As staff I have no right to judge board members, but I owe them my understanding so that the most productive and satisfying board experience may be designed and achieved. A person's needs or motivations must be understood if they are to be balanced against board service demands. Non-balance, whether too light or to heavy will eventually demoralize the organization.

The same understandings are necessary if one is to design appropriate means of demonstrating appreciation. We learn to see self interest from a realistic perspective. If the self interest of an individual is satisfied, and that person has done what was promised, we probably have a good board person.

There is one further consideration if one accepts that board service carries with it a high potential as a human development instrument. Those

motivation needs listed on the right side of Exhibit 8-10 may be divided as
to the probable growth outcome for the individual. Please note Exhibit 8-
11, below.

EXHIBIT 8-11: Static and Growth Facilitating Needs

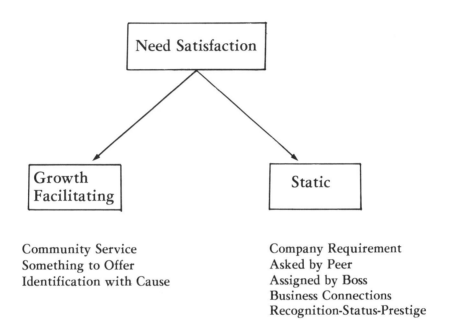

Growth Facilitating

Community Service
Something to Offer
Identification with Cause

Static

Company Requirement
Asked by Peer
Assigned by Boss
Business Connections
Recognition-Status-Prestige

     Some of these needs tend to be "growth facilitating" while others
appear to be "static" in their effects on the lives of people. People do
grow. An experience can be designed so that those who begin board work
with a self serving motivation may become so inspired by what the organization is really doing that they become cause oriented and very dedicated
to the work. Skillful group workers on the staff may sometimes have a
greater impact upon the community by developing leadership than through the
stated purpose of the organization. That is a "fringe benefit." It is
clear that this kind of board and committee work requires a staff willing
to place a lot of attention on building relationships. Promoting this
growth also requires a staff that realizes that their dedication, talent
and training notwithstanding, it is the board which gives the organization
its long term strength and stability.

     A well thought out process is required in order to build the type
of board we have been describing. On Exhibit 8-12 we may observe the
process which all of us pass through on the road to becoming dedicated
board members. Contributions, on the far right, may be time, effort, money
or any type of support that the organization requires to achieve its plan-

ned results. Something must be designed to happen along the horizontal

EXHIBIT 8-12: Involvement — Contribution Ratio

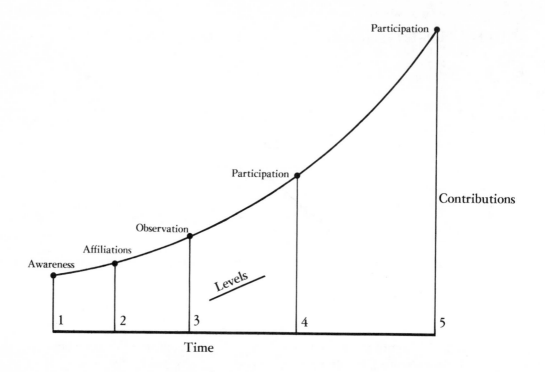

time line. It will not just happen by itself. Note, at the point of
awareness a person is making next to no contribution. To our dismay,
affiliation frequently does not make a very impressive jump on the graph.
If this happens, it is frequently because people don't really know what it
means to join a board. There have been no expectations set. There needs
to be a plan if we are to help a person move quickly from affiliation to
participation. Board volunteers have arrived at participation when they are
integrated into the committee structure and participating in the decision
making process. That second and higher level of participation is reached
when the board volunteers are able to see the "pay offs" in their work.
They see the results of their decisions. They are perhaps having some
contact with clients, or with the product or service of the agency and feel
a warm glow of satisfaction. We are now looking at an organization that is
in balance. The staff and board are a team. They respect each other.
Roles are clear and each side acknowledges that neither staff nor board
could get along without the other.

(The graphics and charts in this chapter are used with the permission of
the Institute for Voluntary Organizations.)

Further Readings

S. Becker and D. Glenn, OFF YOUR DUFFS AND UP THE ASSETS: COMMON SENSE FOR NONPROFIT MANAGERS. New York: Farnswarth Publishing Company, 1984

D. Borst and P.J. Montana, MANAGING NONPROFIT ORGANIZATIONS. New York: American Management Association, 1979

T. Gilmore, "Managing Collaborative Relationships in Complex Organizations," ADMINISTRATION IN SOCIAL WORK. Vol. 3, No. 2, Summer 1979, p.14-18

Robert K. Greenleaf, TRUSTEES AS SERVANTS. Cambridge, MA: Center for Applied Studies, 1974

Pauline L. Hanson and Carolyn Marmaduke, THE BOARD MEMBER: DECISION MAKER FOR THE NONPROFIT CORPORATION. Sacramento, CA: Han/Mar Publications, 1972

Felice Perlmutter, "Citizen Participation and Professionalism: A Developmental Relationship," SOCIAL ADMINISTRATION, Simon Slavin (Ed.). New York: The Haworth Press, 1978

Herman D. Stein, "Board, Executive and Staff," SOCIAL ADMINISTRATION, Simon Slavin (Ed.). New York: The Haworth Press, 1978

Joseph Weber, MANAGING THE BOARD OF DIRECTORS. New York: The Greater New York Fund, 1975

Chapter 9

Overseeing Organizational Operations

Richard J. First, Ph.D.

Most nonprofit organizations are either like the "good old" used car or, the poorly built new one: They need fixing from time to time. In some cases the problems are obvious and the repair work can be done right away. Weak financial oversight, for example, is just plain unsafe at any time or speed. Other problems, such as inadequate personnel polices, require both time and information to fix.

In this chapter, we look at one of the most neglected aspects of the board's business —overseeing organizational operations. We will approach this topic from one basic premise: Without board involvement and "ownership" of evaluation activity, prior efforts in policy making and planning are at risk. Board oversight of operations is critical, since it speaks to the very essence of effective governance in voluntary associations.

Let's begin by looking at some of the choices a board might be called upon to make and how they reflect the need for oversight. The following examples of policy issues for board action are designed to illustrate the major topics which will be addressed in this chapter: a) program monitoring, b) executive performance appraisal; and c) board performance assessment.

Problems in these areas can be prevented by effective and ongoing oversight of programs and people.

A. Your corporation is faced with a shortfall in funds for the next fiscal year. Costs for program operation have increased and the current level of external funding will at best remain constant. The board is presented with a choice of cutting

back on one of two programs currently in place. When the
board meeting is held to consider this issue, reasons are given
for favoring each of the two programs. However, there is
limited hard data on the results achieved by each of the two
programs and some board members are concerned about the lack
of program evaluation activity.

B. The executive committee of the board has received a request
from the staff to schedule a special meeting to discuss
problems in their relationships with the chief executive
officer. The executive has been with the corporation for some
time and is well liked by many of the board members. You have
been told that the staff grievances center around the competency of the executive to manage programs and communicate with
the staff. Some board members are asking why there has never
been any formal system for assessing executive performance.

C. Participation at monthly board meetings has been declining for
the past year. It has finally reached a point where it is
impossible to conduct board business due to low attendance.
Prior efforts of the officers to find new members to serve on
the board have been unsuccessful. In discussing the problem,
everyone present seems discouraged and unsure of how to
proceed. There are indications that the board is not only
inactive but ineffective in decision making.

Each of these hypothetical situations represents a crisis situation.
In this chapter, we are concerned with building systems for continuing
oversight which, at the very least, can provide the board with information
upon which to make decisions on critical issues such as these.

We will begin by looking at the board's role and rationale for
effective oversight of the corporation. A system for identifying and
monitoring potential problem areas will be presented. Next, two critical
assessment tasks that are clearly the responsibility of the board will be
examined. They are evaluation of executive performance and evaluation of
board performance. In our view, these are the two most commonly neglected
practices for preventive health in voluntary organizations.

The Board's Role in Overseeing Organizational Operations

Effective oversight of operations is difficult to achieve in both
the large complex organization and in the small or newly developed
corporation. The common problem or gray area that most corporations face
is how to define the respective roles and responsibilities of the board as
distinct from those of the administrator and staff. Confusion over the
respective roles and responsibilities in overseeing operations can result
in a number of situations where the board and the executive seem to be
working at cross-purposes or just plain getting in each others way. Some
of the more common symptoms that result from a lack of clarity of the

104

board's role in oversight are:

1. The differences between policy determination and policy or program implementation are fuzzy.

2. There is inadequate communication between the administrator and the board.

3. The board does not assume responsibility for assessment of the administrator's performance.

4. Programs are not adequately monitored and evaluated.

5. The organization doesn't know where it wants to go and how to get there.

The effect of being unclear or "fuzzy" about who is responsible for what, is well illustrated in the following fable from Robert Mager's book on Goal Analysis:

Once upon a time in the land of Fuzz, King Aling called in his cousin Ding and commanded, "go ye into all Fuzzland and find me the goodest of men, whom I shall reward for his goodness."

"But how will I know one when I see one?" asked the Fuzzy.

"Why, he will be sincere," scoffed the king, and whacked off a leg for his impertinence.

So, the Fuzzy limped out to find a good man. But soon he returned, confused and empty-handed.

"But how will I know one when I see one?" he asked again.

"Why, he will be dedicated," grumbled the king, and whacked off another leg for his impertinence.

So the Fuzzy hobbled away once more to look for the goodest of men. But again he returned confused and empty handed.

"But how will I know when I see one?" he pleaded.

"Why, he will have internalized his growing awareness," fumed the king, and whacked off another leg for his impertinence.

So the Fuzzy, now on his last leg, hopped out to continue his search. In time, he returned with the wisest, most sincere and dedicated Fuzzy in all of Fuzzland, and stood him before the king.

"Why, this man won't do at all," roared the king. "He is too thin to suit me." Whereupon, he whacked off the last leg of the Fuzzy, who fell to the floor with a squishy thump.(1)

The moral of Mager's fable is: The board that fails to recognize its own role when it sees it, may wind up without a leg to stand on. Roles are often fuzzy in overseeing program operations and this can end up without either the board or staff "having a leg to stand on." So, let's try to clarify the fuzzy aspects of the Board's role and find at least four "good legs to stand on. These roles or steps are shown in Exhibit 9-1.

EXHIBIT 9-1: Building and Utilizing an Assessment System

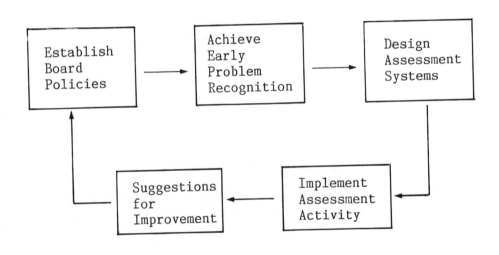

Step 1: Establishing Board Policies on Evaluation and Oversight

Policies and practices which establish the framework for overseeing program operations are the first task and no doubt most common cause of confusion about the board's role in evaluation. What does it mean to have a policy on evaluation and how would we know one if we saw one?

Let's begin with the board's most basic responsibility --effective governance. Governance can be thought of as the means for making sure that the system runs well and that decisions about present or future directions, goals and mission of the enterprise, and ongoing activities are effectively carried out. John Carver, Carver Governance Design, Inc. of Columbus, Indiana, calls the board's role in governance the "moral ownership of the corporation." He sees the board's first job as learning how to "govern by policy" and to succeed at specifying desired ends, rather than becoming mired in the ongoing business of the executive.

Carver defines the goal to be achieved by the nonprofit board as:

> "Governing by policy (explicit statements of board values on various topics) enables a board to attend to the big questions, to focus on the long term, to avoid trivia, to demand excellence in management, and to overcome the non-market dilemma.(2)

For Carver, governance is, "the determination and assurance of values to be served and observed by the organization."(3) For example, an explicit policy on evaluation will say how the board values and intends to adhere to high standards for program effort.

In profit making corporations, values are more explicit and understood by both the board and the chief executive officer (CEO). They revolve around doing those things which stockholders in a corporation can and must do to protect their investment and promote financial success. The board's success in fulfilling this role as owner is observable by both those inside and outside the corporation. Lack of success shows not only in the "pocketbook" but also in the well being and subsequent actions of the stockholders. This kind of built-in feedback on the life and health of the corporation gets lost or left hanging in far too many voluntary associations. Not only the ends, but the means for knowing where to go and how to get there become fuzzy. Thus, the first and most basic step in getting ready to govern the evaluation process is for the board, or committee within the board, to take seriously the mandate to own and oversee the design of ongoing evaluation policies and practices. This is step one and the focal point for subsequent oversight activities.

Step 2: Early Problem Recognition

The second and equally important step for the board to undertake in evaluation is the decider function. According to systems theory, every system must have a decider sub-system or ultimate control mechanism in order for feedback to be received and the parts to operate as a whole. By analogy think of the brain in a human or the thermostat in an electronic heating and cooling system.

In very practical terms, it is frequently the mandate or condition of a funding source that triggers the demand for evaluation and recognition that problems exist. The danger of this approach is that decision making practices can become reactive rather than proactive. A board operating in this manner will have difficulty in charting a course which is free from externally imposed mandates. The options are simply too few and often result in choosing from among a set of equally undesirable alternatives. Prevention of reactive decisions occurs when there is early problem recognition and a system of ongoing performance assessment and monitoring activities.

Proactive decision making as contrasted with reactive approaches is what we expect from a good CEO and from the board. Cyert and March define the task as follows:

> Firms will devise and negotiate an environment so as to eliminate the uncertainty. Rather than treat the environment as exogenous, and to be predicted, they seek ways to make it controllable.(4)

For the nonprofit human service corporation, it is not enough to leave this task to the CEO. The board, as the legal and moral owner, is where the ultimate decider function for oversight must rest. This translates into one critical act: Early problem recognition. Everybody and every organized system for serving people has problems. It is the reason why we advocate board ownership of the evaluation function. Let's look at some examples of what can happen when the board fails to recognize and value early problem recognition.

A neighborhood food cooperative board worked well for about three years and expanded its operations to include a storefront and wider range of products. Eventually the overhead costs were more than the organization could cover. Food stocks decreased due to lack of funds to order and members stopped using the Coop on a regular basis. Meetings were called to address the problem, but members had lost interest and the group was forced to close down. Efforts to solve the problem were too late.

The general hospital is a good example of a large complex organization that must achieve early problem recognition and thereby adapt to changing environmental conditions. In studying the actions of some 121 hospital boards, Ritvo found that when an organization learns of a problem before it becomes a crisis, there is lead time for decision making and coping strategies. (6) A classic example of this failure to achieve early problem recognition occurred in the early 1970's when many hospitals were faced with the problem of declining birthrates and low OB/maternity service utilization. In Hospital A and Hospital B, births declined and resulted in costly empty beds. Whereas in Hospital C the Board used data on birthrates and changes in delivery practices to assess the situation and come up with adaptive solutions early enough to prevent costly mistakes.

This is what the board's job in nonprofit organizations is all about and the information to do it just isn't there without a built-in system for performance assessment. The task of early problem recognition is too urgent to wait for a year long study or, as is more commonly the case, let the chief executive and staff decide what the problems are and "screen" them before the board gets involved. When the chief executive or staff screen out problems that should come to the attention of the board, chances for early problem recognition are missed.

Studies of how top executives spend their time indicate that immediate high-pressure disturbances comprise the greatest bulk of the CEO's available time. Mintzberg's (1975) classic studies of what administrators do indicate that disturbances arise:

Not just because poor managers ignore situations until they reach crisis proportion, but also because good managers cannot possibly anticipate all the consequences of the actions they take.(6)

Some things just have to be decided by the board and this requires information that is concise and reliable, and this cannot occur unless there is a board investment in the oversight role. But how does a diverse group like a board succeed at changing its role from something as fuzzy as reactive to proactive ownership?

Step 3: Design of Assessment and Monitoring System

To be successfully proactive, the board must have a defined means of monitoring or assessing the organization's performance. Systems analysis and the the art of systems thinking revolve around the concept of interdependence. This means that to design a workable system for an organization we have to start by looking at the whole organization, then how the parts, the sub-systems, interact with each other and then we must identify what is problematic or missing. Let's look at an example of how a board might get started in designing a system for monitoring and assessing performance.

The process of systems analysis should begin by doing an assessment of what the whole organization looks like at a given point in time. One way for the board (or a board committee) to begin the process is to carefully review their own organization to see how it operates. In order to break down the entire organization into its parts, the board might use an instrument similar to the one shown in Exhibit 9-2.

EXHIBIT 9-2: Sub-System Assessment Checklist

BOARD PERFORMANCE

1. Appropriate board committees are clearly defined and active.
2. The articles of incorporation (charter) and bylaws are current and the organization is in compliance with their provisions.
3. Composition of the board is appropriate to the mission of the organizations.
4. Board members' attendance and participation are at acceptable levels.
5. There is a clear policy on conflict of interest and complete compliance with the policy.
6. There is a regular board orientation and training program.
7. All directors have been given current board manuals.
8. The board-executive relations are open and interdependent.

ORGANIZATIONAL PLANNING

1. Long term or corporate plans were adopted by the board and are regularly reviewed.
2. The long term plan covers both the internal development of the

Continued

109

organization and external program development.
3. Current program plans and activities are congruent with the longer range plan.
4. The plans are periodically used to assess operations and organizational development.
5. Problems are generally anticipated and planning is seldom done in response to crisis.

FUNDING AND RESOURCE DEVELOPMENT

1. Appropriate committees are active in the design and implementation of resource development programs.
2. Staff provides an appropriate level of support for resource development.
3. The funding base of the organization is diverse and avoids depending on a few sources.
4. There is an acceptable degree of continuity in the funding base; not a series of short term unrelated grants.
5. There is a long term plan for resource development for the organization.

PUBLIC RELATIONS

1. There is a regular assessment of the organization's image in each of its major audiences (clients, funders, other organizations, public officials, etc.).
2. The perceptions of these audiences are generally positive for the organization.
3. There is a planned program that seeks to keep the audiences aware of and informed about the organization.

FINANCIAL MANAGEMENT

1. The board is active in the review and approval of the budget.
2. Sufficient financial information is provided to the board for it to make informed decisions about the financial affairs of the corporation.
3. Appropriate committees exist and are active in the financial management of the organization.
4. An audit is conducted on a regular and timely basis.
5. The board anticipates financial needs and problems.
6. An adequate system of internal controls is utilized.

PERSONNEL

1. Appropriate personnel policies have been adopted by the board and are followed by the executive.
2. There is a position classification and salary schedule policy for the organization.
3. Affirmative action and non-discrimation policies have been adopted and enforced throughout the organization.
4. A current job description exists for each position.

Continued

EXHIBIT: Continued

5. All personnel are evaluated at least annually.
6. Appropriate training is obtained for staff on a regular basis.
7. Appropriate use is made of volunteers.

EVALUATION

1. There is an annual assessment of the results of program activities.
2. Appropriate program data is routinely collected and regularly analyzed.
3. There is a regular assessment of organizational administration.
4. Program and administrative costs, including costs/unit of service, are regularly reviewed by the board.

The data which is collected will indicate where problems might exist in the organization. For example, suppose that ten board members completed this checklist and that nine of them said, in response to Item 2 under public relations, that the organization is generally not perceived favorably by several audiences. This information would indicate that there was a problem with the organization's public relations effort. At this stage, however, the board members probably wouldn't have enough information to know what caused the problem or what they should do about it.

Once the problem area is identified, the board would want to focus on this area in a more detailed way to see why and how the subsystem broke down. After this more detailed study of the problem is conducted, the board should be in position to re-design the sub-system in order to correct the problem or prevent its recurrence. In the latter part of this chapter, we will look in more detail at two areas for system design: assessment of the executive and assessment of board performance.

Step 4: Utilizing Evaluation Outputs for Program Involvement

Briefly, lets turn to the remaining part of the board's role in oversight. So far we have established three roles for the board in oversight: (1) taking ownership of evaluation, (2) achieving early problem recognition, (3) being proactive and anticipating problems. Let's turn now to the output stage or bottom line: Ensuring the utilization of information from the assessment for program and organizational improvement. This is what oversight is all about.

All of us have had the experience of reading or sitting through long and confusing presentations of what a particular monitoring report or evaluation was all about. The fact of the matter is that when it was over we knew very little more about what ought to be done than when we started. To avoid this situation, we advocate that the board change the way the game is played. Specifically, this means seeing to it that board members are actively involved in building the monitoring and assessment system.

Program evaluation, when done well, can and does provide useful information about program effort, effectiveness and efficiency. However, the decision of what to study and how to interpret the findings involves more than facts. Evaluation involves value decisions or choices that must be made by policy makers or key decision makers in conjunction with evaluators. A value is a stated opinion or set of policies which specify what is desirable. Good evaluation work will raise value issues that the board must struggle with and use to modify or extend existing policies about what is good and desirable.

For example, if an evaluation finding shows that program A is not reaching its stated goals but is providing other valued services, choices have to made about how these other or unanticipated outcomes relate to the mission and goals of the organization. They may or may not be the kinds of accomplishments that your corporation wants to focus on.

The point is that evaluation is only a tool for program improvement. It provides a basis on which choices can be clarified and made. Some of these are programmatic or administrative choices, others involve more basic policy choices for the direction and role of the corporation in the community. In the next section of this chapter, we will look in more detail at how the board goes about implementing two special performance assessments: Assessing the executive and itself.

Executive and Board Performance

In assessing both the executive and board, we are looking for some measure of performance based on a standard or set of values which the board establishes. When the board fails to assume ownership of these two evaluation activities, they become lost and subject to "decision by default." In both cases, the goal in the assessment work is to achieve early problem recognition and to initiate corrective action.

What we are concerned with is effective performance and a system for monitoring where we are in relation to where we want to go. Use of assessment techniques implies a concern for performance and a recognition that standards are important. Let's look at the full sequence for building an assessment system as it might be applied in assessing executive performance.

Assessment of Executive Performance

Classical management theory and the principles of good board/staff relations establish the need for a formal and regular system for assessing the performance of the chief executive officer who represents the interests of the corporation and translates board policies into operating programs and practices. Effective leadership is critical in order for the board and staff to fulfill their respective roles.

What are the best ways for the board to establish policies on this neglected aspect of board/staff relations? It is our view that a clear policy statement that is understood by all parties is the first step. However, the purposes for doing executive assessment must be clear before the policy can be developed and implemented. In general, there are two major objectives that have utility for both the individual and the organization:

(1) To enable the manager to identify areas of high per-performance and strengthen areas of administrative weakness as perceived by the board.

(2) To enable the board to measure executive performance and engage in early problem recognition when needed for staff, program and organizational improvement.

The policy statement in this area should be explicit and documented for future reference. For example, the policy mandate might be stated as follows:

A formal assessment of executive performance shall be carried out by the board of directors on an annual basis. The plan for assessment activities to be carried out will be developed in conjunction with the chief executive officer of the corporation and submitted to the board for review and approval ninety (90) days prior to the end of each fiscal year. Assessment criteria and standards for satisfactory performances will be specified prior to conduct of the performance appraisal. Findings will be submitted to the executive committee or other designated board committee and reviewed by the chief executive with opportunity for comment and inclusion of self-assessment data, prior to the beginning of the subsequent fiscal year. In those areas where performance is assessed as below standard, suggestions for improvement shall be developed jointly and reviewed at appropriate future intervals.

As a result of past experience the board may choose to modify its policy statement and or process for implementation. The best test of any policy statement is experience: Did it work well when implemented and if not, why not?

Frequently the problem in doing an executive assessment is not the policy but the lack of a workable system for carrying it out. If the assessment system works well it should provide the board and the executive with information which can serve to answer three questions:

(1) What are the special or unique strengths that this person has demonstrated in this position?

(2) What are the areas for which improvement is indicated?

(3) What are the kinds of management and/or organizational development activities that should be carried out in the future?

Designing the assessment system involves the difficult but necessary task of establishing criteria for performance appraisal. More specifically, what are the competencies necessary for an effective administrator in this job? Board members who have professional experience in personnel management can offer ideas and consulting firms with a good "track record" in working with human service organizations in the area of personnel assessment can provide an element of objectivity at this stage in the process.

One way of establishing the assessment system is to design an appraisal form that reflects the performance categories or areas of the job that are to be assessed. An example of this approach to appraisal is shown in Exhibit 9-2. It is based on the premise that there are three broad areas of competency for the CEO in a nonprofit corporation. The areas are:

(1) Technical Competency. The sum of the knowledge, skills and experience relative to the conditions of people, organizational arrangements and programs that fall within the mission and goals of this organization.

(2) Operational Competency. The technical and behavioral skills demonstrated in current managerial work with the staff, board and others in achieving effective organizational maintenance and growth.

(3) Developmental Competency. The judgment, technical and creative personal capacities (or potential) necessary for future leadership of this corporation.

Exhibit 9-3 is an example of one approach to use in collecting informed judgments in each of the three categories. The instrument can be expanded and adapted to reflect the specific kinds of managerial activities that are viewed as most important for a given nonprofit corporation or dimension of concern to the board.

After the appraisal form is developed, the next task is to determine who should be asked to make the assessments and how the forms are to be used in preparing the report for use by the board and the executive. The decision about who and how many persons should be asked to participate in the appraisal is critical if there are to be constructive rather than destructive outcomes from the process. One guideline that can be used in reaching a decision is to start with the ideal and then work back to a more feasible approach if there are particular constraints or the potential for undesirable consequences.

EXHIBIT 9-3: Executive Performance Appraisal

	Very Weak				Average				Very Strong	
	0	1	2	3	4	5	6	7	8	9

TECHNICAL SKILLS AND COMPETENCIES

1. Knowledge of program area	0	1	2	3	4	5	6	7	8	9
2.	0	1	2	3	4	5	6	7	8	9
3.	0	1	2	3	4	5	6	7	8	9
4.	0	1	2	3	4	5	6	7	8	9
5.	0	1	2	3	4	5	6	7	8	9

OPERATIONAL SKILLS AND COMPETENCIES

1. Leading and motivating staff	0	1	2	3	4	5	6	7	8	9
2.	0	1	2	3	4	5	6	7	8	9
3.	0	1	2	3	4	5	6	7	8	9
4.	0	1	2	3	4	5	6	7	8	9
5.	0	1	2	3	4	5	6	7	8	9

ORGANIZATIONAL DEVELOPMENT SKILLS

1. Board development and training.	0	1	2	3	4	5	6	7	8	9
2.	0	1	2	3	4	5	6	7	8	9
3.	0	1	2	3	4	5	6	7	8	9
4.	0	1	2	3	4	5	6	7	8	9
5.	0	1	2	3	4	5	6	7	8	9

You might decide, for example, to collect data from two groups, the board and the staff reporting to the executive. This would allow for comparison and provide a useful way for staff to have input into the process. However, if the process is being done for the first time, or if there are indications that staff or full board involvement could have a negative effect on the future effectiveness of the executive, a more limited process can be undertaken. The principle to keep in mind is that any appraisal system involves judgment that may or may not be valid indicators of actual performance.

Ample opportunity should be given to the executive to participate in the process. This can be done by:

- having the executive initiate definition of the activities to be assessed;
- building on an existing system for employee performance appraisal, as developed by the executive;
- using self-rating as an additional source of data;
- including reports and external indicators of output and outcomes for the corporation;
- contracting with a firm or individual with expertise in management development for assistance with the appraisal

The point is to be objective, constructive and concerned with the rights of the individual being assessed.

Assessment of Board

Every so often the board as a whole needs to step back and look at itself. This self-assessment process is critical to the development and maintenance of a healthy decision making group. It happens informally when directors get together and talk about individual and board concerns. But, very few policy making groups have a built in process for "taking stock" of its own work.

Such a board self-assessment should be done at least annually, either prior to or in conjunction with the assessment of executive performance. The process doesn't need to drag on forever —it just needs the right first step and can develop from there.

A good beginning is to set aside time at a regular or special meeting to find out where the trouble spots are. Individual members have different experiences and expectations for the board's performance. The task is to identify areas of agreement on what needs fixing. The Board Assessment Questionnaire (Exhibit 9-4) is designed to serve this purpose. It has been designed to identify key areas where board performance is not meeting member expectations.

EXHIBIT 9-4: Board Assessment Questionnaire

DIRECTIONS

The following instrument is designed to help members of a nonprofit board of directors assess their performance. There are no right or wrong answers. The instrument is intended only as an aid to the board in defining areas in which it is not meeting the expectations of its members.

Board performance is divided into sixteen functional areas on the following pages. Each area is defined and accompanied by a scale that ranges from 1-10. There is a description of board behavior at each end of the scale.

Put an "S" above the number on the scale where you think your board's performance should be. Put an "I" over the number that represents where you think the board's actual performance is. Each scale should have an "S" and an "I" marked when you complete the form.

_____An Example:_____

Personal knowledge. The degree to which board members have a real knowledge of each other.

Most board members barely know the names of the others.	I S 1 2 3 4 5 6 7 8 9 10	Board members frequently know each intimately. It's just "one big family."

REMEMBER: I = "is"... S = "should be"

1.   Information. The degree to which board members actively seek information about the operation of the organization's programs and services.

There is a high demand and active search for detailed information about the organization's performance.	1 2 3 4 5 6 7 8 9 10	Board members seek little information about the organization's performance: They simply accept what is given.

2.   Values. The degree to which board members consider the value implications of their policies and organizational behavior.

Values are frequently discussed and considered in decisions.	1 2 3 4 5 6 7 8 9 10	Values are almost never openly discussed.

3. Independence. The degree to which the board depends on staff recommendations and input for its decisions.

The board almost
always follows the
staff's suggestions.

1 2 3 4 5 6 7 8 9 10

The board listens to
staff ideas but fre-
quently reaches dif-
ferent conclusions.

4. Ambassadorship. The degree to which members of the board represent the corporation to others in the community, both formally and informally.

Board members almost
never represent the or-
ganization, seeing this
as a staff function.

1 2 3 4 5 6 7 8 9 10

Board members aggres-
sively represent the
organization to others.

5. Preparedness. The degree to which the board anticipates and plans for the future of the organization.

Board members fre-
quently point out long
range opportunities or
potential trouble spots
for the organization.

1 2 3 4 5 6 7 8 9 10

Board members generally
do not discuss the or-
ganization's future
except when faced by
problem or crisis.

6. Attendance. The degree to which board members actively show concern for ensuring attendance at board and committee meetings.

There is very little
concern or discussion
about individual attend-
ance or absence at
meetings.

1 2 3 4 5 6 7 8 9 10

Members are actively
praised for good attend-
ance or criticized for
poor attendance.

7. Board Orientation. The degree to which the board takes time to provide orientation and training to the members of the board.

Almost no time is devoted
to orientation, training
and briefing of the board
members.

1 2 3 4 5 6 7 8 9 10

Background briefings,
orientation, or train-
ing activities occur
almost constantly.

8. Resource Development. The degree to which the board defines resource development —acquiring equipment, money, volunteers, staff, etc.— as a board or staff function.

Resource development
is almost entirely left
staff.

1 2 3 4 5 6 7 8 9 10

The board takes primary
responsibility for
resource development.

Continued

9. Committee Activity. The degree to which the board carries out activities through its committees.

| Committee activity is rare: The entire board does almost all of the work. | 1 2 3 4 5 6 7 8 9 10 | Almost everything the board does is first re-viewed in a committee. |

10. Formal Leadership. The degree to which the chair and other other officers provide leadership to the board.

| The board's officers take the lead in almost every-thing the board does. | 1 2 3 4 5 6 7 8 9 10 | The officers are passive except in carrying out routine procedural duties. |

11. Special Service. The degree to which the board members volunteer for extra duties in response to organizational needs.

| Members frequently offer assistance and volunteer for organi-zational support activities. | 1 2 3 4 5 6 7 8 9 10 | Board members frequently avoid special services to the organization. |

12. Accessibility. The degree to which the board members are open to the organization's clients or constituents for comments about and criticism of the organization.

| Board members are often used as channels of com-munication by clients and constituents. | 1 2 3 4 5 6 7 8 9 10 | Board members are almost never used as channels of communication by clients and constituents. |

13. Special Interest Representation. The degree to which board members seek to represent special interests on the board.

| Board members frequently speak from a special interest point of view. | 1 2 3 4 5 6 7 8 9 10 | Board members almost never speak for special interests. |

14. Mission Agreement. The degree to which board members agree on the purpose of the organization.

| Board members frequently disagree about the pur-pose of the organization. | 1 2 3 4 5 6 7 8 9 10 | Board members almost al-ways agree on the purpose of the organization. |

15. Initiative. The degree to which board members initiate ideas and action within the organization.

Almost all board actions are in response to staff initiated issues or ideas. 1 2 3 4 5 6 7 8 9 10 Many board actions begin with member or committee initiated issues or ideas.

16. Openness. The degree to which board members are honest in communicating their feelings to other members.

Most board members act as if they have no feelings during a meeting. 1 2 3 4 5 6 7 8 9 10 Board members frequently show their emotions during a meeting.

SCORING: Three issues can be looked at in scoring this instrument: The distribution of the "I" responses, the distribution of "S" responses, and the "gaps" between the I's and S's. For instance, if the board members report a wide range of I's on an item, the board analysis should focus on why people see the board so differently. On the other hand, if there is a wide range of S's on an item, then the board should focus on agreeing on the members' expectation in that area. A wide gap between the I's and S's on an item indicates individual member dissatisfaction with that area of the board's life and the area may be one in which board members are most willing to pursue change.

© Independent Community Consultants, Inc.

Developing a Plan of Action

Now that you have a handle on some problem areas, the next step is to set some realistic goals for change. More specifically, where and how does the board intervene?

Organizational development and change take time and skill. Many of the problem areas that you have uncovered have been there for some time. There is no right way to fix a problem or set of interrelated issues that confront the board. However, there are resources that can be tapped both within the board and outside the organization. The task is to assign priorities and use the interest generated to plan appropriate corrective actions.

Some possible next steps would be to:

(1) Set up a task force that will plan for board development and training activities to achieve the desired changes;

(2) Meet with staff or other community agencies to gain further information about what needs to be done;

(3) Request services from an outside consulting group or individual with experience in organization development for nonprofit corporations.

Muddling through or failing to tackle board and organizational problems is risky when funds are tight and program effectiveness is at stake. Performance assessment is important, but the payoff is in what can be done with the information to develop a more effective system for meeting the goals of the organization and fulfilling its mandate to serve its constituency.

Notes

1. Mager, Robert F. GOAL ANALYSIS. Belmont, California: Lear Siegler, Inc. Fearon Publishers, 1972, pp. V-VI.

2. Carver, John. "Business Leadership on Nonprofit Boards," BOARD PRACTICES MONOGRAPH. National Association of Corporate Directors, October, 1980.

3. Carver, John. " Community Participation." Keynote Address, Board Leadership Program, National Council of Community Mental Health Centers, Annual Meeting, February 21, 1979.

4. Cyert, R.M. and March, J.G. A BEHAVIORAL THEORY OF THE FIRM. Englewood Cliff, New Jersey: Prentice Hall, 1963, pp. 120.

5. Ritvo, Roger Alan. ORGANIZATIONAL AND ENVIRONMENTAL DYNAMICS: A MULTI-HOSPITAL STUDY OF THE ROLE OF BOARDS OF TRUSTEES. Unpublished dissertation, Case Western Reserve University, 1976.

6. Mintzberg H. THE MANAGERS'S JOB: FOLKLORE AND FACT. Harvard Business Review, 1975, 53 (July/August).

7. Rothman, Jack, John L. Erlich, Joseph G. Teresa. CHANGING ORGANIZATIONS AND COMMUNITY PROBLEMS. Beverly Hills, California: Sage Publications, Inc., 1981, p. 11.

Further Readings

C. Clifford Attkisson, William a Hargreaves, and Mardi Horowitz, (Ed.), EVALUATION OF HUMAN SERVICE PROGRAMS. New York: Academic Press, 1978

Lynn Lyons Morris (Ed.), THE EVALUATION KIT (8 volumes). Beverly Hills, CA: Sage Publications, 1978

Donald L. Grant (Ed.), MONITORING ONGOING PROGRAMS. San Francisco: Jossey-Bass, Inc., 1978

William A. Hargreaves and C. Clifford Attkisson (Ed.), RESOURCE MATERIALS FOR COMMUNITY MENTAL HEALTH PROGRAM EVALUATION. Rockville, MD: National Institute of Mental Health, 1977

Ernest R. House, EVALUATING WITH VALIDITY. Beverly Hills, CA: Sage Publications, 1980

William B. McCurdy, PROGRAM EVALUATION: A CONCEPTUAL TOOL KIT. New York: Family Service Association of America, 1979

David Nachmias, PUBLIC POLICY EVALUATION: APPROACHES AND METHODS. New York: St. Martin's Press, 1979

Project Share, PRODUCTIVITY IN HUMAN SERVICES: MEASURMENT, IMPROVEMENT AND MANAGEMENT. Alexandria, VA: Project Share Human Services Bibliography, November 1980

Public Management Institute, EVALUATION HANDBOOK. San Francisco: Public Management Institute, 1980

Leonard Rutman, PLANNING USEFUL EVALUATIONS. Beverly Hills: Sage Publications, 1980

United Way of Greater St. Louis, MANAGEMENT EVALUATION MANUAL: HOW TO MEASURE YOUR EFFECTIVENESS IN FOUR MANAGEMENT AREAS. St. Louis, MO: United Way of Greater St. Louis, 1977

Joseph S. Wholey, EVALUATION: PROMISE AND PERFORMANCE. Washington, D.C.: The Urban Institute, 1979

Chapter 10

Organizational Planning

Earl W. Anthes

Planning is inherent in purposeful action. We all do it every day. If we didn't, we would be wandering around, like the paramecium, in random aimlessness. The only question for nonprofit corporations is whether they plan on a day to day basis or whether they plan over longer periods in order to give themselves a controlled, navigated direction.

It is through planning that the board of directors translates the purpose and essential values of the corporation into consistent policies and targets which can guide the staff in consistent action.

Before looking at the planning process, however, we must make a confession: If planners were the experts they claim to be, they could come up with consistent language of planning. I have suspected for a long time that one of the things that blocks organizations from planning is the confusion engendered when people read more than one book on planning. One planners's "goals" are another's "objectives"; "activities" may be synonymous with "targets" or the "necessary steps in reaching a target." It can get confusing.

The following outline may well add to this confusion. However, the moral of this confession is that the reader must be prepared to use any planning system creatively. Planning is inherently a creative process. While principles can be outlined, their application in the real world depends upon your judgment, intuition and "eye." This is not a "plan by numbers" kit.

The Planning Process: An Overview

A clear mission statement and a set of corporate values are the real beginnings of the planning process. They provide the basic direction and guidelines for the organization. If the corporation is pictured as a mosaic then the mission and essential value policies define only the most crude outlines of the picture. All of the details in the corporate picture are supplied through the planning process.

The planning process may be defined as a series of successively "smaller and smaller" decisions each of which selects the best course of action in order to reach a desired condition or state of being. This definition has several clear implications:

1. You begin the process by defining where you want to be at the end of the process.

2. You continually divide the whole into smaller and smaller parts which are nearer and nearer in time.

3. You make many choices between alternative actions. (To be made rationally these choices must involve a clear comparison and weighing of alternatives.)

An Outline of the Planning Process

The following steps are useful in developing comprehensive, long term organizational plans.

Step 1. Develop or review your organization's mission and essential values.

See Chapter 4 for a detailed discussion of mission and values.

Step 2. Review the history of the organization.

In order to define where the organization should go, you must know where it is today, and where it has come from. Those who will participate in determining the future of the organization need to know and appreciate its past.

Step 3. Develop long range corporate or organizational goals.

These are the long range goals which define the dreams or visions for the organization. They should cover both the results which are sought through program activities and the internal development and maintenance of the organization.

Step 4. Develop a strategic plan outline and goals for meeting the needs.

After identifying current performance levels in the organization and environmental trends, developing the strategic plan involves identifying alternative strategies and selecting the one that is best for your community and organization.

Step 5. Develop operational objectives and plans to achieve the strategic goals.

These multi-year plans specify what will be achieved during the next 3-5 years of operation and define major blocks of activities necessary for achievement of the goals. Estimates of resource requirements and costs are prepared for each major activity and are the basis for developing budget projections.

Step 6. Develop one year implementation or project plans with detailed activity sequences and resource requirements for the first year of the multi-year plan.

These are plans which will be implemented in the coming year. They are specific with detailed cost analysis which are used to develop the organization's budget.

You can think of each of these steps in the full planning process as successively smaller and smaller building blocks for the corporation.

A Goal and Objective Grid

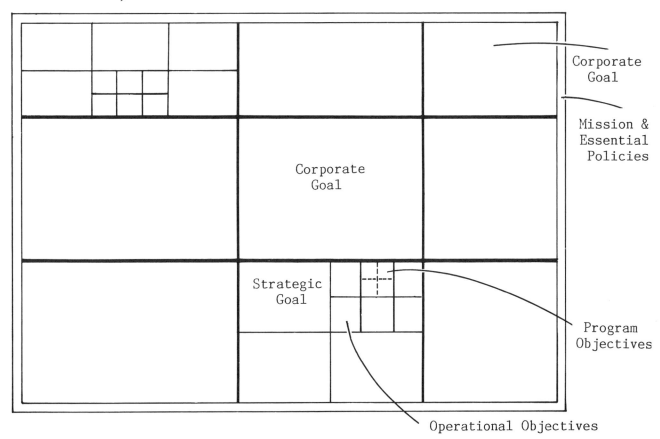

The above illustration shows how a set of annual or project objectives should "add up" to equal an operational objective; a set of operational objectives should "add up" to equal a strategic goal; strategic goals, in turn, "add up" to equal a corporate goal; and all the corporate goals should "add up" to mission fulfillment.

```
┌─────────────────────────────────────────────────────────────────────┐
│                                                                       │
│   EXHIBIT 10-1: Sample Goals and Objectives                           │
│                                                                       │
│      Corporate Goal II.  Avoidance of dependence on funding           │
│         sources.  No single funding source will provide more          │
│         than 25% of our total operating budget.                       │
│                                                                       │
│      Strategic Goal III.  By 1987, annual, externally controlled      │
│         grants (public and private) shall constitute no more than     │
│         50% of our total revenues.  Fifty percent of the budget       │
│         shall be provided by local  contributions, client fees and    │
│         other self-generated sources.                                 │
│                                                                       │
│      Operational Objective II. A. 1.  By the end of 1986, an endow-   │
│         ment fund will have been formed with assets of $100,000.      │
│                                                                       │
│      Operational Objective II. A. 2.  By the end of 1987, an ability  │
│         to pay client fee system will be implemented and producing    │
│         15% of the total program budget.                              │
│                                                                       │
│      Program Objective II. A. 1.b.  By January, 1985, a formal        │
│         announcement of the formation of the endowment will have      │
│         been made along with an announcement that $35,000 has         │
│         been received.                                                │
│                                                                       │
└─────────────────────────────────────────────────────────────────────┘
```

As you can see from this example, the planning process takes us from the general —avoidance of dependence upon funding source— to the more specific announcement of the endowment fund.

There is also a presumption that it progresses from the least changeable to the more changeable. Corporate goals, generally remain stable for longer periods of time while specific program plans and objectives may change quite frequently in response to changing organizational and external conditions. This is a simple recognition that we must maintain flexibility in our strategies, operational objectives and program plans and activities if we are to be assured of reaching our corporate goals. We must constantly operate in a plan-implement-assess-feedback-re-plan cycle. In this sense, we might think of our plan as our theory of the best path to a given result. As our theory or plan is tested by being implemented, it may need to be adjusted for a better fit with the world.

It is worth noting that this progression from general to specific and from relative permanence to relative flexibility has caused some planners to arbitrarily divide the planning process into strategic and tactical planning. Others use the long term and short term categories. Use whatever terms you wish, but it is important to remember that they are part of the same planning process. To often, organizations have a long term or strategic plan which hasn't been out of the file cabinet in the last three years, has long been forgotten, and has absolutely no relationship to the current annual plan except for the name of the organization.

For our purpose, we are dividing the planning process, like all of Gaul, into three parts: Strategic Planning, Operational Planning and Annual Project Planning. Annual planning will be mentioned only briefly.

Benefits of Planning

Given the amount of time and effort needed for this complete planning process, it is reasonable to wonder if planning is worthwhile. There are several ways that organizations benefit from planning.

1. The process of planning helps to give the group a shared sense of direction. This is more a benefit of the planning process than the plan itself because the benefit is derived from the board and staff sitting down and consciously thinking about and discussing where they want to go and how they want to operate. This gives them an opportunity to identify and resolve disagreements and conflicts without the outside pressure of a crisis or deadline.

2. The planning process makes it possible for the organization to control its life and direction. Without a long range plan, groups tend to drift without a sense of direction and then be guided solely by outside forces. These forces may be small groups or cliques in the community, funding sources or other organizations that are more than willing to tell you what you want to do.

3. A plan helps the group avoid wasting effort and money. Without a plan, the group is likely to pursue activities which do not fit together and support one another, or start and stop activities that are the pet ideas of some members, or begin activities which cannot be finished because of resource limits. While none of these can be totally avoided with a plan, wasteful practices can be kept to a minimum.

4. The planning process makes it possible for the organization to be flexible and to move quickly when new opportunities or dangers arise. If you have clearly thought out what you want to achieve as well as your limits, then you are better prepared when faced with something new. Your organization is also less likely to be bogged down in internal conflict when facing new challenges if you have thought through the myriad of organizational issues.

5. Planning makes it easier to get people involved and motivated in the organization. The work necessary to keep your organization afloat may get a little tedious and boring at times, but if members of your board see how their work fits into and contributes to the organization's goals, they will be more motivated. This same ability to show the "big picture" will be important in your fund raising efforts.

Strategic Planning

Assuming that your coporation has defined its mission and essential value policies, then strategic planning can begin with the definition of your corporate goals. Corporate goals are the "eternal truths" of the corporation: If not the truths, then at least the continuing dreams. They describe what your corporation will be like when, at some point in the future, it is complete and perfect.

The general areas in which nonprofits should develop corporate goals are listed below along with some issues frequently addressed in corporate plans.

INTERNAL MAINTENANCE
Finance...budget size, source of revenue, diversity of funding base.

Membership...number, composition, tenure, activity.

Personnel...number, comparability of salaries, diversity of staff backgrounds.

Public Image and Public Relations...type of image, relations with different sectors of the community.

Board Development...number of directors, level of activity, representation.

Facilities...kinds of buildings and equipment, location, condition.

PROGRAM SERVICES
...variety of services, levels of services, distribution of service within service area, size of service area, "share" of need being met, number of new service innovations.

Obviously, these are just some of the possible topics of corporate goal statements. Corporate goals need to be defined for all of the key areas and issues which shape the life of your corporation.

While corporate goals usually do not carry a specific deadline for achievement, they need to be clear, unambiguous statements of desired corporate characteristics and at least a rough measure or indicator of acceptable performance. An easy way to phrase corporate goals is shown below:

INTENT: Maximize accessibility of services to clients

INDICATOR: Clinic facilities shall be located in such a way that 80% of the client population can obtain services with less than 30 minutes of travel time.

This two part construction of a corporate goal allows you to make a clear statement of the goal's intent -- followed by an operational measure or indicator of minimal acceptable performance. This indicator or performance measure will help keep corporate goal statements from being a needlessly long collection of sentiments which are forgotten or ignored as well as help clarify the meaning of the concern or issue expressed in the "intent" statement.

There can be and often should be more than one measure or indicator specified for a goal. For example, if the above clinic were also concerned with financial accessibility, the board could add the following as a second indicator of performance: "Users of the clinic facilities shall be representative of the service area population in terms of income classification."

It is difficult to prescribe a point when you have enough corporate goals. The basic test for completeness of a set of corporate goal statements is done by asking the following questions.

1. Are the goals congruent? Do they fit together and make sense when looked at as a set?

2. Are the goals complete? Are all key areas of corporate life covered by the goals?

3. Is there a consensus on the goals? Do we have a shared dream? Do we agree on the intent of each goal? With the performance measures or indicators?

If your set of goals passes the test on these three criteria, then your corporate goal setting activity has been "successful."

Procedures for Setting Corporate Goals

Since corporate goals are the first detailed expression of the "dream of the corporation," it is usually desirable to develop a first draft of these goals as a full board and staff team rather than simply assigning the task to the executive director or a board committee. A corporate goal setting meeting can be an excellent team and organization building event if it is done in an informal, participatory way. Some corporations not only have board and staff participate, but have "corporate friends" in for the goal setting meeting. These may be former board or staff members as well as people who have supported the organization in the past.

In addition to considering the number and type of participants, the style of the meeting itself must be well thought out. Too often goal setting meetings tend to be operated as formal board meetings: All comments directed to the chairperson and the chairperson recognizing each speaker. This is too restrictive a format for the goal setting function. It is difficult to share your dreams in the formal setting of a parliamentary debate. In order to generate the kinds of interaction needed for corporate goal setting, a more appropriate meeting climate is one characterized by informality, friendliness and sharing. This is far easier to achieve if participants do much of their work in small groups.

The goal setting process can be started by having all of the participants complete a series of simple sentence stems such as the following two examples.

"When our finances are perfect, XYZ,Inc. will be ..."

"My dream for our public image is ..."

These sentence stems can be printed on 3x5 note cards, distributed to the participants prior to the meeting and collected at the start of the meeting. After the cards are collected, they can be sorted by topic and given to small groups to compile into a comprehensive set of goal statements. These lists then can be put on newsprint or prepared forms and passed to another small group for review and comment until each small group has had the opportunity to review and comment on all of the lists. Once the groups have their original goal list back with the comments of all the other groups, they can prepare a tentative draft of the goals for large group discussion and adoption of the intent statements and suggested indicators of success.

The work of all of the small groups can then be typed and circulated for thoughtful review, feedback and adoption at the next board meeting.

Once you have developed a set of corporate goals, the next step in the strategic planning process is to assess where the corporation is at the current time. This provides baseline information for the board and staff. In essence, this is an assessment of the corporation's strengths and weaknesses in the same key areas that were covered in the corporate goals statements. With this information the board can develop a very clear picture of the gap between the "here and now corporation" and the "future corporation" as outlined in the corporate goals.

Some organizations begin their corporate or strategic planning process with the assessment of where they are now. This has the unfortunate tendency to lead the group to develop goals by simply extrapolating from their current status. In order to protect the corporate goal setting process from unconsciously drifting into a "more of the same" plan, it is usually desirable to wait until you have a clear concensus on the goals and their measures of performance before you develop the baseline data on the current status of the corporation. This helps prevent the board from reducing the discrepancy between the current corporate condition and goal condition by "lowering" their goals.

A second advantage in developing the baseline information after corporate goals are set is that the corporate goals and their indicators or performance measures will provide direction and guidance to the staff on what kind of information is needed for a full picture of the current corporation. Without this kind of direction, the staff may (1) give the board more information than it can use; (2) omit important facts because they assume "everyone already knows"; or (3) bias reports in order to lead the board to adopt the staff's pre-determined planning directions. These dangers can be reduced if the goals are determined and then the corresponding baseline data are developed. A form similar to the one illustrated below is useful.

EXHIBIT 10-2: Goal and Current Condition Summary Sheet

Corporate Goal	Current Conditions

Notes:

The third step in strategic planning involves the recognition that the corporation does not exist in a vacuum. This step is the identification of your assumptions about the future environment in which the corporation is to operate. These future trends are the forces which will have an influence on the corporation and its activities over a specified time period. Often a 5-10 year time period is used, but if your environmental forces are highly changeable, you may be forced to use shorter periods.

In identifying these environmental forces, it is important that the board not fall into a "problem-centered" bias. You are not only trying to identify all the forces working against you, but also trying to identify all those forces which may be working with you. One way to make sure you get a complete picture of future trends is to use a chart like Exhibit 10-3 below as a starting point. This chart provides you with a list of eight actors in your environment as well as ways they can affect you.

EXHIBIT 10-3: Environmental Actors and Domain Matrix

Actors	Economic	Technological	Pol/Legal	Social	Physical	Demograph	Other
Clients							
Members							
"Competitors"							
Current Funding Sources							
Government/ Regulators							
"The Public"							
Staff							
Former Funding Sources							
Other							

The board can develop a list of assumptions in several different ways. Members of the board and staff can complete such a sheet and then combine the lists. You could also brainstorm a list of assumptions in a large group.

If there are some areas of your environment with which the board and staff are not experienced, you may want to interview a number of people who can serve as "outside experts." For instance, if your group is concerned with health services to poor people in a rural area, a critical environmental assumption would be "projected economic growth" of the community during the next five years. Interviewing bankers, chamber of commerce officers, regional planning staff and others enables you to develop such information.

Once you have a rough list of assumptions about the future you should look at each assumption in two ways. First, you want to develop some measure of the assumption's uncertainty --the probability of the trend actually developing. This can be done by having people rate each trend on a scale like the one illustrated below or by indicating the percentage of certainty, ranging from 0 to 100%, for each identified trend.

Example of an assumed trend rating instrument.

Assumed trend.	Highly Probable			even			Highly Improbable
By 1990_____	1	2	3	4	5	6	7

The second way to look at each trend is to examine its probable impact on the organization. An impact analysis is an attempt to identify how the trend, if it occurs, will affect the corporation and its activities. This will be important in your later strategy development and selection process since these steps will call for you to make judgments about reasonable "tradeoffs." Therefore, you must know how these trends will influence your operations: Some trends may threaten the life of the corporation while others portend only mild inconvenience or opportunity.

The trends of greatest significance to the board and staff in the strategic planning process are those with both high certainty of occurrence and strong impact. Those trends which have strong impact, but a low probability of occurrence must also be considered by the prudent board.

A simple way to do an impact analysis for the assumed trends is shown in Exhibit 10-4 on the following page.

EXHIBIT 10-4: Impact Analysis Worksheet

Description of Trend	Identified Impacts	Severity of Impact 0 1 2 3 4 5 6 7 8 9 10 (0=none 10=very great)
	1.	
	2.	
	3.	

(repeat for all trends)

All of the previous steps —and the work they entail— finally get you ready to develop a strategic plan. The first step is to carefully define your strategic planning problem. At this step, clarity is of critical importance. For it is in the strategic problem statement that we lay the foundation of the entire strategic planning process. Most bad strategic planning is caused by incomplete strategic problem definition at the start of the process. Either critical environmental trends were omitted or constraints were not specified for the problem. Such shortcomings can be illustrated with two strategic problem statements for the same hypothetical organization. Let's assume that it is a recreation organization.

Statement 1.
> To develop a year round recreation program that will be totally supported by membership and participation fees.

Statement 2.
> Given that the target population will be 30% poor people by 1989, what can we do to develop a year round recreation program which will be totally self-supporting from membership and participation fees but meets the following conditions:
>
> a. provides that no person shall be excluded from participation because of an inability to pay the fees,
>
> b. attracts a representative cross-section of the community in terms of gender, ethnicity and age.

These two simple strategic problems illustrate the need for clarity and completeness in the problem statement. The first may lead the group to develop an exclusive, high membership fee, low intensity use, "country club" strategy and the other probably will lead you to develop a program and marketing strategy based on sliding fee scales, multiple activities and intense use of the facilities.

The second problem statement also illustrates that it is in the problem statement that we first may confront the fact that it is not only external environmental trends, but also our own mix of goals and essential values that contributes to the difficulty of defining our strategy. In short, we will often find that we must make a trade off between corporate goals. Perhaps, in the above example, we would decide that program self-sufficiency was unrealistic, given our conditions and the social and demographic trends in the target area.

If it should turn out that goal or value trade offs are necessary, then this is a critical board policy making responsibility. The danger is that through sloppy, incomplete planning and analysis, the board and staff may make decisions which make the trade-offs but do so without acknowledging and clearly, consciously choosing to do so.

In general, each strategic planning problem statement should specify the following: The relevant corporate goal to be achieved, the environmental trends that either hinder or aid goal achievement in some way, and any constraints which limit your strategic choices. These constraints will normally be generated from other goals or essential values. If all of these parts are contained in your planning problem statement, then you probably have an adequate statement.

Your next step in the process is to define a method and a set of selection criteria for choosing the "best" strategy. This method and set of criteria will define how and on what basis the board can say "this is the best strategy for us."

Defining the criteria before you consider alternative strategies makes it easier for the group or board to agree upon a set of criteria and selection method and helps prevent everyone from biasing their selection procedures to favor their "pet ideas." In decision making, as in any other game, it is usually easier to agree on the rules before the start of the game. Developing the criteria for selection usually is not too difficult because you have already clarified the organization's mission, essential value policies and corporate goals. These provide a natural base for criteria development.

Some general categories of selection criteria to be applied to strategies are listed below. They indicate general decision factors which may be important in many strategic choices.

Certainty of Goal Achievement. What are the odds for or against success?

Cost Effectiveness. Do the promised results justify the cost?

Risk and Regret. What do we lose if we try and fail? What do we lose if we don't try?

Resource Availability. Do we have or can we get the money, equipment and resources to pursue this strategy?

Organizational Strengths and Weaknesses. Do we have the skills, knowledge, reputation, staff morale, etc. necessary to carry out this strategy?

Timing. Given our relative starting point, can we catch the trend and implement the strategy in time to achieve the goal?

Degree of Organizational Change. How will this strategy influence the way we operate? Is this change worth it?

Congruence with Essential Values and Other Goals. Is this strategy supportive of or in conflict with our values and goals?

Since the criteria must be applied to all of the alternative strategies you will develop, an indicator of its comparative importance in the selection and some form of rating scales must be developed so that they can be consistently applied to the alternatives by the members of the board of directors. In addition, each criteria should be assigned a weighting factor since each criteria will not be equally important in the strategic decision.

One good way to develop weights for criteria is to identify the criterion which is most important for selection among alternatives. This is the anchor criterion: Assign 100 points to this criterion. Each of the other criteria in the set is assigned points from 1- 100, based on its relative importance when compared to the anchor criterion. Thus, if a criterion is considered to be only half as important as the anchor it would receive 50 points. Weights can also be assigned by having everyone rate each criterion in terms of a rating scale from 1-10 where "1" represents "not important and "10" represents "extremely important." To develop final weights for each criterion, using this latter method, total the points from all raters on each criterion and divide by the total possible points for an item (ten points times the number of raters). This is the criterion's weight. Exhibit 10-5 shows another criteria weighting system.

The easiest way to develop a method of applying the criteria to the alternative strategies is to use a consistent rating scale from +5 to −5. Under this system, "+5" means a very positive rating and a "−5" means a very negative rating. Obviously the meaning of "very positive" and "very negative" must be defined in terms of each criterion. For example, if one of your critieria was "Probability of developing funding necessary for implementing the strategy," then "+5" might represent "very sure" and a "−5" might represent "very unlikely." Using a consistent scale of this type will make it easier to calculate a total score for each alternative since the total score can be the sum of all of the weighted criteria scale scores times the critieria's weight.

EXHIBIT 10-5: Instrument for Weighting Selection Criteria

Below are six factors that can be used in selecting the best solution of an identified problem or need. The purpose of the ballot is to begin the development of weight for these factors so that the XYZ, Inc. board and staff can agree on the relative importance that should be assigned to each of these factors in our planning efforts.

Please read over the list and add any other factors or criteria which you think should be considered. Space is provided at the end of the list for these additional items.

INSTRUCTIONS. Assume that you have 100 points which can be distributed to the items on the list. The number of points you assign to an item indicates how important you think it should be in our decision making. There are some rules, however.

1. You must use all 100 points.
2. You cannot give more than 30 points to any single item.
3. You must give at least five points to each issue.

Strategy Selection Factors

_____ 1. Certainty of positive outcome from service using this strategy. This can range from "no possibility of success" to "no possibility of failure."

_____ 2. Percent of problem cases that are likely to be reached using this strategy. This can range from 0% to 100% of the cases.

_____ 3. Probability of negative side effects emerging from this strategy. This can range from "no negative side effects are possible" to "absolute certainty of negative side effects" occurring.

_____ 4. Severity of negative side effects if this strategy is pursued. This can range from "very severe side effects" to "slightly inconvenient side effects" may occur.

_____ 5. Availability of required resources to pursue this strategy. This can range from "no required resource is available" to "all required resources are available."

_____ 6. Cost/Benefit ratio. This can range from "costs will grossly exceed benefits" to "benefits will grossly exceed costs."

When you have completed the development of the strategy selection criteria and weights, you are ready to develop the list of alternative solutions to the strategic planning problem. It is at this point that creativity is critical. Unfortunately, the biggest hindrance organizations encounter is that people have a tendency to stick closely to what they have done. This conservative bias means that many possible strategies are omitted from the list and are not given consideration. This, especially in a rapidly or drastically changing environment, is a potentially dangerous form of linear thinking. Careful recruitment of board members to ensure that some members are blessed with the tendency to speak the unthinkable, will help the organization overcome this bias.

Since you have a clearly defined planning problem and a well defined selection procedure for evaluating proposed solutions, you do not need to self-consciously edit yourselves when you are trying to develop solutions. One of the "crazy ideas" you develop, may turn out to be the "best" solution to a complex and difficult planning problem. The benefit of having a well defined selection procedure is that it allows you the luxury of loosening some of the strings on your mind. If some of the solutions do turn out to be impractical, they will be easily spotted and rejected as you evaluate all of the proposed solutions.

You are now ready to compare and evaluate the alternative strategies by applying the previously agreed upon selection criteria. This may entail more work than initially appears because an evaluation of some of the alternatives may require information which your organization does not have. If successful implementation of one of the strategic alternatives depends, for example, on client acceptance of a new service, product or treatment modality, then you may not be able to make a strategy decision until an information base is available concerning client acceptance.

Whether you should invest staff time and money in information collection in the process of evaluating strategy alternatives depends on a number of factors. A helpful rule is to compare the probability and risk of making a bad decision without information against the cost and delay of getting the information. While it may be true that "fools rush in where angels fear to tread," if a careful, prudent board is comfortable with making a strategic decision, then it probably has enough information.

With enough information to comfortably compare the alternative strategies, you finally must select a strategy for implementation. The implementation of strategic plans begins with the translation of your strategy into clear, time phased and at least roughly measurable strategic goals. The realization of these strategic goals becomes the task of operational planning.

Operational Planning

The middle of the planning process is "operational planning." It is a conversion of your strategy into a multi-year plan of operations. While strategic planning will have a 5 - 10 year time frame, operational planning will normally have a 2 - 5 year time frame. The outcome of operational planning is a set of operational objectives and resource requirements which can be thought of as medium range benchmarks and rough budget projections established to give you a clear means of evaluating your progress and making resource allocation decisions.

Developing operational plans is a more structured and defined process than your strategic planning because it involves "smaller" decision fields. This is because the strategic goals already define many theoretically possible operations as inappropriate for your organization. Thus, in operational planning, you start with a narrow and clear planning problem and you probably have fewer alternative solutions available. The other side or the coin, however, is that operational planning requires far more information support and the decision making criteria must be more finely tuned than in strategic planning.

In essence, the process of developing operational plans follows the same decision making model as that used in defining and selecting your strategic options. The important points of each step are noted below.

1. Define each operational planning problem.

    Again, the problem statement must specify the
    goal to be achieved, the relevant environmental
    and organizational trends, and the constraints
    under which the solution must be found. The
    environmental trends will be less global in
    operational planning than was the case with
    strategic planning. Here you must try to identify
    more specific forces which may be a hindrance
    or an opportunity.

2. Develop and weight selection criteria for evaluating
    alternative operational plans.

    This step will also require more effort and precision.
    Costs and benefits may be important and highly weighted
    criteria during operational planning. Other criteria
    which may be important at this level of analysis are
    system reliability; system maintainability and system
    capacity to meet needs.

3. Develop alternative operational plans.

    The range of alternatives is more restricted since
    all alternatives must be consistent with the strategy.

4. Evaluate alternative plans.

    At this point some cost estimates and analysis
    of projected benefits should be attempted on
    many of your options.

5. Select the best alternative.

6. Develop specific operational objectives.

7. Identify major activity blocks and resource requirements necessary for achievement of operational objectives.

   As noted above, your operational objective is a guidepost on the way to your strategic goal. An operational objective is much more detailed and specific than corporate and strategic goals. Objectives should be measurable, quantifiable, time framed and state an acceptable level of performance.

   An example of an operational objective which is broken into its different parts is shown below:

   At the end of 3 years...........time frame
   300 members of DC/CDC...........quantified
   will actively support the
   organization by contributing....measurable
   at least $25.00 annually in
   cash or in-kind................level of performance.

Once the board and staff have defined their three year operational objectives, you must consider the major activity blocks for accomplishing your objectives. Here again you should see if there are alternative ways of reaching your objective and, if there are, select the one that you think best fits your community and organization.

A three year period is frequently used as the time frame for operational planning. A three year plan is most easily constructed by listing in chronological order each major set of activity blocks which must be carried out to achieve the objective. Exhibit 10-6 is a completed example of such a plan. You will note that the form calls for specifying when each activity will be completed, the resources necessary for carrying out the activity, and a cost estimate. Generally, groups find it easier to complete the activity and time columns and then go back and figure out resource requirements and costs. If you try to do it all at once you tend to get bogged down in determining costs and lose the flow of activities.

The full collection of these forms for your organization's internal development and external programs should represent a comprehensive three year plan. As you look at Exhibit 10-6, notice a couple of things:

1. The cost figures on some of the items during the second and third years get to be pretty rough estimates. These estimates will be tightened up and corrected when you update your plan each following year so the rough estimates should not be a major concern. The one year for which you do have to be accurate in your estimations is the first year. But even

EXHIBIT 10-6: Sample Three Year Operational Plan

Objective: At the end of 1986, a separate nonprofit corporation will have been incorporated and will have acquired title to land and a commitment for construction funds sufficient to construct 150 units of low and moderate income rental housing.

Major Activities	Month of completion	Required resource	Cost
YEAR 1			
Identify, inform and recruit persons who will form nonprofit housing organization	6	staff time, meeting supplies, refreshments	1,200
Incorporate, write bylaws, get tax exempt status	9	attorney time, filing fees, technical assistance, staff time	500
Develop board knowledge and DC/CDC staff skill in housing programs	10	travel to other programs, training, technical assistance	2,000
Do detailed research on rental housing needs through survey	11	survey forms, 15 volunteers with 20 hours each, 5000 miles of travel, training and survey supplies	1,500
Complete preliminary feasibility study	12	staff time, consultant	1,000
Recurring Monthly Costs		Monthly Costs	
1/2-time staff person		541.66 x 12	6,500
fringe benefits		70.42 x 12	845
Phone, supplies, other overhead		150.00 x 12	1,800
Mileage costs at 1000 miles/ @ $ .20		200.00 x 12	2,400
		ESTIMATED FIRST YEAR TOTAL:	17,745

143

Major Activities	Month of Completion	Required Resources	Cost
YEAR 2			
Identify possible sites and obtain rough site cost estimates	14	staff time, board time	500
Develop funding plan and mechanism for land purchase	14	staff time, technical assistance	1,000
Retain architect and initiate site preparation	15	staff time	
Obtain land option or outright purchase contract	18	staff time, attorney	250
Obtain funds for land and close purchase	24	board and staff time, other depends on funding strategy	not known
		land cost estimates	30-40,000
Recurring Monthly Costs:		Monthly Cost	
1/2 time staff		541.66 x 12	6,500
fringe benefits		70.42 x 12	845
Phone, supplies, other overhead		150.00 x 12	1,800
Mileage costs at 1000/miles @ $.20		200.00 x 12	2,400
		ESTIMATED SECOND YEAR TOTAL:	43,295-53,295

144

Major Activities	Month of Completion	Required Resources	Cost
YEAR 3			
Identify possible funding sources for construction	25	staff time	
Obtain final architectural and engineering workups and cost estimates for the project	26	architect time	5,000
Close negotiation with sources for funding construction	32	technical assistance, attorney time	3,000
Obtain construction financing	33		
Advertise for necessary contractors	33	prepare specifications for bids, advertising costs	1,300
Select contractors	36	not known	not known
Recurring Monthly Costs		Monthly Cost	
1/2 time staff		541.66 x 12	6,500
fringe benefits		70.42 x 12	845
Phone, supplies other overhead		150.00 x 12	1,800
Mileage costs at 1000 miles @ $ .20		200.00 x 12	2,400
		ESTIMATED THIRD YEAR TOTAL	20,845

here you should not get too detailed or you will get bogged down. Detailed cost analysis gets done during the next step of the process when you do the one year implementation or project activity analysis and budgeting.

When you have completed your detailed one year plan, go back and verify the figures for the first year in your three year operational plan.

2. Note how regular and routine costs are shown on the three year plan. This is the easiest way to show all of these costs without trying to show, for example, how many miles the staff might have to drive to perform each of the things listed in the three year plan.

You can also use this technique to show continuing costs for a program which might become operational in the first year and where the second and third years would be just continued operations with no other special activities and costs. In this case, you can simply write "continued operation" in the activity block and breakdown the monthly costs. However, if you do this, be sure to review your plan to see that you have not omitted some special events such as staff training, special travel or program changes.

Although the basic planning process is similar in strategic and operational planning, the procedures which are used by the board in operational planning can be very different from those used in strategic planning. During the strategic planning process, most of the work was done by the board and staff working as a "committee of the whole." In operational planning, most of the work will be assigned to board committees or task forces with specific mandates for staff support. A recommended process for operational planning is shown in Exhibit 10-7 on the following page.

This chart indicates several specific differences between the procedures employed in strategic and operational planning. Most important, perhaps, is the role of staff. In strategic planning, the staff participated as "members of the family"; everyone participated as equals --people equally involved in defining how they can best cope with an uncertain, ambiquous, changeable environment in order to achieve their shared dream.

In operational planning, on the other hand, it is probably more important to maintain clearer role differentiation between staff and board. A major factor in this need for increased role distinction is the nature of operational planning problems and analysis. Operational planning gets into a middle area of normative vs. instrumental planning. As such it is made up of about equal parts of "should we? ... Is this good?" and "can we? ... Is this possible?" The role of the board is fundamentally centered on the normative, or value, questions confronted in the operational planning process. The staff to a great extent, must be depended upon to provide the instrumental, technical background information needed in the process.

EXHIBIT 10-7: Operational Planning Flow Chart

Steps in the Process:

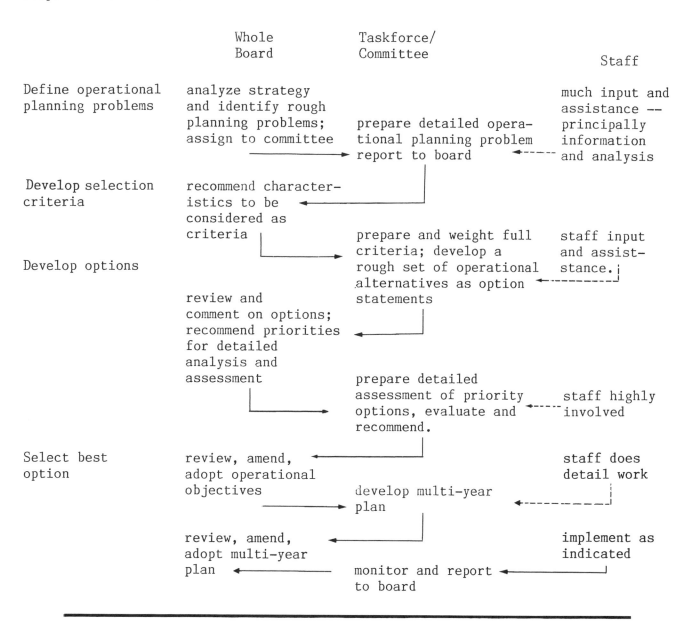

	Whole Board	Taskforce/ Committee	Staff
Define operational planning problems	analyze strategy and identify rough planning problems; assign to committee	prepare detailed operational planning problem report to board	much input and assistance -- principally information and analysis
Develop selection criteria	recommend characteristics to be considered as criteria		
Develop options	review and comment on options; recommend priorities for detailed analysis and assessment	prepare and weight full criteria; develop a rough set of operational alternatives as option statements	staff input and assistance.
		prepare detailed assessment of priority options, evaluate and recommend.	staff highly involved
Select best option	review, amend, adopt operational objectives	develop multi-year plan	staff does detail work
	review, amend, adopt multi-year plan	monitor and report to board	implement as indicated

Given the more "technical" nature of operational planning and the need for much more information and analysis, it will probably be necessary to have more than the executive director involved in staff support for the board in this process. In fact, it is likely that a staff "team" may be needed in order to generate the kinds of assistance and support required by the committees or task forces on some operational planning projects.

Also obvious from the above procedure is the increased use of committees and task forces to do most of the analysis and preparation of operational plans for the board. Whether operational planning problems should be assigned to a standing committee or an ad hoc special committee depends on the workload of existing committees and the "fit" between the planning problem and a committee's normal domain.

Annual Implementation or Project Planning

The final step in the overall planning process is the development of annual implementation or project plans. This is essentially the job of staff in conjunction with various board committees. Annual implementation planning, when the strategic and multi-year operational plans are in place, is basically a detailed breakdown of the first year of the multi-year plan. Generally, the completion of each of the major activity blocks becomes your project objectives for that year. Again, these objectives should be measurable, time framed, quantified, and should state an acceptable level of performance.

Organizational Planning Calendar and Procedures

On the next several pages are two schedules or calendars for the planning process. The first one is for the organization that is developing its first organizational plan. The second is a calendar for reviewing and updating the plan each following year. The schedules assume that the organization uses a January through December fiscal year for budgeting and accounting. All of the planning for the following year should be done by late November. By ending in November, you can avoid many scheduling conflicts when your committee and board members have other things to do during the holidays. This schedule also gives you one month of "catch up" time which may be needed if you run into planning problems or conflicts.

If your organization operates on a different fiscal year, you will need to make the appropriate calendar changes so you can complete your planning at least one month before the start of your fiscal year.

Calendar and Procedures for the First Organizational Plan

Step	Month	Procedure and Participants
Review and write mission, history and philosophy	July	Board, staff, and key members of the organization should participate equally in this first step. This can be done either by: (1) having a committee draft these documents, circulate them fully for review and then hold a group discussion to modify and

148

adjust for group consensus; or (2) hold a one day meeting where these issues can be discussed and resolved. The one day meeting will probably require an outside facilitator or moderator so all group members can participate.

Prepare long range, corporate goals

Board members and staff are the primary participants in drafting and adopting the long range goals of the organization.

These can be prepared in either of the two ways listed above. If the all day meeting is used for the mission, etc., it is usually possible to complete a rough draft of the goals in the same meeting. These can then be written up and submitted to the board for modification and adoption.

July

Strategic "problem analysis" and environmental assessment

A rough draft of problems and needs can be developed at a meeting where board and staff participate. Different problem areas should then be assigned to temporary "problem area" committees to do more detailed problem analysis and data gathering. Each of these committees should have staff support. After the committees have analyzed their problem area, they should report their findings to the board (see next step).

Early
August

Strategic planning

After the board of directors has reviewed the analysis of each committee, the board should discuss and give directions to each committee for strategic planning.

Mid-
August

The committee operating with the advice of the whole board will prepare a draft strategic plan outline and submit it to the board for amendment and adoption.

Late-
August

Operational planning

Upon adoption of a set of strategic plans, the board assigns the task of

149

	Late-August	operational planning to a committee, or a set of committees. The board can assign all three year plans to the planning committee or to a number of "program" committees (such as the children's services committee, housing committee, etc.)
	Mid-September	These committees should submit a set of proposed three year plans to the board at the following board meeting. The board reviews, modifies, rejects, or accepts the plans.
		If accepted, the three year plan is given to the staff so they can develop and draft one year project plans.
One year project implementation planning and budgeting	Early October	Staff develops detailed one year project plans and cost figures and submits these to the planning committee for review. The planning committee modifies or accepts the plans and submits them to the board for review and comment.
	Mid-October	After review and comment by the board these plans are sent back to the committee and staff to modify as directed by the board. The modified plans are then submitted to the board for final review.
One year project implementation planning and budgeting	Mid-November	Prior to adopting the plans, the board assigns all one year implementation plans to the budget committee for financial review and the development of the overall organizational budget.
		The budget committee reports to the board at the next meeting with a proposed organizational budget and recommends project changes or deletions if planned activities exceed projected revenues.
	Late November	The board adopts or modifies the budget committee's recommendations and approves the next year's budget.

Calendar and Procedures for the Annual Organizational Plan Review

Review mission, history philosophy, long range goals	July	Board and staff discuss needed changes. Board adopts.
Review and update strategic analysis	July	Planning committee, with staff help, does detailed review and recommends changes and additions to the board.
	August	Board modifies and adopts committee recommendations.
Strategic planning review	August	Planning committee, with staff help, modifies and adjusts strategic plans to reflect project experiences and changed conditions. Recommends changes and adjustments to the board.
Review and update of three year operational plans	July, August	Planning committee performs detailed review of past and current year performance. Reports these findings to the board. Along with recommended changes and adjustments in the three year plan.
	August	Board reviews the recommendation and provides directions to the planning committee for development of the revised three year plan.
	Early September	Planning committee prepares and submits the revised three year plan to the board of directors. The board adjust and adopts the three year plan.
Prepare new one year project implementation plans and budget	Mid- September	Upon adopting the three year plan, the board directs the staff to prepare detailed one year plans. Staff submits these plans to the planning committee for review.
	Early October	The planning committee reviews and modifies the plans and submits recommended plans to the board of directors. The board reviews and comments on the plans.

Prepare new one year project implementation plans and budget		
	Mid-October	After review and comment by the board these plans are sent back to the committee and staff to be modified as directed by the board. The modified plans are then submitted to the board for final review.
	Late October	Prior to adopting the plans, the board will assign all one year implementation plans to the budget or finance committee for financial review and the development of the overall organizational budget.
	Mid-November	The budget committee reports to the board at the next board meeting with a proposed organizational budget and recommends project changes or deletions if planned activities exceed projected revenues.
	Late November	The board adopts or modifies the budget committee's recommendations and approves the next year's annual budget.

Further Readings

William H. Brickner and Donald M. Cope, THE PLANNING PROCESS.
Cambridge, MA: Winthrop Management Series, 1977

New England Municipal Center, COMMUNITY PLANNING FOR HUMAN SERVICES:
AN INTRODUCTION TO NEEDS ASSESSMENT, PRIORITY ASSESSMENT AND
PLANNING. Durham, NH: 1978

Stephen M. Drezner and William B. McCurdy, A PLANNING GUIDE FOR
VOLUNTARY HUMAN SERVICE DELIVERY AGENCIES. NY, NY: Family Service
Association of America, 1979

Donald R. Fessler, FACILITATING COMMUNITY CHANGE: A BASIC GUIDE.
La Jolla, CA: University Associates, 1976

Christopher Hodgkinson, TOWARD A THEORY OF ADMINISTRATION. Oxford:
Basil Blackwell, 1978

James Hardy, CORPORATE PLANNING FOR NONPROFIT ORGANIZATIONS. NY, NY:
Association Press, 1972

Armand Lauffer, SOCIAL PLANNING AT THE COMMUNITY LEVEL. Englewood
Cliffs, NJ: Prentice-Hall, 1978

Richard O. Mason and Ian I. Mitroff, CHALLENGING STRATEGIC PLANNING
ASSUMPTIONS. NY, NY: John Wiley Interscience, 1981

Dale McConkey, MBO FOR NONPROFIT ORGANIZATIONS. New York: American
Management Association, 1979

National Health Planning and Information Center, METHODS FOR SETTING
PRIORITIES IN AREAWIDE HEALTH PLANNING: AN ANNOTATED BIBLIOGRAPHY.
Rockville, MD: National Health Planning and Information Center,
1978

New England Municipal Center, COMMUNITY PLANNING FOR HUMAN SERVICES:
AN INTRODUCTION TO NEEDS ASSESSMENT, PRIORITY SETTING AND PLANNING.
Durham, NH: New England Municipal Center, 1977

A. Richards, NEEDS ASSESSMENT HANDBOOK. San Francisco: Public
Management Institute, 1980

Allen D. Spiegel and Herbert Harvey Hukman, BASIC HEALTH PLANNING
METHODS. Germantown, MD: Aspen Publications, 1978

Gerald Zaltman, Robert Duncan, STRATEGIES FOR PLANNED CHANGE.
Somerset, NJ: John Wiley and Sons, 1974

Chapter 11

Managing Finances

Christopher T. Callaghan

Nonprofit organizations face increasing financial vulnerability. The challenges facing directors and managers in the years to come will surpass anything seen to date. In the face of increasing demand for services, the nonprofit sector is also confronted with escalating costs, increased regulation, limited resources, and, perhaps most importantly, rising expectations.

The current and future environment also presents many opportunities. The nonprofit organization requires more and better management, and it requires different management. Yesterday's way of doing things becomes inappropriate if not counter-productive. While this is the case in nearly every aspect of managing a nonprofit organization, it's particularly true with regard to managing finances.

Board Responsibilities

Boards are often thought to have only policy making responsibility. However, as expressed elsewhere in this book, board responsibilities are much broader. In terms of financial management, the responsibility for insuring the organization's long term financial viability must be reinforced. This responsibility, of course, embraces policy making, but also includes financial planning which is critical for insuring long term financial stability.

Confusion often reigns with regard to accountability and reporting responsibilities. Except in instances of outright negligence, especially where collusion exists, the accountability buck stops with the board. So board members should not only be concerned with their general financial management responsibilities, but should be confident that day-to-day financial operations are both efficient and effective.

Management Responsibilities

In order to ensure effective performance, management must have sufficient prowess in handling financial affairs. This is a special challenge when you consider financial management as one of the many tasks and responsibilities required in effectively operating an organization. Without adequate financial management capability, an organization will be hard pressed in its efforts to pursue program planning and development, resource development, marketing, and evaluation. All of these responsibilities have financial overtones.

Financial management, however, should not be considered an end in itself. It is really a tool, a means, for accomplishing the program priorities set forth by management and the board. Like anything else, preoccupation with any one element of management causes suboptimization. Financial management needs to be kept in perspective, should not be feared, and should be considered a genuine tool that, when implemented well, strengthens the overall ability of the organization to meet its primary charge.

Objectives

The purpose of this chapter is to acquaint board members with the basic elements of financial management. Covered below, these elements include: Financial Planning and Control; Budgeting and Cash Management; and Accounting and Financial Reporting.

The principal concerns regarding each of these elements will be reviewed with special emphasis on their applicability in managing the organization as a whole. It is hoped that this material will whet board appetites for increased awareness and understanding of some financial management principles, and to focus attention on the financial arena as a haven for opportunities. It is hoped, too, that this material will eliminate the mystique generally attached to financial management. A working knowledge of all information provided will equip the board for meeting the highest of expectations.

Financial Planning and Control

Financial Planning is a responsibility that threads through each of the traditional duties of management – planning, control, and evaluation. Traditionally, financial planning incorporates two other major aspects. These are resource allocation and budgeting. The ability to effectively link the three distinguishes the best managed from the better managed nonprofits. And when appropriate consideration is given to the related aspects of resource development and marketing, genuine focus for directing and creating tomorrow is well within reach.

Although few will argue the significance of controls, or how management control can enhance effectiveness and overall productivity, few seem to recognize the importance of control in financial terms. Basically every organization needs to operate with both administrative and financial controls. Here we'll focus on organizing, staffing and directing the financial function, with special emphasis on the role of the treasurer. Additionally, we'll address internal financial controls essential to the safeguarding of assets and reliability of financial reports. Then, under budgeting, we'll address the monitoring, evaluation and reporting of financial control.

Understanding the relationship between planning, resource allocation, and budgeting is critical to the effective management of finances and financial planning. When carried out in a timely and responsible fashion, the planning, resource allocation and budgeting process holds the potential for combating financial instability and vulnerability. It also helps guard against reacting to, instead of creating, the organization's future.

Strategic Planning

The organization must think through the changed circumstances in which it operates. In a changing and unpredictable environment, board and management must continually ask "What is our business?" And so the importance of strategic planning. The organization must periodically ask the unpopular question: "Knowing what we now know, would we get into this activity, this service if we were not already in it?" At the very least, board and management should ask whether methods should be changed to accomplish what the organization originally set out to accomplish. This line of questioning and reasoning is the heart of program planning and resource allocation. These functions are the backbone of a stable, responsible and dynamic organization and are essential to financial planning.

Once the organization is confident that its mission is in focus and its line of service is responsive, resource development and marketing responsibilities can be assumed more productively. As with evaluation, marketing and resource development are inextricable to the planning/resource allocation/budgeting cycle.

The most critical element in strategic planning is program planning and development. This aspect of planning, of course, is at the core of marketing since the latter requires a firm grasp of needs assessment, identification of alternatives to meet real needs, and in turn, program design. With these in focus, pricing, promotion, and distribution of services can then be given due consideration.

As to resource development, today's environment requires two basic objectives --financial stability and self-sufficiency. While these have always been ideals, most organizations need to place these concerns at the fore in their planning, resource development, and marketing activities. Unfortunately, all too often there is a tendency to develop programs in response to funding; as a result, organizations find themselves out of focus and vulnerable. To guard against this predicament, board and management must come to grips with the organization's overall mission and

157

program priorities. Only then should it search for funds.

An overall program must be in place before considering the desirability and composition of restricted, unrestricted, and endowment funds, and whether these should come from foundations, corporations, government contracts, fees, or memberships. A carefully articulated plan of matching the organization's priorities to those of prospective funders, and not vice versa, is of utmost importance and will yield the highest long term return.

Resource Allocation

Resource allocation is a most difficult task: It is also a critical element of the financial planning process. Resource allocation serves as a bridge between planning and budgeting. It begins where program planning and development leaves off by identifying priorities based upon a cost-benefit analysis.

Present practice leaves much to be desired. In fact, many organizations, while financially stable, lack sufficient financial mobility largely because of inadequate analysis of program priorities. Once a program is established, it is very difficult, if not impossible, to eliminate it.

Cost-benefit analysis is another illustration of where nonprofit organization management is more difficult. In the private business sector, cost-benefit analysis is much easier since a business can use a desired minimum rate of return which matches or exceeds the organization's cost as its cost-benefit gauge. Generally, no such gauge exists in the nonprofit sector since the profit motive usually isn't operating. However, the principal concepts of cost-benefit analysis remain the same whether applied in the nonprofit, private business or public sector.

Popular resource allocation concepts are PPBS (Program, Planning, and Budgeting System) and Zero-Base Budgeting. In both cases, the spirit is more important than the letter. Some organization practice both without knowing it; others go through all the formal motions without coming near them. The spirit of both of these concepts is a marriage between program planning and budgeting. Because resources are limited, they must be allocated based upon some priority scheme. Just as one's personal time and energy is allocated based upon priorities, so must an organization's financial resources. Attempts at being all things to all people is a trap all organizations must escape.

For an organization to be effective, its long range plan must remain in focus, and such factors as policy, market strategy, objectives, and levels of operation required to achieve objectives must be defined prior to any budgeting. Then a budgeting process must be engaged that will align all operating plans with the overall organizational plan. The resource allocation must present alternatives, possible reductions, and necessary expansion, before the traditional budgeting process begins. This is where zero-base budgeting is extremely valuable to management; it sets a logical resource allocation framework.

A systematic resource allocation process linking planning and budgeting must be in place in order for the organization to maintain its focus and efficiently distribute its limited resources, while maintaining both financial stability and flexibility.

Effective resource allocation requires keeping in mind a number of key points. First, while the second half of the cost-benefit equation is largely subjective, an organization should have ready access to relevant and critical information necessary to assess relative strengths and weaknesses of alternative programs and options. The management information system that generates this data is largely the same required to provide input in marketing, evaluation and resource development efforts. Secondly, board and management must keep in mind that cost-benefit analysis is a disciplined manner of reasoning and nothing more than that. Resource allocation should not be a cumbersome mathematical exercise; rather it requires a reasoned approach to assessing strengths and weaknesses.

A third consideration is that board and management must continually access more than just financial resources. By definition, resource development embraces more than just cash. The organization must maximize available resources by giving appropriate consideration to the potential for accessing and marshalling donated services and material. In determining capital requirements, management has a basic responsibility to identify any and all significant in-kind support.

Budgeting

As discussed below, budgeting picks up where resource allocation leaves off. The budgeting process should be more routine once program priorities are identified, and decisions are made on how monies and other resources will be allocated in carrying out stated program goals and objectives.

Most importantly, budgeting is a control function. It's one thing to plan one's work, its quite another to actually work the plan. Budgeting allows the organization to state its organizational plan in financial terms, but beyond that, it allows management and board alike to monitor efficient and effective use of resources.

The "how to" of program and operational budgeting is discussed further below.

Financial Planning — A Systems Approach

Further confusion in applying some financial planning concepts rests in the misuse of programming and budgeting concepts. While programming and budgeting are inextricable to planning, they are so only in the largest context of planning; namely, in carrying out the organizational plan. But first a corporate strategy or plan must be adopted which addresses fundamental goals and objectives, as well as the levels of operation required to achieve objectives. All phases of the planning process must be understood both independently and interdependently.

In summary, the financial planning system should include the following steps:

1. Clarify, review, and re-establish the mission and values of the organization.

2. Establish corporate goals which give long range direction to the organization. These comprise program goals which relate to the constituency for whom the organization exists and organizational goals which relate to the organization's internal structure and process. It's only through the accomplishment of both program and organizational goals that the image of the future can be realized.

3. Identify alternative strategies for achieving corporate goals. Attention must be given to program and administrative options.

4. Identify the organization's short term and long term capital requirements as a basis for gauging economies of scale and identifying strategies to insure financial mobility.

5. Analyze cost-benefit of alternative courses of action and rank program and administrative options accordingly.

6. Design programs or operational objectives to accomplish the strategic goals relative to available resources.

7. Mold the organizational structure (delivery system) to compliment the programs. This necessarily focuses on the allocation of all available resources.

8. Budget allocated resources over a reasonable operating period as a basis for controlling and monitoring results.

9. Determine the implementation plan and evaluation system with which to carry out and monitor the plan.

10. Provide a fully operational financial control system to insure safeguarding of assets and reliability of financial reports.

Financial Controls

One of the underpinnings of any organization's ability to operate effectively and efficiently is its financial control system. The system affects, in one fashion or another, all phases of operation including planning, administration, resource development and evaluation. Because the basic nature of internal control is so pervasive, it is all too often taken for granted.

The basic objectives of financial controls are safeguarding the organization's assets, and insuring the reliability of financial records and reports. Without having the "house in order" in this regard, the organization is hard pressed to meet rising expectations and accountability. But beyond that, financial controls are necessary in carrying out policy and in keeping the operation running efficiently and effectively. Financial controls are important because through them financial and other resources are safeguarded and we can insure the accuracy of accounting records on which we base reports for our own decision making.

An effective financial control system, when properly set and enforced, comprises a set of procedures and cross checks which, in the absence of collusion, minimize the likelihood of misuse of assets or misstatement of the accounts and, if misuse occurs, maximize the likelihood of detection. If the organization's objectives of internal control are to be fulfilled, the system needs the following characteristics:

1. Competent, trustworthy personnel with clear lines of authority and responsibility.

2. Adequate segregation of duties.

3. Proper procedures for authorization.

4. Proper procedures for record keeping.

5. Physical control over assets and records.

6. Independent checks on performance.

7. Complete and accurate documentation and a sufficient audit trail.

Appendix A provides a self-evaluation checklist for financial controls. This serves as a comprehensive review of the essential ingredients for a genuinely effective internal control system. Careful boards will use this checklist to test its controls. The Finance Committee can be charged with reviewing internal controls and reporting the results to the entire board.

As with any service organization, nonprofits must be especially concerned about personnel. The role of the treasurer and the financial responsibility of management take on special importance in the area of financial control. Exhibits 11-1 and 11-2 provide sample job descriptions for the treasurer and staff accountant. These two job descriptions should aid in clarifying financial tasks and responsibilities for the two positions, but should only be considered as guides.

EXHIBIT 11-1: Responsibilities of Treasurer

A. Inventory organization's staff capability in managing finances and ascertain gaps.
B. Arrange job descriptions for all financial personnel including CEO.
C. Provide training for the CEO and other financial personnel.
D. Ensure that a sound system of internal control is operating.
E. Ensure:
   1. Accurate financial records.
   2. Timely variance analysis.
   3. Preparation and effective use of operating budget.
   4. Effective cash management practices.
   5. Compliance with any and all financial reporting requirements – federal, state and local.
   6. Compliance with contract requirements and special features of funding agreements.
F. Anticipate financial problems and difficulties. This requires performing periodic but timely financial analysis.
G. Assist CEO in ensuring accounting records provide timely and accurate management information related especially to:
   1. Functional reporting.
   2. Program cost data.
H. Effectively communicate the organization's financial affairs to other board members.
I. Maintain liaison with the Resource Development (fund raising) Committee to ensure complete understanding of unique features of, among other things, prospective contracts, other funding agreements and capital fund drives.
J. Maintain sufficient knowledge of tax laws pertaining to nonprofits.

EXHIBIT 11-2: Sample Staff Accountant Job Description

Reports to: Executive or Administrative Director.

General Scope and Function: Overall administration of internal accounting and financial matters.

A. Maintain updated cash flow analysis.
B. Review short and long term investments on a timely basis.
C. Review work performed by bookkeeper.
   1. Review all receipts and disbursements ascertaining correct account distribution and ensuring all supporting documentation is accurate and in order.
   2. Review and initial trial balance, general journal and drafts of financial statements.
D. Prepare financial budget analysis (budget vs. actual) at least each quarter.

Continued

E. Determine compliance with master reporting and activity calendar.
F. Ensure maintenance of effective internal controls to ensure safeguarding of assets and reliability of financial statements.
G. Ensure accurate and timely completion of staff time summaries for functional reporting.
H. Ensure complete and up-to-date Standard Operating Procedures Manual for all accounting and financial reporting matters.
I. Ensure compliance with local, state and federal reporting requirements.
J. Resolve unusual accounting and financial problems as they arise which could not otherwise be delegated to bookkeeper.
K. Prepare special cost studies as required.
L. Facilitate preparation for annual audit.
M. Perform monthly bank reconciliations.
N. Furnish personnel evaluations of bookkeeper on at least a semi-annual basis.
O. Perform additional duties as requested by the agency director and treasurer.

Qualifications

A. Thorough understanding of nonprofit financial accounting and control.
B. Ability to analyze problems and resolve with dispatch.
C. Available average of 15 - 25 hours each week.

Budgeting and Cash Management

The core to managing finances is budget preparation and use of the budget as a control tool. Budgeting is the third leg of the financial planning process. Once the organization's strategic plan is solidified (mission evaluated, goals and objectives identified and programmed, and administrative options clarified), and resources allocated, the budgeting process is ready to begin.

Budgeting in Perspective

Exhibits 11-3, 11-4 and 11-5 place budgeting in proper perspective. Exhibit 11-3 sets forth, in general, where the organization intends to be in financial terms over a five year period. Such a five year master plan gives focus and serves as a springboard for thinking through and maintaining priorities. Additionally, it establishes a framework for resource development and marketing efforts. Intended only as a guide, the five year financial plan is invaluable in establishing direction and in addressing policy and resource allocation concerns.

Note that as a tool, the master plan is very selective in the information it portrays. It does not illustrate normal budget details but instead focuses on key summary financial information. The objective of the tool is to map, in capsule form, expected costs for both program and supporting services, as well as estimating revenue and support.

EXHIBIT 11-3: Five Year Financial Master Plan

	19 x 1	19 x 2	19 x 3	19 x 4	19 x 5
GOALS/OBJECTIVES:					
Conduct Research	$55,400	$62,000	$70,000	$70,000	$70,000
Counseling Program	97,600	102,000	110,000	120,000	120,000
Education Program	57,515	61,000	75,000	90,000	100,000
Medical Services	87,810	93,000	100,000	115,000	115,000
Supporting Services	134,025	140,000	155,000	170,000	175,000
Explore Project "A"	-------	10,000	5,000	-------	-------
Establish Branch Off.	-------	-------	-------	60,000	75,000
Establish Vol. Prog.	-------	-------	20,000	24,000	30,000
Donated Materials/ Services	114,700	130,000	160,000	220,000	230,000
Total	$547,050	598,000	695,000	869,000	915,000
SOURCES OF INCOME					
Corporate Support	69,000	75,000	95,000	95,000	100,000
Private Foundations	83,500	95,000	65,000	45,000	45,000
Government Grants	135,000	175,000	180,000	180,000	185,000
Individual Donations	18,000	24,000	30,000	32,000	35,000
Donated Materials/ Services	114,700	130,000	160,000	220,000	230,000
Investment Income	5,000	6,500	10,000	12,000	12,000
Program Income:					
Gov't Contracts	88,000	95,000	105,000	110,000	110,000
3rd Party Payments	28,000	35,000	40,000	45,000	50,000
Other Fees/Sales	20,500	22,500	24,000	26,000	30,000
Capital Fund Drive	------	------	40,000	60,000	------
Total	561,700	658,000	749,000	825,000	797,000
PROJECTED SURPLUS (DEFICIT)	14,650	60,000	54,000	(44,000)	(118,000)
BEGINNING FUND BALANCE	13,600	28,250	88,250	142,250	98,250
ENDING FUND BALANCE	28,250	88,250	142,250	98,250	(19,750)

Such a plan cannot be developed without a good deal of forethought and analysis of past experience and priorities for the future. This requirement, of course, reinforces the need for careful strategic planning and resource allocation. The master plan should be supported by detailed analysis of, among others, goals and objectives, program evaluation data, resource development plans, and marketing plans. Additionally, detailed program budgets outlining minimum and maximum personnel and other costs are essential.

Management and staff are responsible for initiating the master plan in a timely fashion. The treasurer, however, should play an integral role as a devil's advocate, in reviewing the final product before it's presented to the board. The plan should then be updated during the last quarter of each year.

The Budgeting Process

Since the budget is an important monitoring and control tool, its development should reflect considerable, but reasonable, time, energy and effort. Exhibit 11-4 outlines the major steps required in developing the annual budget. The basic purpose of the Master Budget Calendar is to guide management and staff in addressing the most important steps or events required to launch an effective financial operations plan.

As a calendar, this tool should assure that all major financial planning considerations are given their due in a timely fashion. Exhibit 11-4 assumes the organization operates on a calendar year. Obviously, organizations having a fiscal year ending other than on December 31 can adapt the same budget calendar to their fiscal year.

Exhibit 11-5 illustrates the final product which pulls together the entire budgeting process. As the final product, it captures all the elements affecting the subsequent year's financial operations. The following points require special attention in connection with Exhibits 11-4 and 11-5.

Program Versus Supporting Services

While woefully lacking in practice, perhaps the most important aspect of budgeting for nonprofit organizations is program budgeting. Nonprofit organizations cannot effectively plan and manage their operations without having an ability to distinguish between program and support services. Beyond having an understanding of the distinction, management must be able to allocate costs to its various programs and be able to think of its operations not only as a whole, but in terms of specific programs and supporting services.

Long range planning, resource development, marketing and evaluation cannot be addressed properly without an effective program budgeting system. Resource allocation is hopeless unless management has the ability to access both financial and nonfinancial data related to its program and supporting services. Without program budgeting and accounting, there is no logical basis for cost accounting.

Key to the ability to program budget is an understanding of program and supporting services. According to the Institute of Certified Public Accountant's definition, supporting services include general administrative and fund raising activities. Program services are those activities and costs which are neither general administration nor fund raising.

EXHIBIT 11-4: Master Budget Calendar

Key Events   J F M A M J J A S O N D

Re-evaluate organization mission   ———•

Develop long range objectives   ———•

Prioritize long range objectives in terms   ———•
  of both programs and organizational goals

Identify options for accomplishing stated   ———•
  goals and objectives

Evaluate existing programs   ———•

Consider new programs   ———•

Determine short and long term financial   ———•
  requirements

Analyze cost-benefit of alternative program   ———•
  and administrative options and rank
  accordingly

Design programs based on available resources   ———•

Develop and disseminate budget guidelines   ———•

Prepare program budgets   ———•

Prepare budgets for supporting services   ———•

Develop capital budgets   ———•

Develop revenue budgets   ———•

Review all **budgets** and adjust as appropriate   ———•

Develop **operational (summary) budget**   ———•

Board review   ———•

Board approval   ———•

Summarize financial operating plan   •

166

EXHIBIT 11-5: Sample Revenue and Expenditure Budget

Funds / Source	Program (Restricted & Self Generated)				General Operating	In kind	Total
	Research	Counseling	Education	Medical			
Contributions, Gifts, Grants							
Corporations	5,000	---	16,000	---	48,000		69,000
Private foundations	12,000	---	7,500	---	64,000		83,500
Government grants	10,000	---	12,000	8,000	105,000		135,000
Individual donations	---	---	2,000	---	16,000		18,000
Donated Materials and Services						114,700	114,700
Investment Income					5,000		5,000
Program/Business Income							
Government contracts	---	24,000	---	64,000	---		88,000
3rd Party payments	---	12,000	---	16,000	---		28,000
Other fees/sales	8,000	---	12,500	---	---		20,500
Other	---	---	---	---	---		---
Total Expected Revenues	35,000	36,000	50,000	88,000	238,000	114,700	561,700
Beginning Fund Balance	---	1,500	2,000	1,600	8,500		13,600
Total Funds Available	35,000	37,500	52,000	89,600	246,500	114,700	575,300
Allocation of General Operating Funds	22,000	62,000	7,000	2,500	<93,500>		
Funds Adjusted for Transfers	57,000	99,500	59,000	92,100	153,000		
Total Expected Expenditures	55,400	97,600	57,515	87,810	134,025	114,700	547,050
Expected Surplus <Deficit>	1,600	1,900	1,485	4,290	18,975		28,250

EXHIBIT Continued

Functional Classification Object Classification	PROGRAM				SUPPORTING		In kind	Total
	Research	Counseling	Education	Medical	Administration	Fund raising		
Employee Wages & Salary								
Executive Director	1,800	3,600	7,600	2,700	13,100	7,200	---	36,000
Assistant Director	3,500	2,700	3,400	2,000	14,000	2,400	---	28,000
Program Managers (4)	16,000	16,000	15,000	17,000	6,000	2,000	---	72,000
Psychologist	---	13,000	---	---	3,000	---	---	16,000
Nurses (2)	---	---	---	25,000	3,000	---	---	28,000
Counselors	---	25,000	---	---	2,000	---	---	27,000
Office Manager	---	---	---	---	13,500	2,500	---	16,500
Clerical	---	---	---	---	12,000	2,000	24,000	38,000
Bookkeeper/Billing Clerk	---	---	---	---	12,000	1,000	3,500	16,500
Part-Time Program Support	6,000	7,000	3,500	3,000	---	---	7,000	26,500
Volunteer Services	---	---	---	---	---	---	60,000	60,000
Sub-Total: Empl. Wages	27,300	67,300	29,500	49,700	64,600	17,100	94,500	350,000
Employee Benefits	3,850	10,600	3,600	7,500	11,000	2,500	---	39,050
Consultants & Contr. Fees	12,000	4,500	8,500	14,000	---	2,500	12,000	53,500
Occupancy	1,600	4,500	2,800	5,300	3,000	800	3,000	21,000
Utilities	300	750	450	900	450	150	---	3,000
Office Supplies	1,800	1,000	1,100	1,500	2,000	600	1,200	9,200
Telephone	2,000	1,500	1,800	1,100	1,600	500	---	8,500
Printing & Postage	2,700	1,050	2,600	1,050	2,800	1,300	2,000	13,500
Transportation	950	800	1,650	1,100	1,000	1,050	---	6,550
Equip Rent & Maintenance	1,250	1,800	3,600	2,800	1,400	600	2,000	13,450
Conferences & Conventions	400	750	500	650	450	250	---	3,000
Miscellaneous	300	675	275	500	850	200	---	2,775
Contingency	950	2,375	1,140	1,710	2,755	570	---	9,500
Total Expenditures	55,400	97,600	57,515	87,810	91,905	28,120	114,700	533,025

Management and general administrative costs are considered those costs not identifiable with a single program or fund raising activity, but which are indispensable to the conduct of those activities and to an organization's existence. These costs include expenses for overall direction of the organization's general board activities, business management, general record keeping, budgeting and related purposes. Costs of overall direction usually include the salary and expenses of the chief officer of the organization and his or her staff. However, if such staff spend a portion of their time directly supervising program services or categories of supporting services, their salaries and expenses should be prorated among those functions. The cost of disseminating information to inform the public of the organization's stewardship of contributed funds, the publication of announcements concerning appointments, the annual report, and so forth, should also be classified as management and general expenses.

Fund raising expenses are a very sensitive category of expense because a great deal of publicity has been associated with certain organizations that appear to have very high fund raising costs. The cost of fund raising includes not only the direct costs associated with a particular effort, but a fair allocation of the overhead of the organization, including the time of top management. Additionally, if fund raising is combined with a program function, such as educational literature which also solicits funds, the total cost should be allocated between the program and fund raising functions on the basis of the use made of the literature, as determined from its content, reason for distribution and audience.

In order to have an effective allocation system for charging costs to their appropriate categories --program, fund raising and general administration-- the organization needs to have a clear understanding of what activities constitute program verses supporting services. Since the largest share of any organization's budget is comprised of personnel and personnel related costs, such as fringe benefits, a time budget spelling where each staff person will spend their time is enormously helpful. Then a periodic reading (at least monthly is desirable) of how time is actually spent can be used not only as an effective monitoring tool, but also for purposes of allocating costs. Other line items, such as occupancy, telephone or printing, have to be allocated on a rational basis. The audit guides noted in "Further Readings" at the end of this chapter suggests methods of computing the allocation of certain types of expenses.

Who Prepares the Budget?

Exhibit 11-4 suggests budget preparation is a comprehensive process. Indeed it is. And while the board has final responsibility for approving the operating budget before it is put into action, management has primary responsibility for its development. However, throughout the budget process, management should seek board input as appropriate.

The board also must be involved in the re-evaluation of the organization's mission, particularly in identifying long range objectives, and in identifying options for accomplishing goals and objectives. This requires management to seek input in a systematic fashion perhaps through a long range planning subcommittee or by involving interested board members in meetings designed for addressing the elements contained in the Master Budget Calendar. To the extent a finance committee has been established to address the operating budget, its role should be carefully spelled out in the larger context of accomplishing the steps outlined in Exhibit 11-4.

Historical Data and Documentation

Specific schedules that detail past expenditures and receipts for all line items must be developed as support analysis before outlining the following year's budget. Past budgets and expenditure records are invaluable in budget preparation.

If budgets are being prepared for the first time, attempts should be made to secure necessary information from organizations that do similar work or from people who might have experience in such matters, such as foundation executives, government funding agencies, professional consultants, university professors, or private business people.

Selecting a Budget Period

The budget period deserves careful consideration. The periods most often chosen are the calendar year (January - December) and fiscal year that begins July 1. But the budget period can close at the end of any month as long as it is a logical twelve month period.

The period selected should be one that allows the best presentation of a full period of activity. If, for example, the organization offers its services from October to December and from March until August, a period with the month end falling at other than the peak times may be desirable. At least, the fluctuation from month to month would be easier to plan and report.

In some instances it may be desireable to align the budget period with that of the most significant funder. If a large percentage of finances comes from one source, it may be logical to be in line with that source.

Estimating Costs

The best predictor of costs is what has been experienced in preceding years. But just as importantly, the most appropriate basis for estimating costs is through program planning which identifies the exact nature of the activities and resources required to accomplish the program goals and objectives. In this fashion, it is much easier to identify personnel, equipment, printing, postage, supply requirements, and other expenditures necessary for the program: Rather than assume that the organization can simply add a certain percentage increase over the preceding year's budget, a "fresh look" will go a long way in ensuring that not only all costs have been considered, but that consideration is given to minimizing costs.

Varying economic conditions, uncertainty, and seasonality should be given thought when estimating costs. Certainly staff should be invited to participate for the benefit of their experience and, most importantly, their ideas.

It's been suggested that organizations would be wise to begin estimating revenues before estimating costs, since estimating revenues first may lead to too much wishful thinking. However, a preoccupation with revenue before having a full sense of costs could cause suboptimization by having those who provide funds dictate or otherwise shape the compostion (and therefore costs) of programs. This can be dangerous. What's important is to avoid wishful thinking as well as situations in which funders potentially dictate policy.

Estimating Revenues

Often a good deal of uncertainty surrounds the estimation of revenues. This can be due to varying economic conditions, but more often is due to general uncertainty. One tool that can be used in estimating revenues for budgeting purposes is the calculation of expected values. This causes management to consider not only amounts proposed from funders, but the probability of receiving the full amount requested. In some cases, the organization can expect to receive the full amount requested. In other instances, there may be only a slight probability of receiving the award. Yet revenues must be budgeted in order to plan and operate effectively. Expected value calculation aids in determining amounts of revenue which should be reflected in the operating budget for planning purposes. Expected values are calculated by multiplying the full amount of the request by the probability of receiving the full amount. For example, if you have requested $ 50,000 but feel you have only a 50 % chance of receiving that amount, then you would budget only $ 25,000 ($ 50,000 x .50 = $ 25,000).

As Exhibit 11-5 indicates, special consideration must be given to the type of funds expected. Some funds will be for general operations; others will be restricted for specific purposes. Additionally, certain programs will generate funds on their own through fees for service. In all cases, the board and management must have a clear understanding of the different types of funds available --unrestritced, restricted, endowment, etc.-- in order to plan their use in line with expectations, contracts and grant agreements.

Contingency Planning

A continually changing environment requires management to be responsible and prudent in response to significant changes, whether favorable or unfavorable. Every financial operating plan should, therefore, reflect the organization's plans for responding to unforeseen happenings.

The contingency plan has to be much more than a "fudge factor" in an annual operating budget. While the contingency shown in Exhibit 11-5 reflects a specified amount, the amount should be determined by careful planning and resource allocation decisions. Every budget should have a contingency reserve, the size of which depends on a variety of circumstances. The line item should be thought of as a hedge against decreasing revenue, completely unexpected expense, or an unexpected rise in cost. It's proper size depends on predictability of income, relative stability of the organization, extent to which expenditures are fixed in advance, and age and experience of the organization.

Many board members request the elimination of contingency reserves especially when funds are tight and a deficit is looming, because they feel, "we can't afford it." But this is improper reasoning since the purpose of the contingency is to provide for an expense that cannot be avoided but also cannot be predicted. In the absence of the reserve, the expense will still occur.

Flexible Versus Static Budgets

The importance of considering a budget as a guide instead of a rule cannot be underestimated. All too often an organization becomes its own worst enemy because it considers the budget as the end all. As a tool, the budget should aid in planning and operating the organization. While all personnel should be urged to stay within general parameters, the operating budget should be flexible. To the extent they're static, they no longer serve as a guide and can make the organization inflexible. This situation is obviously counterproductive and can be avoided by the board adopting a workable budget amendment procedure.

Donated Material and Services

Many organization would flounder without the in-kind support they receive from volunteers, corporations, and other providers of resources. Yet many of these same organizations never address the financial implications of in-kind support. Not surprisingly, donated materials and services are often a significant portion of an organization's financial operations.

Note that the sample budget accommodated donated materials and services. In this example, it becomes apparent that the organization's total operating budget is considerably larger than what would otherwise be the case if in-kind support was not shown. Of course, in-kind support must be reflected as both revenue and expense in order to keep the "bottom line" unaffected. This form of presentation is consistent with that required by generally accepted accounting and reporting practices.

All organizations are wise to show prospective funders or donors the value of in-kind support in order to show how donations are leveraged.

Pulling It All Together

The end product of the budgeting process is the annual financial operating plan. Note that Exhibit 11-5 is not only a total budget (receipts and expenditures) but also shows individual program and supporting services budgets as well. Critical to this analysis is an understanding of the resources required to operate the individual program services, as well as administrative and fund rising activities. Additionally, in-kind support is shown in the revenue and expense budgets. Regarding revenues, restricted and self-generated funds need to be identified before general operating funds are allocated to program and supporting services. In fact, resource allocation decisions are shown in the "allocation of general operating funds" line. The organization must decide to what extent program and supporting activities are deserving of general operating funds.

As for expenditures, some basis must again be found for allocating costs to program and supporting services. Without such an allocation, it would be most difficult to determine the true cost of operating the individual program and supporting services.

Budget as a Control Tool

Management and the board generally agree about the importance of program evaluation, recognizing this form of feedback is essential to program planning and development, resource development and marketing. But financial evaluation is important, too. Board and management should be interested in how the organization is operating relative to its plan. To get this feedback, management should prepare a Budget Variance Analysis report on a periodic but timely basis.

In order to monitor financial activities, the board should request a comparison of actual revenue and expense to that budgeted for the same period. This is not unreasonable since management should generate the same information in order to maintain control of the financial operation.

Exhibit 11-6 illustrates a variance analysis. Note that it compares actual to budgeted expenditures for the first nine months of operation. This analysis should be done at least quarterly and more frequently as circumstances dictate. A more frequent comparison will be more costly in time and energy, but in some instances this may be justifiable.

Just as important, the analysis builds in appropriate planning considerations by requiring management to react to changed circumstances and forecast the full impact such changes will have on the annual financial operating plan. This should be of special interest to the board.

Obviously, the analysis is useful only to the extent it is accurate and timely. Accuracy rests largely on the reliability of the accounting and bookkeeping system and the competency of financial personnel. Timing should be addressed by both management and the board by requiring that the

EXHIBIT 11-6: Sample Budget Variance Analysis

Revenues/Expenditures	Approved Annual Budget	Actual to Date	% Budget	Projected to Year End	Expected Favorable or (Unfavorable) Variance	Note
Corporations	$ 60,000	$ 42,000	70	$ 22,000	$ (4,000)	1
Private Foundations	40,000	30,000	75	10,000	-----	2
Government Grants	60,000	35,000	58	20,000	5,000	3
Fees	50,000	44,000	88	4,000	2,000	
Investment Income	6,000	2,000	33	2,000	2,000	
Donated Materials/Services	40,000	30,000	75	12,000	(2,000)	
Total Income	256,000	183,000	75	70,000	3,000	
Personnel	125,000	94,000	75	26,000	5,000	3
Fringes	22,000	8,800	40	7,200	6,000	3
Donated Materials/Services	40,000	30,000	75	12,000	(2,000)	
Occupancy	14,000	10,500	75	3,500	-----	
Utilities	1,000	700	70	500	(200)	
Printing/Postage	6,000	4,800	80	2,400	(1,200)	
Travel	8,000	4,800	60	2,000	1,200	
Equipment	10,000	5,000	50	2,000	3,000	4
Office Supplies	6,000	5,100	85	1,200	(300)	
Miscellaneous	2,000	1,400	70	600	-----	
Contingency	6,000	1,200	20	2,000	2,800	
Total Expenses	240,000	166,300	69	59,400	14,300	
Net	$ 16,000	$ 16,700		10,600	($11,300)	

NOTES: (1) Grant expected in subsequent year received in current year. (2) Amount held back until auditors complete routine audit; expected completion date first quarter next year. (3) Resignation of program manager expected November 1 this year. Fee income and fringe affected accordingly. (4) Due primarily to unanticipated donation.

analysis be developed at specific intervals. For example, if the Executive Committee meets monthly, a standing Treasurer's Report item in the month following the end of a quarter should be a review of the variance analysis. The treasurer should, of course, review the analysis with management prior to the Executive Committee meeting.

To make the analysis complete, management should document explanations for significant variances. Obviously some variances require investigation; others do not. The threshold for materiality will vary by organization, but a good rule of thumb is to prepare explanations for variances of more than 8 or 10 %. Even when a budget is expected to be balanced, or when favorable and unfavorable variances offset one another, prudent management and control calls for adequate explanation.

Cash Management

Everyone agrees with the importance of an operating budget. But another type of budget which is most useful to management is the cash budget. Unlike the operational budget, the cash budget focuses strictly on the "in and out" of the organization's cash. Since cash is the most important financial resource, it deserves special attention.

Exhibit 11-7 illustrates a cash budget or cash flow analysis. The basic objective of this budget is to identify borrowing needs and opportunities for maximizing available resources. Even though an organization may expect to balance its budget by the end of the year, there may be times during the year when there is an unusually large amount of cash available beyond short term operating needs, or conversely, a shortage of funds may occur. As a management tool, the cash budget or cash flow analysis allows management and the board treasurer to react responsibly and in a timely fashion to either situation.

When there is a shortage (as in April in our example), advance knowledge will permit management and the treasurer to plan well in advance on how to make up the deficit. Depending on the situation, available investments could be sold, perhaps expected donations or grants could be accelerated, or financing through borrowing might be arranged. In any event, responsible management calls for signaling deficits far enough in advance so appropriate action can be taken on a timely basis.

In the event excess cash is available, that is monies not needed to meet short term operating expenses, management has a responsibility to funders and the public at large to capitalize on this opportunity. But without a carefully constructed cash budget, it will be difficult to pinpoint these opportunities. In our example, there is approximately $25,000 at the end of June which will not be required to meet general operating expenses for at least two months. Rather than have this money sit idle in a savings account, the organization may give consideration to short term investments. The opportunity cost involved in not channeling the money elsewhere could be very high. When passbook savings earn 5.25% and Treasury Bills yield 10.25%, the opportunity cost is 5%.

EXHIBIT 11-7: Sample Cash Budget

SIX MONTHS ENDED JUNE 30

	JAN	FEB	MAR	APR	MAY	JUNE
Beginning Cash	$10,000	$17,100	$10,250	$ 4,400	$ 2,600	$15,300
Receipts						
Accts Receivable	6,000	4,000	3,000	----	----	----
Donations	12,000	----	----	4,000	4,000	6,000
Fees	1,000	2,000	2,000	3,000	3,000	6,000
Grants	----	----	4,000	----	10,000	11,000
Contracts	----	----	----	----	10,000	20,000
Other	----	----	----	1,500	2,000	2,000
Total Available	29,000	23,100	19,250	12,900	31,600	60,300
Disbursements						
Accts Payable	3,000	2,000	----	----	----	----
Personnel	6,000	6,000	8,000	8,000	8,000	8,000
Fringes	750	750	750	750	750	750
Rent	1,000	1,000	1,000	1,000	1,000	1,000
Utilities	250	250	250	300	300	300
Printing	400	400	400	600	600	600
Local Transpo.	150	150	150	150	150	150
Supplies	200	200	200	400	400	400
Equipment	----	2,000	4,000	4,000	----	----
Other	150	100	100	100	100	100
Total	11,900	12,850	14,850	15,300	11,300	11,300
Net	17,100	10,250	4,400	(2,400)	20,300	49,000
Financing	----	----	----	5,000	----	----
Repayment	----	----	----	----	5,000	----
Ending Cash	17,100	10,250	4,400	2,600	15,300	49,000
Investments	----	----	----	----	----	25,000
Available for Operations	$17,100	$10,250	$4,400	$2,600	$15,300	$24,000

One important and related aspect of cash management is working capital management. Working capital is an organization's cash and near-cash items such as accounts receivable, inventory, short term investments, less its current obligations such as accounts payable or short term loans. Like cash, other working capital items require proper management. For example, collection policies and procedures reflect the organization's ability to manage its accounts receivable. Similarly, when the group pays its bills and whether it takes quantity and other discounts demonstrates its ability to manage accounts payable. In some organizations current assets and current liabilities will be immaterial; in others, especially if service fees are a significant portion of total revenue or a significant proportion of purchases are made on account, working capital management can be very important.

The notion of opportunity cost arises again. Not to be taken lightly, these costs, while not directly out of pocket, are costs just the same. An organization channeling funds to an investment when an alternative investment yielding higher returns exists (with other things being equal), has incurred a cost. These are the kinds of costs that are inexcusable.

Another way to manage cash effectively, and address, in part, financing needs, is to stretch payables. This simply means making arrangements with creditors to accept payment at a later date because of cash timing differences. Most vendors, being business people themselves, understand these situations. Even if they require payment of interest, this additional cost may be appropriate when alternative arrangements are more costly.

Accounting and Financial Reporting

Accounting is the language of business and is a most useful tool for effective nonprofit management. Just as effective planning cannot take place without first asking the question "What is our business?", any organization must be able to express its business in financial terms. The organization's financial history, present and plans should be of interest to management and the board and is unquestionably of interest to funders, regulators and the public at large.

While generally thought of in terms of accountability, accounting and financial reporting involves much more. Without underestimating the importance of accountability, the organization must think beyond this notion and view accounting from a management perspective. Management must come to understand how knowledge of accounting can strengthen the ability to plan, allocate scarce resources, budget, control and evaluate.

In order for an accounting system to be useful, a well conceived and thorough bookkeeping or record keeping system must be in order. Even with the best of intentions, management and the board are unable to access information needed for decision making when the record keeping system is incomplete or inaccurate.

177

Importance of Record Keeping

If the record keeping system is not defined carefully, many pitfalls can arise which serve to debilitate effective management decision making. Timely and reliable information is a must if management and the board are to carry out their stewardship responsibilities. Effective decision making is based on a complete and accurate management information system which can generate data related to program and financial activities. For example, without a carefully designed system, it is difficult to determine the cost of running a particular program or how services should be priced. Efficient operation also requires the organization to have information and records readily available when needed. Additionally, a reliable record keeping system enables the organization to adequately meet the expectations of funders and others who rely on information regarding the use of resources and program accomplishments. As will be reinforced below, the cost of audits in terms of money, time, and energy can be inordinately high if an audit trail is lacking in the records.

The backbone of any record keeping system is the organization's chart of accounts. This is simply a detailed listing of the organization's assets, liabilities, revenue, expenses and funds (unrestricted and restricted). Information must be retrieved along these lines to satisfy financial reporting requirements --both internal and external. Without a carefully designed chart of accounts, the record keeping system can become quite cumbersome and inadequate. The accounts must be based on carefully assessed needs regarding both internal and external requirements. A carefully designed chart of accounts enhances efficiency and strengthens the management information system required for budgeting, planning and control.

Another important aspect of record keeping involves the accounting bases used in recording and reporting financial activities. Financial information reported on an accrual basis is required by generally accepted accounting principles, but this does not mean that the record keeping system has to be maintained on an accrual basis. A cash basis record keeping system is appropriate in most instances. However, in order to give a complete financial picture, reports must reflect any necessary accruals. This simply means giving due recognition to significant amounts owed to the organization as well as amounts it owes others so that a complete economic picture of the organization's assets, liabilities, revenues and expenses can be drawn.

As with any system, record keeping should be tailored to the appropriate set of circumstances and flexibility should be maintained.

Financial Statements

Financial statements required to satisfy generally accepted accounting principles are set out in the American Institute of Certified Public Accountants (AICPA) Audit Guides. In all instances, nonprofit organizations are required to present a Balance Sheet and a Statement of Revenue, Support and Expenses if it intends to convey to others a complete financial picture of the organization. For organizations covered by the Voluntary Health and Welfare guide, A Statement of Functional Expenses is also required.

The purpose of any set of financial statements is to communicate an accurate and complete picture of the organization's financial status. Financial statements intended otherwise are next to useless. Financial statements should provide the primary vehicle for informing others of the total resources available to carry out various program services and activities, and the use made of these resources. They should also give a reading on the organization's general "well offness" in the form of a statement of financial position (balance sheet).

When carefully designed, these statements will be meaningful and accommodating to the needs of the organzation's board, funders, government, the general public and management. Critical decisions shaping the future of any organization are based in part on financial data. Knowing how resources were allocated in the past is important information in planning future use and is discussed in the budget section, timely access to reliable financial data is a must if board and management are to fulfill their stewardship responsibilities.

Exhibit 11-8 provides illustrative financial statements for an organization, 11-8a is a balance sheet (at the end of the six months) showing the status of both the restricted and unrestricted funds. The traditional name for this financial statement is balance sheet simply because, as the exhibit indicates, total assets equals total liabilities and fund balances. The statement's utility is not in its mathematics, but in what it conveys. A comparative balance sheet is a statement of the organization's financial position at two points in time.

Note the distinction made between current and long term assets. As defined previously, current assets are cash or near cash items. The latter, by definition, must be easily converted to cash generally within a year's time. Fixed assets simply reflect the organization's ownership in furniture, equipment, and other property.

Liabilities also should be divided between current and long term. As discussed previously, the distinction is important in order to compute the organization's working capital. As for fund balance, this basically represents the organization's "equity" (assets minus liabilities). Changes in fund balances from year to year generally reflect the results of operations between the two years. This is why ending fund balances cross-reference to Exhibit 11-8b. The distinction between restricted, unrestricted and board designated accounts are explained in detail below.

A statement of Revenue, Support and Expenses (11-8b) is essentially the organization's financial operating statement. But unlike the typical operating statement, expenses in this statement do not detail the conventional line items; rather, only the organization's program and supporting services. The distinction between program and supporting services was defined earlier in connection with our discussion on program budgeting.

EXHIBIT 11-8a: Sample Balance Sheet

XYZ COMMUNITY CENTER

FOR THE SIX MONTHS ENDING JUNE 30, 1983

	General Fund	Restricted Fund	All Funds
ASSETS			
Current Assets:			
Cash in bank	3126.86	1027.49	4154.35
Savings	8000.00	----	8000.00
Petty Cash	50.00	----	50.00
Investments	9000.00	----	9000.00
Grant Receivables	2500.00	5632.15	8132.15
Employee Receivables	300.00	----	300.00
Pledge Receivables	505.00	----	505.00
Pre-Paid Expenses	667.45	864.23	1531.68
Total Current Assets	24149.31	7523.87	31673.18
Fixed Assets:			
Land & Buildings	---	26000.00	26000.00
Less accum. depr.	---	<7600.00>	<7600.00>
Equip & Furniture	1650.00	2350.00	4000.00
Less accum. depr.	<569.27>	<804.76>	<1374.03>
Net fixed assets	1080.73	19945.24	21025.97

LIABILITIES AND FUND BALANCES

	General Fund	Restricted Fund	All Funds
Current Liabilities:			
Accrued payroll taxes	318.70	282.00	600.70
Wage payables	180.00	----	180.00
Vendor payables	2368.33	248.12	2616.45
Contract/grant adv.	---	3631.15	3631.15
Deferred gifts	500.00	----	500.00
Total current liab.	3367.03	4161.27	7528.30
Long term debt	---	18400.00	18400.00
Total Liabilities	3367.03	22561.27	25928.30
Fund Balance:	21863.01	4907.84	26770.85
Total Liabilities & Fund Balances	25230.04	27469.11	52699.15

EXHIBIT 11-8b: Sample Statement of Income, Expenses and Changes in Fund Balance

XYZ COMMUNITY CENTER

STATEMENT OF INCOME, EXPENSES AND CHANGES IN FUND BALANCES
For the six months ending June 30, 1983

INCOME:
Contributions and gifts	9212.50	
Bequests	5763.99	
Special event income	1286.45	
Membership	9655.00	
Participant fees	8012.00	
Contract income	12267.23	
Grant income	10632.15	
Investment income	1002.78	
TOTAL INCOME		57832.10

EXPENSES:
Program services:
Child care program	13268.15	
Youth recreation program	12008.20	
Total program services		25276.35

Supporting services:
General administration	14364.68	
Fund Raising	7147.71	
Total supporting services		21512.39
TOTAL EXPENSES		46788.74
Excess of income over expenses		11043.36
Fund balance, beginning of year		15727.49
Fund Balance, end of period		26770.85

EXHIBIT 11-8c: Sample Statement of Functional Expenses

XYZ COMMUNITY CENTER

For the six month period ended June 30, 1983

| | Program Services | | | Support Services | | | All |
	Child Care	Youth Recreat.	Total Program	Fund Raising	Gen. Admin.	Total Support	All Expenses
Salary/wages	6000.00	6000.00	12000.00	3777.33	5207.81	8985.14	20985.14
Payroll taxes	576.00	576.00	1152.00	362.63	499.95	862.58	2014.58
Contract Serv.	---	---	---	---	300.00	300.00	300.00
Mileage	2548.40	1126.40	3674.80	482.20	2122.80	2605.00	6279.80
Food/lodging	386.30	370.83	757.13	228.00	687.30	915.30	1672.43
Supplies/acces.	1432.20	1824.21	3256.41	489.20	1034.69	1523.89	4780.30
Space rental	---	---	---	270.00	1230.00	1500.00	1500.00
Maint./repair	311.43	346.15	657.58	41.49	188.96	230.45	888.03
Utilities	418.93	465.63	884.56	---	---	---	884.56
Building deprc	225.00	250.00	475.00	---	---	---	475.00
Equip/frn. lease	86.50	54.00	140.50	400.00	350.00	750.00	890.50
Equip/frn. maint	128.00	105.68	233.68	---	160.25	160.25	393.93
Equip/frn. deprc	123.37	22.95	146.32	---	87.58	87.58	233.90
Phone	209.97	207.12	417.09	374.33	573.80	948.13	1365.22
Postage/shipping	20.00	18.89	38.89	105.15	163.22	268.37	307.26
Printing/copying	35.75	29.25	65.00	420.10	448.16	868.26	933.26
Dues/membership	50.00	50.00	100.00	---	50.00	50.00	150.00
Subscrp/public.	420.00	100.00	520.00	80.00	435.93	515.93	1035.93
Ins/bonding/lic.	248.30	419.15	667.45	40.00	824.23	864.23	1531.68
Miscellaneous	48.00	41.94	89.94	77.28	---	77.28	167.22
Total Expenses	13268.15	12008.20	25276.35	7147.71	14364.68	21512.39	46788.74

Classifying expenditures in this fashion allows the organization to focus on key financial information in capsule form. But the detailed line item expenditures are also important and these are outlined in 11-8c. Note that the total figures cross reference to 11-8b. Most importantly, it should be noted that the functional expense summary, in effect, represents program budgets.

The balance sheet and operating statement should be prepared monthly. The statement of functional expenses should be prepared at least annually. All three statements are required for full compliance with generally accepted accounting principles and, therefore, would be required to accommodate an independent audit. The usefulness of the functional expense summary is clear. Whether the summary should be prepared more frequently than on an annual basis is a cost-benefit decision.

Standards and Guidelines

The attitude of the accounting profession toward nonprofit organizations in this country has historically been one of benign neglect. While accounting firms concentrated their energies on business, where the big bucks are, nonprofits struggled along with no direction or guidelines, borrowing methods where they found them. But without uniformity in accounting and reporting practices, neither contributors nor creditors could tell how much of an organization's revenue was actually expended on its programs. Confusion reigned and credibility suffered.

In recent years, as it became apparent that nonprofits control and spend millions of dollars annually, the AICPA issued "audit guides" for the four largest categories of nonprofit organizations: Hospitals, colleges and universities, voluntary health and welfare organizations, and state and local governments. More recently, standards for "all other" nonprofits have been developed and summarized in the AICPA Statement of Position 78-10. These guides are listed in "further readings" and thoroughly discuss accounting and financial reporting requirements for each type of nonprofit organization. For this reason, the guides serve as excellent resource materials for board and management.

All nonprofit organizations must comply with some basic accounting principles and standards. These include fund accounting, accrual accounting, historical costs, consistency, fair and complete disclosure, investments, donated services, fixed assets and pledges. These and other concerns are covered in the AICPA guides.

The most important accounting principle for nonprofits is, of course, fund accounting. In many cases, restrictions have been placed on resources which prohibit their use directly or currently for operating purposes. This situation requires separate accountability for these funds which is generally accomplished by the use of fund accounting - maintaining a separate system of accounts so that the restrictions can be recognized. Under the fund accounting concept, separate accounting entities, or funds, are established as needed to achieve a proper segregation and fair presentation of those resources available for use at the discretion of the governing board (unrestricted funds), and of those resources over which the board has little, if any, discretion as to their use because of externally imposed restrictions (restricted funds). The most commonly used funds are:

Unrestricted funds – account for all resources (e.g., contributions, bequests, program service fees, dues and investment income) over which the governing board has discretionary control to use in carrying on the operations of the organization in accordance with the limitations of its charter and bylaws, except for unrestricted accounts which may be land, buildings, and equipment that may be accounted for in a separate fund.

Restricted funds – established to account for resources currently available for use, but expendable only for operating purposes specified by the donor or grantor. These resources may originate from gifts, grants, income from endowment funds, or other similar sources where the donor has specified the operating purposes for which the funds are to be used.

Land, building and equipment fund – is often used to accumulate the net investment of fixed assets and to account for the expended resources contributed specifically for the purpose of acquiring or replacing land, buildings, or equipment for use in the organization's operations. Conventionally a separate fund was established to account for such resources even when their use is unrestricted. In other words, an organization choosing to allocate or designate a portion of its unrestricted funds towards the acquisition of significant amounts of property may find it convenient to maintain separate accounting for such funds by establishing a separate fund.

Endowment fund – represents the principal (or face) amount of gifts and bequests accepted with the donor's stipulation that the principal be maintained intact in perpetuity or until a specified time or event takes place. Generally the income derived from the investment of the principal is expendable for general purposes or for purposes specified by the donor.

Custodian funds – are established to account for assets received by an organization to be held or disbursed only on instructions of the person or organization from whom they are received. Unlike other funds, custodian funds are not assets of the organization; therefore receipts of income that might be generated from them should not be considered as part of the organization's revenue or support.

Resource development plans should articulate very carefully the desirability of obtaining each and every type of the funds described above. In addition to considering the impact that the various sources can have on financial stability and mobility of the organization, due consideration must be given to the related accounting once the funds are obtained.

Compilations, Reviews and Audits

Managing finances is certainly a challenging task. It's one that the board and management cannot afford to abdicate. If done with care and prudence, financial management will strengthen the organization's ability to face challenges and maximize resources.

An effective financial management system relies heavily on reliable and timely accounting information. Some organizations seek outside assistance since they do not have the staff capability to handle accounting and financial reporting requirements.

Recently the accounting profession issued standards which should prove helpful to any organization. Previously, accounting firms could not express an opinion about a financial statement unless a full scale audit had been performed. Services other than a full audit required a disclaimer of opinion such as: "We did not perform an audit and we don't express an opinion on the financial statements."

To many users, the meaning was unclear. It seemed like the accountants had done a great deal of work on the financial statements; yet the report said nothing was done. Now there's an alternative. Accountants can provide the same basic services without the negative sounds of the "unaudited" label. The options available now include (1) limited assurance as a result of review; (2) a compilation service which provides no assurance to those requiring such; and, of course, (3) the positive assurance of an audit.

Compilation

A compilation is essentially a service in which the CPA presents financial data supplied by management in financial statement format. Because the scope of this service is so limited, a CPA does not express an opinion or any level of assurance on the financial statements, either to the organization or to other users of the statements. The service can be performed monthly, quarterly or annually.

Where an organization is without sufficient staff resources to have financial data prepared on a timely basis, the compilation service is most useful. Although the CPA will not give an in-depth analysis of the system, he will be able to furnish a reading of the organization's current financial position and results of operation. This should aid management and governance, particularly that of the board treasurer, in fulfilling stewardship responsibilities and making effective financial decisions.

The CPA performs three basic steps in a compilation:

1. Becomes knowledgeable about the accounting principles and practices of the organization's industry and acquires a general understanding of the company's business transactions and accounting records.

2. Prepares the financial statements from the organization's records and reads the statements for appropriate form and lack of obvious material error.

3. Issues a report, stating that the financial reports were compiled, but because they were not audited or reviewed, no opinion or any other form of assurance is expressed.

There may be further warnings (additional paragraphs in the report) if the statements are issued to outsiders without certain explanatory footnotes required by generally accepted accounting principles.

Review

A review is appropriate for an organization when the users of the financial statement need some degree of assurance from the CPA that the financial reports require no material changes. While it may include a compilation, the review requires the CPA to go several steps further by:

1. Obtaining a working knowledge of the company's industry.

2. Acquiring a detailed understanding of the company's business
   —Its organization, operations, products, and services.

3. Making inquires of company personnel, such as:
   —Have bank balances been reconciled with book balances?
   —Have receivables considered uncollectable been written off?

4. Performing analytical procedures on certain financial data, such as:
   —Percentage analysis – e.g. fund raising costs as a total percentage of costs.
   —Financial ratio analysis – e.g. current period's accounts receivable turnover.

5. Issuing a report, stating that the financial reports were reviewed, but because they were not audited, no opinion is expressed. However, the CPA's report also describes the nature of the procedures performed and indicates that the CPA is not aware of any material changes that should be made to the financial statements.

Since a review is generally more expensive than a compilation it is important to know what you pay for. The inquiries made by the CPA are an important aspect of the review process inasmuch as they form collectively an investigation of significant matters which could affect the reliability of financial statements.

Audit

Audits provide a thorough analysis of the supporting evidence underlying financial data and lead to an opinion by the CPA regarding the data's "reliability." Implicit in deciding to have an audit is a basic need to obtain independent assurance on the completeness and credibility of the financial information.

An audit must be performed in accordance with generally accepted auditing standards. These standards require the CPA to perform procedures not fully embodied in either a compilation or review, by:

1. Obtaining a comprehensive understanding of the organization's industry and business operations to enable the auditor to plan and perform the audit.

2. Analyzing the organization's financial data to identify unusual relationships that would affect the emphasis of the audit work.

3. Studying and evaluating the organization's system of internal accounting control to determine the amount and type of audit procedures needed.

4. Preparing an audit program to document the procedures necessary to accomplish the audit objective.

5. Making inspections, observations, inquires, and confirmations with third parties to corroborate data received from the non-profit such as:

    -Confirmation of receivables
    -Physical inspection of securities
    -Detailed tests of selected transactions

6. Issuing a report stating that financial reports were audited and whether or not they are fairly presented.

The most desirable end product is an unqualified or "clean" opinion. If a qualified or adverse opinion is furnished, a "warning signal" automatically surfaces. In these latter instances, the auditor's report will explain the auditor's exception.

Like so many decisions requiring the investment of resources, the choice of which service you need is one involving cost and benefits. Any organization must weigh carefully the additional benefits which accrue from varying levels of assurance needed by the organization's board, management and third parties. In some instances, a combination of services may be desirable, such as an annual audit with quarterly reviews, or an annual review with monthly compilations. The important thing to remember is that the level of service should meet the specific needs of the organization.

Appendix A: Financial Controls Self-Evaluation

Instructions. When an area or question is not applicable, mark N/A in the status column and footnote reasons why it is not applicable. Generally, a "no" response indicates a financial control weakness which should be weighed carefully and resolved as appropriate.

Status

LEGAL CONSIDERATIONS

1. Do the organization's bylaws

    A. Address fiduciary responsibilities?

    B. Outline the specific duties and responsibilities of the treasurer?

    C. Restrict powers on use of monies or other properties received by the corporation?

    D. Restrict corporation from carrying on any activities not permitted to be carried on by a a 501 (c)(3) corporation?

    E. Require annual reports summarizing preceding fiscal year's receipts and expenditures and statement of position (balance sheet) for its annual board or membership meeting?

    F. Provide for a separate article on financial procedures and restrictions on transactions and which address the following matters:

        (1) Nature and timing of financial report summaries?

        (2) Deposits and withdrawal of funds?

        (3) Loan procurement?

        (4) Execution of contracts?

        (5) Compensation of directors?

        (6) Contracts with officers and directors?

    G. Provide an article addressing dissolution and disposition of corporate assets?

    H. Address indemnification of officers and
       directors?

2. Does adequate fidelity insurance (bonding) exist
   for those entrusted with the handling of cash
   and other assets?

3. Has the organization provided for adequate
   liability insurance for corporate directors?

4. Is there a need for liability insurance to cover
   the organization's volunteers?

GENERAL MATTERS

1. Are the treasurer's specific responsibilities
   outlined in the organization's bylaws or
   elsewhere?

2. Are there clear lines of authority and
   responsibility documented in an organization
   chart?

   A. Executive director

   B. Financial personnel

3. Are there job descriptions covering all fiscal
   duties?

4. Are there clear management policies establishing
   responsibilities for purchasing, recording
   transactions, reporting, budgeting, payroll
   processing, etc.?

5. Are all employees aware of their duties and
   responsibilities?

6. Does the board require an annual audit on a
   timely basis?

7. Does the board approve the appointment of the
   auditors?

8. Does the board have an audit committee?

9. Does the audit committee have defined duties
   and responsibilities?

10. Are those duties and responsibilties

documented in a board resolution or
otherwise?

11. Does the audit committee meet with the
    auditor to discuss the audit report?

12. Does the Board cause effective actions to
    be taken where indicated by the auditor's
    report?

13. Does the director respond to deficiencies
    in internal controls pointed out through
    audit reports or other monitoring visits?

14. Has the board given consideration to arranging
    compilation and/or review services in lieu of
    (or partial substitution for) audit services?

15. Has a master reporting calendar been effected
    for each fiscal year?

FINANCIAL PLANNING

1. Does the organization's financial planning
   process:

    A. Begin with enough lead time prior to
       completing current fiscal year?

    B. Include a master planning calendar?

    C. Consider program evaluation data in
       allocating financial resources?

2. Does the director keep on hand a current
   copy of applicable financial regulations
   or guidelines?

3. Is there 3 - 5 year financial forecast of
   revenues (by type) compared to expected
   program and supporting expenditures?

4. Before an annual operating budget is
   designed

    A. Is the organization's purpose or
       mission statement re-evaluated?

    B. Is consideration given to the nature and
       magnitude of planned activities which
       might be classified as "unrelated

business income"?

 C. Are the following year's operating goals and objectives identified?

 D. Is there a re-evaluation of the range of programs (services) for accomplishing the subsequent year's goals and objectives?

 E. Are all existing and proposed programs subjected to a cost-benefit analysis?

 F. Are funds budgeted (receipts and expenses) for individual programs and supporting (fund raising and general administration) services?

5. Does the treasurer play an active role in the financial planning process?

6. Does the program staff play an active role (have input) in the budgeting process?

7. Is the proposed operating budget approved by the board?

8. Does the board require a periodic reporting against the budget at least quarterly?

9. Are significant variances (favorable or unfavorable) documented?

10. Do financial reports (budgets, operating statements, balance sheets, etc.) meet management's need to know

 A. Cost center information?

 B. Funding source information?

 C. Total program information?

11. Are allocations of costs made where it may result in fuller utilization of funds? from all funding sources?

12. Is unit (service) cost information developed and analyzed on a timely basis?

TRANSACTION CONTROLS

General

1. Is there a standard operating procedures (S.O.P.)
   manual outlining all bookkeeping, accounting and
   financial reporting procedures?

2. Does the S.O.P. manual identify specific
   accounting controls to be maintained?

3. Is there a standard reporting system
   requiring
   A. Operating statement (receipts and
      expenses) each month?

   B. Balance sheet (statement of financial
      position) at least quarterly?

4. Is a 12 month cash budget in place to
   forecast borrowing needs and investment
   opportunities?

5. Is the cash budget updated at least quarterly?

6. Is adequate separation of duties maintained
   to ensure the safeguarding of assets (i.e.,
   persons responsible for recording of cash,
   property and other assets - e.g. marketable
   securities, do not also have access to the
   assets)?

CASH RECEIPTS

1. Is mail opened by persons with no bookkeeping
   duties?

2. Is a record of cash received established as
   soon as the cash or cash item is received?

3. Are all checks restrictively endorsed "for
   deposit only" by the person opening the
   mail?

4. Is cash received and deposited intact and on a
   timely basis?

5. Are deposits made to a savings account in
   lieu of general checking to maximize
   earnings?

6. Are all receipts recorded in a journal which lists
   check number, amount, payroll and purpose?

7. Can cash received be traced from the initial listing to the bank statement and to the posting in the general ledger?

8. Is the cash receipts journal posted currently?

CASH DISBURSEMENTS

1. Are purchase approval procedures adequately documented and communicated?

2. Are invoices internally checked for accuracy before being paid?

3. Are invoices marked "paid" or otherwise cancelled to prevent duplicate payment?

4. Are all checks signed by an individual(s) authorized by the Board of Directors?

5. Are all disbursements (other than petty cash) made by prenumbered checks?

6. Does a policy exist requiring that no checks be made payable to "cash"?

7. Has an efficient method been established to initially record and categorize disbursements for purposes of recording in the general ledger and management reporting?

8. Is there an organized filing method for paid vendor invoices.

9. Are adequate property records established which maintain accountability for purchases of fixed assets?

10. Does the subsidiary property record agree with the general ledger?

11. Is there a periodic inventory of property with comparison to the subsidiary property ledger?

12. Is the cash disbursements journal posted currently?

BANK ACCOUNTS

1. Is each bank account authorized by the board?

2. Is there sufficient justification for using
   more than one bank account?

3. For any accounts not used, has the bank been
   notified in writing to close the account and not
   to process any subsequent transactions?

4. Has the board authorized check signers and
   identified check amount (e.g. $ 500) above which
   a board signature is required?

5. Have bank statements been reconciled monthly to
   the general ledger?

6. Is the reconciliation reviewed and approved by a
   responsible individual and such review
   appropriately documented?

7. Have all required adjustments to the general
   ledger cash balance identified through the
   reconciliation procedure been posted promptly?
   (The adjustment should be posted through the
   general journal.)

PAYROLL

1. Does the payroll register list the name,
   check number, gross pay, withholdings and
   net pay of each employee?

2. Is an attendance record maintained for each
   employee and approved by the employee's
   supervisor?

3. Is a record of vacation, sick and leave time maintained
   for each employee? Does it include the time accrued,
   taken and the available balance?

4. Is a record of cumulative individual earnings (gross,
   net, withholding) maintained for each person on the
   payroll?

5. Does each employee have a personnel file with
   documentation concerning appointments,
   position reclassification, salary rates and
   terminations?

6. Are salary and wage rates approved in writing
   by an authorized individual? Are procedures

adequate to provide that employees are paid in accordance with approved wage and salary plans?

7. Are adjustments to payroll disbursements approved by an authorized individual independent of payroll preparation?

8. Are payroll checks signed by persons having no part in preparing the payroll?

9. Are employees furnished information on their gross earnings, deductions from earnings, etc., with their payroll checks?

10. Is the proper withholding and prompt payment of applicable federal, state and local income and payroll taxes evidenced by quarterly or monthly withholding reports sent to the appropriate authorities?

GENERAL JOURNAL

1. Is every entry to the general ledger not originating from the Cash Receipts Journal, Payroll Register, Cash Disbursements Journal or any other record of original entry posted to the General Journal?

2. Is each entry to the General Journal

   A. Fully described?

   B. Adequately documented?

   C. Sequentially numbered?

   D. Approved by an authorized individual?

GENERAL LEDGER

1. Is the general ledger posted monthly and on a timely basis?

2. Is the general ledger posted on a double entry system?

3. Does the general ledger design accommodate fund accounting or cost center accounting requirements in accordance with the most expedient procedures under the circumstances?

4. Is the cost center or fund accounting requirements (whichever is not incorporated into general

ledger) provided for outside of the confines of
the general ledger?

5. Is the chart of accounts adequate to provide general
   ledger detail sufficient to easily generate needed
   management information?

TRIAL BALANCE

1. Is a trial balance of the general ledger prepared
   monthly?

2. Are out of balance conditions identified and
   corrected?

3. Are all trial balances kept on file until the audit
   for that fiscal year has been completed and the audit
   report issued?

Further Readings

GENERAL REFERENCES

Tracy D. Connors, Editor in Chief, THE NONPROFIT HANDBOOK. New
York, NY: McGraw-Hill Book Company, 1979

Tracy D. Connors and C.T. Callaghan (eds.), FINANCIAL MANAGEMENT
FOR NONPROFIT ORGANIZATIONS. New York: American Management
Institute, 1982

Malvern J. Gross and William Warshauer, FINANCIAL AND ACCOUNTING
GUIDE FOR NONPROFIT ORGANIZATIONS. Revised Third edition, New
York: Ronald Press (John Wiley & Sons): New York, NY, 1983

A.J. Olenick and P.R. Olenick, MAKING THE NONPROFIT ORGANIZATION
WORK: A FINANCIAL, LEGAL AND TAX GUIDE FOR ADMINISTRATORS.
Englewood Cliffs, NJ: Institute for Business Planning, 1983

United Way of America, ACCOUNTING AND FINANCIAL REPORTS. Alexandria,
VA: United Way of America, 1974

STANDARDS FOR ACCOUNTING AND FINANCIAL REPORTING FOR VOLUNTARY
HEALTH AND WELFARE ORGANIZATIONS, revised. New York: National
Health Council

William H. Daughtrey and Malvern Gross, MUSEUM ACCOUNTING
HANDBOOK. Washington, D.C. American Association of Museums

Paul Bennett UP YOUR ACCOUNTABILITY. Washington, D.C.: Taft
Corporation, 1973

FINANCIAL MANAGEMENT FOR THE ARTS: A GUIDE FOR ARTS ORGANIZATIONS.
NY, NY: ACA Publications, 1976

AICPA GUIDES

AICPA VOLUNTARY HEALTH AND WELFARE ORGANIZATIONS. NY, NY: AICPA,
1974

AUDITS OF COLLEGES AND UNIVERSITIES. NY,NY: AICPA, 1973

HOSPITAL AUDIT GUIDE. NY,NY: AICPA, 1972

ACCOUNTING PRINCIPLES AND REPORTING PRACTICES FOR CERTAIN NONPROFIT
ORGANIZATIONS. Statement of Position 78-10, December 31, 1978.
NY, NY: AICPA, 1978

FOR THE FEDERALLY FUNDED

      -------FEDERAL FINANCIAL MANAGEMENT: ACCOUNTING AND PRACTICES.
        Washington, D.C.: Office of Management and Budget

      -------UNIFORM ADMINISTRATIVE REQUIREMENTS FOR GRANT AND AGREEMENTS
        WITH INSTITUTIONS OF HIGHER LEARNING, HOSPITALS AND OTHER
        NONPROFIT ORGANIZATIONS, Circular A-21. Washington, D.C.: Office
        Of Management and Budget

      -------UNIFORM ADMINISTRATIVE REQUIREMENTS FOR GRANTS AND AGREEMENTS
        WITH NONPROFIT ORGANIZATIONS, EXCEPT HOSPITALS, AND COLLEGES AND
        UNIVERSITIES, Circular A-122. Washington, D.C.: Office of
        Management and Budget

      -------BCHS ACCOUNTING MANUAL: ILLUSTRATED ACCOUNTING PRACTICE SET
        FOR FEDERALLY FUNDED HEALTH CENTERS AND INSTRUCTION MANUAL FOR
        THE BCHR COMMON REPORTING REQUIREMENTS. Rockville, MD: Bureau
        of Community Health Services

      -------ACCOUNTING GUIDELINES FOR MENTAL HEALTH CENTERS AND RELATED
        FACILITIES. Rockville, MD: The National Institute of Mental
        Health, 1972

ARTICLES

      Christopher T. Callaghan, "New Math for Nonprofits," GRANTSMANSHIP
        CENTER NEWS. March/April, 1979

      Neil Churchhill and Luis A. Werbeanett, Jr., "Choosing and
        Evaluating Your Accountant," HARVARD BUSINESS REVIEW. May/June,
        1979

      E.O. Henke, "Performance Evaluation for Not-For-Profit Organiza-
        tions," JOURNAL OF ACCOUNTANCY. June 1972

OTHER REFERENCES

      BOOKKEEPING PROCEDURES AND BUSINESS PRACTICES FOR SMALL HOSPITALS.
        Chicago: American Hospital Association, 1969

      CHARTS OF ACCOUNTS FOR HOSPITALS. Chicago: The American Hospital
        Association, 1976

      Malvern J. Gross, Jr., "Nonprofit Accounting: The Continuing
        Revolution," JOURNAL OF ACCOUNTANCY. (June 1977), p. 66-74

      Leon E. Hay and R.M. Mikesel, GOVERNMENTAL ACCOUNTING. Homewood,
        IL: Richard R. Irwin, Inc., 1974

      Harry D. Kerrig, FUND ACCOUNTING. New York, NY: McGraw-Hill Book
        Company, 1969

Chapter 12

Fund Raising: The Board is the Key

Stephen Hitchcock

In the Mind's Eye: Picturing the Board's Involvement in Fund Raising

Nonprofit organizations are on a rough road these days. Making the road even rougher is that some of us don't know where the road leads.

In working with nonprofit organizations --their staffs and their boards of directors-- I've found it helpful to have some "road maps" to guide us on this rough and winding, complex and uncertain road. These road maps or pictures are visualizations of both the destination for our journey and the techniques that will help us stay on course.

We know that effective athletes, artists, and crafts persons are able to visualize in this way, to have "in their mind's eye," a picture of what it is they're trying to accomplish. So in the sometimes frantic rushing of events and effort, these effective persons are able to stay on course. They're able to keep their balance and not lose sight of their goal.

Let's look, then, at three pictures of nonprofit organizations as they engage in fund raising. First is the "nonprofit solar system:"

The Nonprofit Solar System

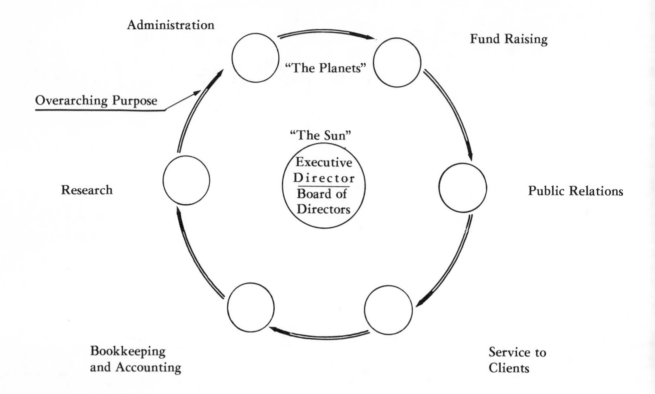

Effective nonprofits, in my opinion, have a strong board and a strong executive director. Together, they act as the "sun" in this solar system. Like the sun, they set the orbit --the direction, the boundaries, the pace-- for the planets or components of an organization. This orbit is the driving force, the mission, or overarching purpose of the nonprofit. In other words, the orbit or mission is the ultimate reason for the organization's existence; it is an expression of the board and executive's vision of how society will be better because this nonprofit organization exists.

What does this have to do with the board's role in fund raising? Fund raising is most effective when it serves the organization's mission. It is ineffective when it tries to become the "sun," when it tries to set the orbit of the entire organization. When that happens, board members and contributors get wrapped up in fund raising techniques and strategies. They lose sight of the ultimate purpose of their giving, and we know that this ultimate purpose is the driving force --the most effective motivator-- for charitable giving.

Now we'll view a second picture: the frosted layer cake.

The Frosted Layer Cake

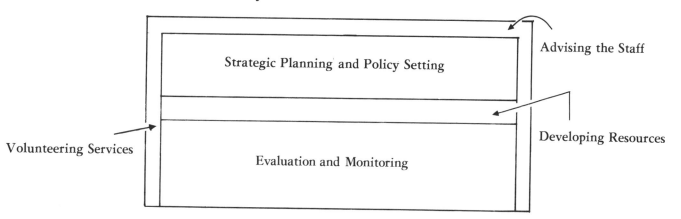

This picture helps us see the five roles of an effective nonprofit board of directors. The substance of the "cake," the primary reason for the board's existence, is to establish the nonprofit's orbit, its mission and then to set policies that express and fulfill that mission. Secondly, the board evaluates and monitors how well that mission is being carried out.

The "frosting on the cake" is the legitimate, necessary, enjoyable --yet secondary-- role of advising the executive director as she or he implements those policies. Some board members also like the frosting on the side of the cake: They roll up their sleeves and pitch in as volunteers. They help out in the kitchen, sit at the desk in the clinic waiting room, spend their Saturdays making repairs to buildings or use their law offices to draw up legal papers for the nonprofit organization.

Finally, the "frosting" between the two layers of the cake, the stuff that stays all moist and gooey, the stuff that really makes the cake, is resource development. That's helping the staff as they bring together the facilities, equipment, expertise, and money necessary to carry out the organization's overarching purpose.

With these two pictures in mind, we're eager as nonprofit staff and board members to get on with fund raising. We know what our goal and roles are. Now how do we do it? A third picture, "the fund raising radar scope," helps provide the answer.

In this picture, the nonprofit's mission or driving force becomes the "scope" in which the board and staff "sight" the four key components of fund raising. In other words, fund raising is most effective when boards and staff seek to identify funding sources (individuals, corporations, foundations), organizational needs (What are we going to use the funds for?), donors' needs (sense of participation, need to express compassion, need to join, prestige), and specific fund raising techniques (direct mail, phonathons, bake sales, grant proposals) that are within the scope of the organization's mission and purpose. That means certain sources of funds (federal funding, for instance) or techniques (benefit rock concerts) might be outside the scope of a particular organization's mission.

The Fund Raising Radar Scope

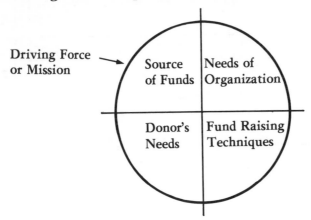

This "radar scope" model also reminds us that effective fund raising brings all four components together, as the board and staff make sure all four interact to contribute to one common purpose or goal.

Now that the "picture show" is over, we are ready to target those fund raising techniques that are within your organization's scope, that best fulfill your organization's purpose. In what follows, I'll be talking about non-governmental sources of funds. That's because I believe individuals, foundations, and corporations are going to be the critical fund raising challenges for nonprofit boards in the years ahead.

The Board Plans and Evaluates Fund Raising Efforts

The reason I get so excited about fund raising for nonprofits is that it is a critical test of the validity of the organization's mission and of the executive director's ability to implement that mission. If the organization is serving a valid purpose, then donors will want to support that purpose. This is true, however, only if the staff and volunteers are effectively implementing that purpose and if donors are being given avenues to channel their financial support to that implementation.

The board needs to know more, though, than whether the organization's fund raising efforts work or don't work. The board needs to know more about all four components of fund raising so it can set policy, those broad guidelines that keep programs and activities focused on the organization's overarching purpose, and so it can evaluate whether specific fund raising techniques are the best for that particular organization.

All this is especially helpful when the board is faced with setting the organization's budget or initiating and reviewing feasibility studies for capital campaigns or major fund drives. The board also needs this information so it can decide how the board, and the individual members, will actually be involved in fund raising.

The following list and chart (Exhibit 12-1 and Appendix A) should help the board as it attempts to find out more about those four components of effective fund raising.

EXHIBIT 12-1: Principles of Fund Raising

1. In shaky financial times, those organizations with involved boards will come through better than those with uncommitted boards.

2. An organization's annual giving goal should be the total of all goals plus a 10-15% contingency fund. (See Chapter 11)

3. Fund raising volunteers don't have to be board members, but, like board members, they should have personal goals and should be kept well informed of the progress of the campaign.

4. As government funding increases, private donations decrease.

5. To keep your donors and get them to increase, try this: Send a receipt, thank them, communicate with them, cultivate them.

6. A good image will not raise funds for you, but a poor image can hinder your fund raising.

7. Don't expect that for which you didn't ask.

8. Ask for contributions to a program. Don't ask for an amount of money. Suggest a level of contribution.

9. Prospective donors are increasingly interested in proof that their money is producing the results that you promised during the solicitation.

10. People give to people, not causes. Face to face is the best solicitation method.

11. Break your program into components, each of which can be funded separately.

12. Tax considerations are seldom the basic motivation for giving.

13. Contributions from individuals account for almost 90% of all non-governmental funding of nonprofit organizations.

Continued

---

14. The size of contributions tends to relate directly to the size of the fund raising goal.

15. The more sources of funding you have, the more stable your funding.

16. Put a specific amount of your fund raising revenue toward new fund raising activities.

17. Start with low risk fund raising (annual giving) and then move into more sophisticated methods (deferred giving).

18. Know in advance how much money you want to raise with each method during the next 1, 2 and 5 years.

19. Research who your donors are, test new methods on some of them, monitor your success rate.

20. Ask donors to help with fund raising.

21. Ask for money with the conviction that the agency is doing an outstanding, important job for its clients. You're not asking for money for yourself. Do not beg. Remember: You are looking for people to invest in your future.

22. Fund raisers often play one of four roles that discourage donors: The "bill collector" (its that time of year again); the "slick salesperson" (solicitation is seen as a battle which you can only win with a hard sell); the "cry wolf" (if you don't give, we will surely die); and the "flagellant" someone has to do it, so it might as well be me).

23 Fund raisers are: brokers, wholesalers, subdividers, executors, evangelists.

- Brokers – A broker puts the needs of a buyer and seller together to create a situation where both parties get what they want from the exchange. That's what you do when you ask for a donation.

- Wholesaler/Subdivider – You are giving your donors an opportunity to share in your good works for a very modest investment. Rather than "wholesaling" good works, many organizations retail their organization with hefty mark-ups based on their growing financial problems.

- Executor – An executor administers an estate on behalf of another. You are an executor for your donors' money; you make sure it gets spent as wisely and efficiently as possible, to the benefit of the greatest number.

Continued

- Evangelist - You are literally the "bringer of good news." You have a mission and you are helping your donors "hear the good word" and join that mission.

24. Before you hire a professional fund raiser, develop your goals and action plans. The professional can help you meet your goals.

25. Professional fund raisers will give you the tools to make effective presentations. They will not do the asking for you.

© 1980, Board Member-Trustee Handbook, Public Management Institute. Used with permission.

All Board Members Contribute

One of the important areas in which boards set policy is that of how the board itself will operate: Who can serve on the board, how long they can serve, what to do with board members who are absent repeatedly, and so on. One of the important policies about board operation is, in my opinion, the policy that describes the amount of contribution expected from each board member.

I'm not sure that's a good fund raising strategy: It certainly doesn't give you a board focused on policy setting and evaluation. Nevertheless, I do feel very strongly that all board members should be expected to contribute to the nonprofit organization they govern, even if the organization is flush with cash and the board is composed of poor or unemployed people.

This goal of 100% financial participation by board members is important for at least three reasons:

1. Board members won't be able to ask others for contributions unless they, themselves, have made a contribution. Many wealthy individuals and foundations will want to know if the board has contributed.

2. Contributions from board members provide needed income for the organization's projects and programs. Board members do make valuable contributions of their time and knowledge, but their financial contributions are also needed if there is to be an organization for them to govern.

3. In our society, financial investments are a symbol and vehicle of deeper emotional and intellectual involvement. Thus, when board members contribute, they tend to have a deeper stake in the organization's total success.

Well, if your goal is to get all board members to contribute, how do you go about it? The following checklist provides suggestions that might be useful for your board.

EXHIBIT 12-2: Encouraging Contributions from Board Members

Item or Suggestion

1. Emphasize the act of giving, not the amount given.

2. Devote a session of a board meeting to discussing the pros and cons of board member contributions to the organization. It soon becomes apparent how many good reasons there are for board members to give.

3. Make contributing to your organization, without specifying the amount, one of the qualifications for membership on your board.

4. Have the board chairperson send a letter to each board member requesting a contribution. Follow-up with at least three letters if the board member does not respond.

5. Ask board members to host a luncheon or meeting of potential donors. They'll want to make a contribution before they talk to others about becoming donors.

6. Start a giving club, such as the "President's Roundtable" or "Founder's Society," which publicizes the names of donors. Board members will want to make sure their names are on the list.

7. Have a board member who has already contributed speak about his or her decision to contribute at one of your board meetings.

8. Send board members all brochures and fund raising materials as they are produced. Attach a note indicating you just wanted them to see what's going out to other donors and potential donors. Be sure to enclose a return envelope.

9. Invite board members to include your organization in their wills and to name your organization as a beneficiary in their insurance policies.

Board Solicitation of Contributions

A sociological study divided persons into two groups: One group was asked to put a small sign in their front window advocating environmental action and then later asked to have a large billboard planted in their front yard. The second group was approached right away with the billboard request. Guess which group was more likely to put the billboard sign in their front yards?

I think board members are too often asked too soon to take the big fund raising step: To go out there and ask Ms Grande for the Really Big Contribution. Then we wonder why board members say, "I'll be glad to serve on your board, but I don't want to get involved in fund raising."

One of the most valuable --and least demanding-- ways board members can assist the staff in fund raising is to identify contacts and make introductions. This can happen through the simple, non-threatening request that each board member provide the names and addresses of persons they know who might be interested in learning more about the organization. The contact lists can be made using the "webbing form" shown on the following page as Exhibit 12-3.

When the staff and board members use these webbing forms, an amazingly fruitful list of foundation trustees, corporate executives, politicians, and wealthy individuals may emerge. Then board members can make the phone calls, set up appointments, and write letters of introduction for staff and volunteers who will approach these major gift prospects.

There are other small, first steps that board members can take. These actions will help board members to better understand the fund raising process and lead the board members to deeper involvement in asking others for financial support. Some good ideas include:

- Arrange a lunch meeting for three or four major donors in
  order to brief them on developments in the organization.
  Have a board member assist the staff in giving the briefing.

- Divide the top 200-300 donors from your list among the board
  members. Ask the members to write brief personal letters
  of thanks and appreciation to the donors. Board members should
  use their own stationary.

- From time to time include on your letterhead that you use to
  solicit contributions a list of your entire board.

- When you receive a new or sizeable donation, ask a
  board member to write an extra letter of thanks to
  that donor.

- Have a board member sign one or more of the direct mail
  fund raising appeal letters.

- Ask board members to accompany a staff person or volunteer
  on a major gift solicitation visit. Emphasize that it is
  just to observe and the board member won't have to ask for
  the gift.

EXHIBIT 12-3: Webbing Form

Instructions: Please answer these questions as completely as you can. If you need more space, please use additional sheets. Return the completed form to .... Your answers will remain confidential.

1. Name_____Address_____

2. What is your business and title?_____

3. Your business address?_____

4. Are you on the board of any grant making foundations?_____

5. If so, which one(s)?_____
    _____

6. Are any of your business associates, friends or acquaintances on the boards of grant making foundations or corporations? _____

    Name   Foundation/Corporation
    _____
    _____
    _____

7. Which of these people would you be willing to see on our behalf?
    _____

8. To which social, fraternal, athletic or other clubs do you belong?_____

9. Briefly outline your educational background (college, date of graduation, degrees, etc.)_____

10. What is your military background (branch of service, outfit, etc)? _____

11. Have you ever helped this organization, or any other, obtain a grant?_____

12. Is so, who was it for, who was it from, and how much was the award?

    Organization Funded   Funding Source   Size of Award
    _____
    _____

And Now the Big Step

Every executive director and board chairperson dreams of a board filled with individuals eager to make face-to-face calls on wealthy individuals, foundation trustees, and corporate moguls.

Those are worthy dreams. Nonprofits need more major gifts, larger foundation grants, and greater corporate support if their vital services are to survive and thrive in the years ahead. Board member involvement in face-to-face solicitation is absolutely essential if the solicitation is to be successful. Indeed, you can't have capital campaigns or major fund appeals without that board involvement.

I'm committed to this because I have participated in face-to-face fund raising and I've watched board members and other volunteers do it well. For me and for them, these solicitation interviews were some of the most exciting and thrilling events in our association with nonprofit organizations. These interviews are great opportunities to find out why donors care for and want to support your organization. You'll have to go a long way to get more telling "soft market research data". In addition, board members, as they reflect on the reasons they ask someone else to support an organization, discover new reasons and grounds for their own involvement in the organization's governance.

I've found that the major gift solicitation process is most effective and least threatening to board members when it is described as a series of interviews. Board members are encouraged to get to know the needs, interests, and concerns of persons capable of making major gifts. A friendship inevitably develops, based on a mutual commitment to your organization's mission. Finally, the major gift becomes a tangible and natural expression of that common bond.

The following two worksheets, Exhibits 12-4 and 12-5, will be helpful as board members are trained and prepared for fund raising.

EXHIBIT 12-4: What Volunteer Solicitors Need to Know

Information	Source of Information	Location
1. Amount of money to be raised		
2. How it will be spent		
3. History of the organization		
4. Case statement for the organization		
5. Organization's purpose and policies		

Continued

---

6. Timeline for campaign

7. Financial summaries for
   the last five years

8. Any direct mail and
   fund raising appeals

9. Any public relations
   materials or publicity

10. Your long range plan
    and your "wish list"

11. Background information
    on your service and its
    importance to society

12. Endorsement letters
    from clients and
    community leaders

13. Board membership list

14. Annual reports for
    last five years

15. One page description of
    your present program

16. Background sheets on
    prospects to be con-
    tacted - interests and
    previous contributions

17. Techniques for making
    appointments and inter-
    viewing prospects

EXHIBIT 12-5: Tips for Interviewing a Major Gift Prospect

Steps	Tip or Technique
1. Preparation	• don't prepare a presentation of your projects
	• prepare information on what you have to offer the donor: tax deductions, liquidity of frozen assets, security and income for life, estate planning aid
	• ask for big money first. If one big donor gives, others will follow.
2. Beginning the interview	• get her to talk about herself
	• ask for his help. "we have a problem and we know you are the best one to help us solve it."
	• inform them. "Folks, I know your grandmother died of lung cancer. Would you be interested in knowing a way we may cure cancer in five years?"
	• ask open ended questions for fact finding. "How do you feel about...? Is there anything so far that seems unreasonable?
	• paint pictures with stories about people and with the use of dialogue.
3. Conducting the interview	• use what you hear to tailor your appeal
	• acknowledge the objections
	• restate objections as questions
	• answer the questions
	• get to know the prospect. Talk about those aspects of the project she is interested in. Ask opinions. Get her to ask how much money you want.
	• ask for another time to see him
	• always ask for gifts other than cash
4. Closing the interview	• have amount you want in mind
	• ask for enough, never too little

Continued

EXHIBIT: Continued

- if the amount he offers is too small, ask
  if it would be all right if you check with
  President of your board. Prolong negotiations.

- it is very difficult to get a prospect to
  increase her gift after a pledge is signed

5. Following up
   the interview

- second call: have answers ready to questions
  or objections raised on first call. Take some
  one else along.

- refresh prospect's memory

- talk about other pace setting gifts

- ask for the gift and leave soon after
  you get it

6. After the
   gift

- ask for names of other potential donors

- ask new donor to make calls with you

- keep new donors involved in your organization

- send a personal letter of thanks

- send a 6 month progress report to brief the
  donor

- if possible, get a major donor to join your
  board

Appendix A: Funding Source Information Chart

Source and Definition	Considerations	Reasons for Giving
1. Board Members Can include advisory and auxiliary members	• every board member should give something • community representatives or client board members can contribute to raffles, bake sales, etc. • requirement to give is spelled out in recruitment phase before member comes on board and in board manual. • a large number of small contributions is a better base than a small number of large contributions.	• because they believe in the organization and its purposes • peer pressure • desire for recognition and prestige • tax reasons • because they are asked
2. Individual donors (source of greatest amount of giving) • those who have given in the past • beneficiaries • expand list by asking your donors to refer you to others	• most donations go to religion • the wealthy give to hospitals, colleges, cultural organizations • middle class givers give to local arts, youth services, drug and alcohol abuse counseling, etc. • people give more if they're married, and as they get older • sell the benefits of your organization, not the organization itself • in personal solicitation, each board or fund raising volunteer can effectively approach 5 other people	• opportunity to reinforce their self-images as people helping solve a problem in society • because money will be well spent • the gift makes a difference to society
3. Membership program • donor belongs to	• state level of gift required • state level for upgrading gift	• same as for donors • member has sense of

Source and Definition	Considerations	Reasons for Giving
organization and receives benefits in exchange for newsletter, sticker, tours, books, etc.	--different benefits for different levels. • good renewal rate if donor feels he or she belongs • costs of operating can be higher due to cost of benefits • revenue high over time • start a special $100 club (Guardian Club or Century Club) to upgrade membership	identification; therefore it is easier to solicit major and deferred gifts
4. Annual Giving • yearly appeal to a fairly large number of donors	• any gift acceptable • upgrade to next level is left up to donor • many small gifts • renewal rate is usually 50-60% • cost of operations includes only appeal --no member benefits • renewal mailings may bring in lower revenue over time • fewer repeat donors	• same as for individual donor • mailing must be eye catching
5. Direct mail solicitation • (large mailing with carefully designed appeal and envelope)	• use your "house list" --people whose names you have, who have used your services • return will be approximately 3% to to 20% with a "house list" • if you rent a list and mail to 25,000 people you will probably get 750	• if receiver doesn't throw away your letter, he/she will respond to the same appeal as an individual donor

Source and Definition	Considerations	Reasons for Giving
6. Major gifts • anything over $1,000 from an individual solicited in person	• potential large returns for small expenditures of time and money • 1/3rd of money will come from top 10 gifts • prepare case statement and long range plan • do your homework on prospects • major gift committee members should all be donors and should be on same cultural and intellectual level as prospect and should not be a close friend of prospect • use third party linkage to introduce prospect to solicitor (see Webbing worksheet) • ask for too much rather than too little	• the project will solve a problem the donor is very concerned about
7. Foundations • over 26,000 private foundations, biggest 2500 make 80% of the grants • half of all grants are under $1,000 and 80% are less than $5,000 • community foundations have funds from many sources	• recent trends in foundation giving show more giving to health, welfare and humanities, although greatest amount still given to education • community foundations are responsive to local needs, may fund "bricks and mortar" • corporate foundations fund urban affairs, anti-poverty, programs for employees and community residents • approach family foundations as you would individuals • split your program into different	• fund projects (not organizations) that are new, forward looking, very visible • fund projects in special interest area • corporate foundations fund projects that have something to benefit the corporate body

Source and Definition	Reasons for Giving	Considerations
• corporate foundations are vehicles for corporate giving, generally will follow the corporation's giving goals • family foundations make up most of all foundations—are controlled by donor or family	components to be funded individually. Show how you will fund the part of the program left out of your proposal • persevere --go back again and again	
8. Corporations • generally, only the largest give (50% of corporate gifts are from largest 1,000 firms)	• corporations give most when profits are going up; grants drop sharply when profits fall • like to give close to corporate plant sites or headquarters • conservative givers, not interested in breaking new ground--your first corporate grant is the hardest • give mostly to health, welfare and education • look for linkages in community and work your way up to decision makers	• project helps in corporate goal attainment • benefits to employees and community residents • improves political, social, natural environment • increases citizen productivity • improves corporate reputation • interests of corporate officers and executives are served

216

Source and Definition	Considerations	Reasons for Giving
9. Memorial, honor and gift memberships • donor gives you money in the name of someone else, often in lieu of giving money or a gift to that person	• start a gift program with brochures, newsletter, regular donors, ads in newspapers • enclose postage paid return envelopes and recognize gifts on plaque or in newsletter or memorial book • the amount of the gift is not revealed to the public • giver receives tax deduction, honored person receives a card • follow up on donor as a prospect for future giving • program can be done by volunteers	• honors a loved one or • helps organization continue good work • it is easy and convenient for donor to give
10. Deferred or planned giving • giving that is not an outright, current donation • an endowment fund can be established to handle various types of giving	• bequests through wills to organization • start program with board members' gifts--use a board committee • many different types of annuities and trusts that provide significant present tax advantages to donors and that result in sizable donations to your organization • publicize your program --pamphlets, newsletters, newspapers, mailings to current donors, notices to legal and financial communities • must have successful annual giving program before you start deferred giving program (need to cultivate current donors)	• for those who can't afford a large gift now • may strengthen donor's financial security • aid in tax planning • no pressure on donor to give now • can relieve older donor of burden of juggling assets, and provide steady income

Source and Definition	Considerations	Reasons for Giving
11. Capital campaign • raises large sums in limited time —usually for construction	• need many board and other volunteers —one person can contact 5 others • have major part of goal on hand before you start public solicitation (at least 15% from board members) • 80% of contributions will come from 20% of donors • one time pledge for donations to be given over a 3–5 year period	• peer pressure • importance of capital program • area of concern and interest to donor • "bandwagon" approach— everyone's giving
12. United giving • donations from individuals and businesses to a federated campaign.	• good for annual giving once you are accepted as a recipient • annual review of your budget, program, staffing and client patterns • may prevent you from soliciting corporations that give to umbrella agencies or whose employees give to umbrella agencies	• established organization with proven track record of responsible service
13. Special Events • balls, benefits, bazaars, seminars, lecture series, marathons, goods sales, garage sales, seasonal appeals, open houses, house tours, etc.	• gets members involved • need one ongoing fund raiser —don't rely on special events • repeated events bring in more money • seek sponsors from business community to underwrite expenses • needs many volunteers • allow ample planning time • seek advice from others who have held similar events.	• a good time is had by all

Further Readings

William Balthaser, FRI MONTHLY PORTFOLIO. Ambler, PA: Fund Raising
  Institute ($48 annual subscription)

Daniel Lynn Conrad, HOW TO SOLICIT BIG GIFTS. San Francisco: Public
  Management Institute

Daniel Lynn Conrad, SUCCESSFUL FUND RAISING TECHNIQUES. San
  Francisco: Public Management Institute

Joan Flanagan, THE GRASSROOTS FUNDRAISING BOOK: HOW TO RAISE MONEY
  IN YOUR COMMUNITY. Chicago: Contemporary Books, Inc., 1982

Tom Hopkins, HOW TO MASTER THE ART OF SELLING, New York: Warner
  Books, 1982

David Owen, "State of the Art Panhandling," HARPER'S, August 1982,
  pp 35-45

Michael Phillips, THE SEVEN LAWS OF MONEY. World Wheel and Random
  House, 1974

A.C. Podesta, RAISING FUNDS FROM AMERICA'S 2,000,000 OVERLOOKED
  CORPORATIONS. Hartsdale, NY: Public Service Materials Center, 1984

Public Service Material Center, THE CORPORATE FUND RAISING DIRECTORY,
  1985-86 EDITION. Hartsdale, NY: Public Service Materials Center,
  1984

Robert Sharpe, PLANNED GIVING IDEA BOOK. Memphis, TN: Robert Sharpe
  Company, 1978

Chapter 13

Public Relations: Letting Them Know You're There

Bonnie Bernholz

Described as the most characteristically American institution, the nonprofit organization presents unique challenges in the area of public relations. Serving social, cultural and humanitarian concerns, such organizations rely largely on a belief in their purpose and a willingness of the public to commit resources to that purpose.

Although social conscience and tax credits provide a basis for charitable giving, the most powerful motivation for involvement is pride of association. People desire affiliation with concerns and individuals that reflect their own particular interests. Effective public relations can channel this desire towards a specific organization.

An objective of any public relations effort for a nonprofit organization must be to perpetuate and increase the organization's ability to attract voluntary support. There is not a nonprofit organization in existence that does not need volunteerism. The scope and nature of volunteers may vary, but inherent in a nonprofit organization's existence is some dependency on volunteered dollars, skill, time, and effort.

Effective public relations requires work and planning to occur. The worthiest of causes, if poorly represented or barely visible, cannot gain long term support. Creating a positive environment that encourages participation is a function of public relations and can be a powerful tool for an organization's longevity and success.

Public Relations and the Board of Directors

The public relations of any nonprofit begins with the board of directors. Board members are selected for their particular interest in the organization and their ability to positively influence others in the community. The knowledge and enthusiasm represented by the board will directly affect the communications activities of the organization. Because of this influence, a planned public relations program that involves board members will ensure that external communications are not left to chance.

The first component of effective external communications is cohesive internal communications. Exhibit 13-1 is an audit questionnaire designed for a nonprofit organization's board. Each board members should answer the questionnaire separately and anonymously, and allow a staff member to compile the answers. Through careful review of this compilation, the board will gain a sense of the effectiveness of the organization's internal communications system. If the answers are extremely divergent, it is probable that the organization's external communications are also divergent and even confusing to its various audiences.

EXHIBIT 13-1: Sample Internal Audit Questionnaire

* 1. Describe the history of the organization.

  2. Describe the organization's performance last year. (number of new members, funds raised, expansion of services, increased public awareness, new volunteers recruited, etc.)

  3. What are the organization's short term goals?

  4. What are the organization's long term goals?

  5. If you were preparing a five year plan for the organizations what would be the components of such a plan?

* 6. What are the organization's present objectives?

* 7. What are the characteristics of the organization? (What comprises the organization's identity?)

  8. Envisioning the organization at its greatest maturation, describe the organization.

* 9. What are the fund raising vehicles of the organization? (Corporate/foundation donations, special events, annual donations by individuals, etc.)

  10. Who are the organization's present audiences? needed audiences?

* 11. What level of general public awareness exists, in your opinion, regarding the organization?

* 12. How did you find out about us (if you know us)?

It is vitally important that the board also recognize the public relations impact of board policy decisions. Decisions must be weighed and considered in the light of their implications to the organization's audiences. Occasionally, decisions must be made which are controversial or represent drastic change. Announcement to the media of such a decision by the board, even if unpleasant, will reduce or avoid the potentially negative consequences of coverage that could result from withholding information. It is usually more beneficial to take the "proactive" approach: Serving as a source for the media rather than answering accusations in a "reactive" manner.

The planning and development of a successful public relations program must be based on a clear definition of the organization's mission stated in a way that is concise, insightful and reflective of the organization's function. The program must, of course, be mindful of the organization's various audiences, including staff, publics served, or clients, members, related organizations, volunteers, contributors, media, and the general public. Audiences for different organizations vary depending upon who has an interest in or potential impact upon the organization. Consider these questions in review.

> Does the organization's purpose present an accurate and easily comprehendible picture to its audiences?

> What opinions would the organization like the audiences to have?

> What are existing opinions within each of the organization's audiences toward the organization?

> Is each audience aware of the organization's history, purpose and present goals?

Further internal review of the organization will lead the board to examine the organization's communication pieces (brochures, annual report, logo, stationery, forms, slides, video, etc.). These pieces are vehicles for presenting the organization and its purpose. If not carefully designed and periodically reviewed, such tools of communication can lead the organization's various audiences to inaccurately perceive the organization and the messages it is trying to communicate. Overall graphics and design of various pieces should lend a sense of credibility and give the audiences some understanding of the function and purpose of the organization. If the organization's graphics are incorrect, inconsistent or outdated, the audiences' impressions of the organization will be also. Attention must be given to the redesign of communication pieces and graphics before any effort is begun in the area of external communication.

EXERCISE 13-1

Gather all the organization's visual communication pieces and answer the following questions.

Is there a single, common logotype?

Does the logo provide an immediate identity for the organization?

Are the typefaces, design, paper choices, color and layout consistent? Do they work well with each other?

Are the organization's statistics and background information current?

After evaluating the organization's internal communications and the design and graphics of existing and planned pieces, a comprehensive plan to increase public awareness can be devised. Within the board of directors, a public relations committee can be designated and assigned the function of designing and implementing the public relations program. The committee must continue to promote the importance of public relations through involvement of the remaining directors in public relations decisions and discussions at board meetings and periodic informational meetings. Responsibilities of the public relations committee should include the following:

1. Coordinate and design surveys to monitor existing and ongoing public attitudes toward the organization.

2. Develop a comprehensive public relations program.

3. Direct public relations activities to the organization's various audiences.

4. Serve as a news source, if necessary, for media inquiries.

5. Develop, if possible, a relationship with resources such as public relations, advertising and/or marketing agencies, printers, typesetters, photographers, designers, etc.

6. Maintain a reporting system for review of qualitative and quantitative progress.

Many of these responsibilities, inherent in a well planned public relations program, can be implemented by administrative staff if the organization has the in-house capacity. Often the executive director of a smaller nonprofit organization will function as the board's public relations specialist. The board, however, should not avoid its responsibility for public relations planning and monitoring.

The planning of a public relations program may at first seem to be an awesome task. However, the following components and accompanying exercises and exhibits will enable a board of directors to not only develop a public awareness program, but develop a sense of the scope and importance of public relations.

The first component of a public relations program must be the identification of the organization's various audiences and the messages that need to be communicated to each of those audiences. The messages that are communicated by the organization must be understood by and be compatible with the various audiences and with the nonprofit's mission.

External Surveys

External surveys will allow not only identification of audiences, but also identification of what messages and information need to be projected, and what vehicles must be utilized to reach those audiences. Depending on time and financial constraints, representatives of important audience may be interviewed personally, by telephone, by direct mail or some combination of these methods. Through external survey, an organization can identify the information needs of audiences and decide what communication vehicles are appropriate for satsifying those needs.

Questionnaires can be designed by the public relations committee incorporating many of the questions offered in Exhibit 13-1 for the internal audit. (Appropriate questions for external surveying are indicated by an *.) Additional questions can be designed to determine and assess current audience awareness such as "What are the organization's purposes?"

After assessing and identifying the importance of these audiences to the organization and defining the messages that must be communicated to each, the information disseminated by the organization from that point forward should show sensitivity and awareness of the audiences' particular informational needs.

Publicity

The next step in the development of a public relations program is the process of directing these messages to the various audiences. A publicity plan for the organization should be devised and updated at least quarterly and should include both print and electronic media.

In order to design a publicity plan for a one-year period, a calendar of events for the organization should be utilized. The timing of events (membership drives, fund raising, special events, volunteer recruitment) will be tied in to specific publicity surrounding these activities. Publicity tools, which are discussed in detail below, include press kits, press releases, feature stories, public service announcements, and mailing lists.

Press Kit

Before building relationships with the media, a useful but not mandatory consideration is the development of a press kit. The press kit is a folder in which various communication and background pieces can be inserted and serve as a source of information for a variety of audiences. It can be tailored through use of specific pieces to accomodate a particular audience and/or event. The press kit will also serve as a source of support material for the organization's staff and volunteers who are involved in the organization's management, fund raising and promotion. Exhibit 13-2 provides a list of various pieces that can be utilized in a press kit.

EXHIBIT 13-2: Press Kit Contents

* Annual Report

* Brochure (statement of organization purpose, programs, services, organizational structure)

* List of major contributors to the organization, particularly corporations and foundations

* Reprints of selected newspaper and magazine articles about the organization.

* Endorsement of programs by corporations through sponsorship or involvement of employees

* Press release or press invitation to event, if appropriate

* 8" x 10" black and white glossy photographs pertinent to the organization and event

* If the organization does not have the first two pieces, the following information should be covered by topic on the organization's letterhead:

  Background information about the organization
  Board of Directors roster
  Financial statement/funding necessary (by objective)
  Programs, services, etc. offered by the organization

Press Release

The press release serves several purposes. It can announce an event, issue a policy statement, or provide information about the progress or accomplishments of the organization and individuals associated with it.

A scarcity of information may allow other, better reported

organizations to gain support from many of the same audiences vital to your organization. It is important that your publicity plan be continual: The media should receive something regarding your organization, associated individuals or events at least once every three months. This does not mean that the media will necessarily print each of these releases, but the media will become increasingly familiar with your organization. Often, this awareness will allow a publication's editorial staff to remember the organization for possible inclusion in round-up stories or other pieces initiated by the publication.

It is also important to note that the placement of a release does not depend on advertising or other financial considerations to the publication. In most papers, there is no relationship between the advertising and editorial departments. An editor will be discriminating on the basis of a release's accuracy, timeliness and interest to readers.

The key to a well-written press release is the opening or "lead" paragraph. Traditionally, the lead sentence would contain the "five W's and H": who, what, when, where, why and how. A polished release, however, may only answer the most important question in the lead, leaving the others to be answered in the body of the copy. An interesting, well thought out lead paragraph will have much greater acceptance than one that is crammed with nothing but the five W's and H.

The body of the press release will follow the lead with other essential information. The structure of the press release should follow the model of an inverted pyramid. An editor should be able to pick up the important facts in the first two or three paragraphs. If necessary, an editor should be able to cut from the bottom of the story to accomodate newspaper space with little or no rewriting or loss of important information.

A press release should be written in short, concise sentences and must be accurate. Paragraphs should be limited to approximately five lines. Double space all copy. A one page release is best; two pages should be the maximum. Other do's and don'ts of a press release include the following:

1. Avoid using jargon, opinion or excessive adjectives.

2. Proofread carefully for typographical errors or incorrect information.

3. If in doubt about the proper way to present names, titles, numbers, etc., consult the ASSOCIATED PRESS STYLE BOOK.

4. All quotes and facts must be attributed to appropriate sources.

5. Do not overwrite. Write as concisely as possible, without leaving out relevant data or congesting your release.

6. Never serve the same story to two editors on the
    same papers. Getting caught could ruin media
    relations.

7. Do not load your story with so many brand names and
    commercial plugs that it is difficult to use with
    reasonable credit mention. In other words, do not
    overload.

There is a set format to be followed for all press releases. Exhibit 13-3 provides guidelines for a release, and Exhibit 13-4 illustrates the format with a sample release form.

EXHIBIT 13-3: Press Release Format

1. Releases should be typewritten on plain, white 8 1/2" x 11"
    paper.

2. Always include the organization's name, phone number and the name
    and home phone number of the person to be contacted for more
    details.

3. Always use specific day and date on the release.

4. Indicate when the release may be used. "FOR IMMEDIATE RELEASE"
    indicates that the editor may use the material at any time. If a
    specific publication date is needed, say "FOR RELEASE ON OR
    AFTER_____DAY_____, _____MONTH_____DATE_____, 19__.

5. If the release is only being given to one media outlet, indicate
    that with "EXCLUSIVE".

6. Begin typing approximately one third of the way down the first
    page. Double space the copy, leaving margins of about 1.5" on each
    side of the copy. Type on one side of the page only.

7. Do not continue a paragraph from one page to the next.
    Successive pages should be numbered.

8. Write "more" at the bottom of every page except the last. On the
    final page, type "###" after the last paragraph of the release.

9. If using a photo with the release, have a "CONSENT RELEASE"
    signed by the individuals in the photo(s). A description of the
    photo (a "cutline") should be typed and pasted on the back of the
    photo for the editor's information. Do not type or write
    directly on the back of the photo.

EXHIBIT 13-4: Sample Press Release ────────────────

FOR: ON YOUR TOES BALLET COMPANY   CONTACT: Mr. Pierre deDeux
                                           713-555-3333 (office)
                                         713-555-9564 (home)

FOR IMMEDIATE RELEASE

HOUSTON IS OFFICIAL COMPETITION SITE

HOUSTON, February 8, 1984. Officials of the On Your Toes Ballet Company announced that it has been selected as one of the six official dance organizations sponsoring preliminary competitions preceeding the IV En Pointe Competition in Hampton. The IV En Pointe Competition, announced yesterday in Hampton, will be September 11-30, 1984. It will bring together dancers, teachers and choreographers from all over the world to compete in what has been termed the "Kentucky Derby of Dance". It was also announced yesterday that Hampton, Arkansas, which in 1975 sponsored the first En Pointe Competition, will be the permanent site for the En Pointe Competitions in the United States.

"We are delighted to make this announcemet," said Pierre deDeux, president of the On Your Toes Ballet Company. "These competitions not only broaden the opportunity for American dancers to participate in the En Pointe Competition, it also gives them a choice of competition sites."

                                 - more-

EXHIBIT: Continued

To be eligible for the IV En Pointe Competition, an American dancer must either compete successfully in a regional competition or be nominated by the director of his or her dance company.

Other sites are Tampa, San Francisco, Chicago and Anchorage. The regional competitions are planned for April and May, 1984.

The On Your Toes Ballet Company, a nonprofit organization, was formed in 1965 to promote dance as an art form and a means for encouraging physical fitness in youth. Located in Houston, Texas, it has over 150 members.

# # #

EXERCISE 13-2

1. Study for a seven-day period the local news section of a daily newspaper published in the city. Analyze the nature and amount of stories which seem to come from publicity and/or public relations sources.

2. Write a press release for tomorrow's paper assuming that Ms Sherry Helms, chairperson of the organization's board, has received an "Outstanding Citizen" award. Consider additional information about Ms Helms for possible inclusion in the release. Name additional print media that might be interested in such a release and why they would be interested.

3. Your organization's board has determined that a number of broad organizational and program changes are necessary. Write a two page media release explaining the changes, the rationale for making the changes, and how these changes will affect the organization. Will the release need an "IMMEDIATE" or "SPECIFIC" date release? What sections of the newspaper(s) will be interested in the release? Is there a specific quote that can be attributed to the chairperson of the board?

After distributing a media release, an individual within the organization should be assigned the responsibility of monitoring the media. Whether it is print, radio or TV, monitoring should be done by the organization and not by calling the editor to determine if and when the story will run.

In addition to distributing a press release to a publication news editor, many publications have "Things To Do" columns. These columns can be utilized by sending a separate release to the "Community Listings" editor or other appropriate individual on the publication's staff.

Feature Story

Feature stories are another publicity tool which requires greater research and preparation time. Magazines and newspapers are full of features. These media outlets are usually interested in a feature story idea if it is timely, has an element of special human interest and is localized/personalized for the publication's readership.

Feature story placement can be approached by two separate avenues. One is writing the article personally and the other is by interesting a member of the publication's staff in writing the article for you. Often, because of the research and preparation necessary for a good feature story, editors prefer to assign the task to a member of their own staff. However, many magazine and newspaper publications, especially small or weekly papers, will encourage feature story ideas by contributors.

After a potential source for an article is located, it is appropriate to send the editor or other specified staff member a "query" letter. This letter should present a simplified explanation of the purpose of the article, an outline of the content, why it is appropriate for the publication and whether photographs will be available. If the publication is interested in pursuing the article, the editor will determine whether the article is to be contributed or assigned to a staff member.

EXERCISE 13-4

1. Assume that a member of your organization has been asked to address the United Nations about a particular service your organization offers to elderly people. Develop a query letter to appropriate newspaper and magazine editors. What are the possible elements of human interest? How is the purpose of the article related to the publication(s) and its readership(s)? Are there different photos that can be used if more than one publication expresses interest in the article?

Before proposing a feature story idea, it is necessary to become acquainted with the format, style, editorial policies, content and readership of the publication. Reference materials such as the WRITER'S MARKET (published annually by the Writer's Digest) will provide such information regarding magazines and Sunday newspaper supplements. Criteria for selecting a publication, if not covered adequately in the reference source, can be ascertained by simply calling the publication and requesting editorial guidelines. Stories that are inappropriate for a publication or its readership will wind up in the trash, and can serve as a source of unnecessary irritation to the editor.

Electronic Media

Broadcast media, like the print media, provide their audiences with news, information and entertainment. Before making contact with a television or radio station, study the type of programming offered by the station, and whether and how the organization's activities would be of interest to the station's audience. Formats to be considered for presenting the organization include interview shows, panel discussions, special topic shows, talk shows, newscasts and community calendars. These types of programming are excellent to seek out for coverage of special events that are colorful, unique, successful and generate public interest. A good reference source of radio and television programming is the annual TALK SHOW DIRECTORY FOR RADIO AND TELEVISION.

Again, monitoring coverage should be assigned to an individual within the organization. Most large cities have electronic news clipping services which will provide the organization with a tape of the broadcast. As the organization grows, a library of broadcast coverage will provide the organization with materials for films, slides and other presentation tools. (Legal counsel should be consulted to insure that copyright laws are not violated by such usage.)

Public Service Announcements

Public service announcements are free air time devoted to nonprofit organizations by both public and commercial radio and television stations. They are usually no more than 60 seconds in length and provide the public with either specific or general information about a service, program and/or need of the organization.

Start a "resource" file on radio and television stations of interest to the organization. Contact the station and get the name of the person responsible for public service announcements and to determine the station's requirements for public service announcements. Please recognize that each station may well have very different requirements governing use of PSA's.

Exhibit 13-5 is a copy of a video public service announcement ready for submission to a station.

EXHIBIT 13-5: Sample Video Public Service Announcement

Children's Museum
4201 Little Feet, Houston, Texas 77056

Contact: Ann Parsons
(713) 961-3256

SUMMER PROGRAM CAMPAIGN

TV - AS RECORDED
30 second spot

1. OPEN ON SCENE OF TWO BOYS
   PLAYING WITH TOY SOLDIERS
   IN CHILDREN'S ROOM

1. AL (OC): did you
   know that when
   statues are built
   with the horse's
   hooves in the air,
   like this, it means
   the soldier won the
   battle?

2. CUT TO CLOSE UP OF KIRKIE

2. KIRKIE (OC): It
   does not.

3. CUT BACK TO AL AS HE
   ANSWERS

3. AL (OC): It sure
   does. I learned
   that today

4. PULL OUT TO MEDIUM SHOT
   OF BOTH

4. KIRKIE (OC): Where?
   Not in school.

5. TIGHT SHOT OF AL AS HE
   EXPLAINS

5. AL (OC): I learned
   about it in this
   brochure for the
   Children's Museum.
   My mother signed me
   up for their summer
   program.

6. CUT BACK TO KIRKIE

6. KIRKIE (OC): Oh,
   wow, how can I sign
   up?

7. PULL OUT TO MEDIUM SHOT
   OF BOTH

7. AL (OC): Have your
   parents pick up
   a brochure or call
   555-1101 for more
   information on class
   schedules and
   enrollment. Classes
   start June 15, so
   tell them not to
   wait!

SUPER :   CHILDREN'S MUSEUM

In addition to what has been said, consider also the following items when writing public service announcements. Adherence to these few simple rules will help make your publicity efforts more successful.

1. Remember that with radio and television copy, the message will be seen and/or heard and not simply read. Television copy will have to be paced more slowly to allow the viewer to coordinate two senses, sight and hearing.

2. For television copy, what is said should not duplicate what is seen.

3. Use simple, descriptive words. Repeat the important information at least twice in different ways.

4. The first words of radio and television copy should be attention getting, **"settle-in-to-listen"** words.

5. Television public service announcements require visuals. A portfolio of about ten slides, including an "ID" slide with the organization's name should be sent to the station contact. The slides should be of good quality and be updated with each of the stations every six months to a year.

EXERCISE 13-3

1. Assume your organization is sponsoring an arts and crafts fair as a fund raising event. Write a 30-second radio spot to be used as a public service announcement. After reading the spot aloud, does it comfortably fill thirty seconds? Is thirty seconds enough or too much time for the information to be delivered? Is the opening attention getting, but lacking important information? Is the date, location and time repeated at least twice in the spot? Is the name of your organization mentioned at least twice in the spot?

2. Now using the same special event, write a 30-second television spot. Is the video or slides and the voice-over (VO) synchronized properly? Do the visuals provide an additional dimension to the copy or are they redundant?

Mailing List

The development of a media mailing list is not as difficult as it may sound. Utilizing the following references as well as knowledge of local media, an organization's mailing list should include the appropriate daily and weekly and suburban newspaper editors, regional magazines and newspapers, radio and television station news editors, in-town college papers and business journals, corporate contributors' in-house newsletters, and local/state/national nonprofit organization association newsletters.

As time permits, personal contact with local media staff should be
developed by members of the board and/or organization staff (particularly
the organization's executive director). Reference materials for compiling
a mailng list include BACON'S PUBLICITY CHECKER, EDITOR AND PUBLISHER
YEARBOOK, and, in most cities, there is a citywide and/or area media
directory. (To determine if such a directory is available, call a local
public relations or advertising agency.)

Proper and professional use of the media can provide an
organization with the necessary tools to begin and continue building an
environment of public awareness. Working with the media can be an
educational and enjoyable function of public relations. A relationship of
respect can be developed with the media through reliability of information
and a sensitivity for the publications' editorial requirements.

Fund Raising

Another function of public relations is the development of fund
raising programs and their positioning and promotion relative to funding
sources. Basically, two major types of fund raising efforts will benefit
from aggressive public relations --annual appeals and major campaigns.

Annual appeals are year-to-year funding drives conducted to
attract the money necessary for the organization's operational budget.
Annual appeal techniques include small group presentations to corporations,
foundation, direct mail and special events. Tools to be considered in
annual appeals include a folder similar to the press kit with background
material and information regarding the fund drive, film and/or slide
presentation, newsletters to contributors, media publicity, reprints of
articles, speeches and letters.

Special events are not only an annual appeal technique but an
opportunity to generate public awareness. Special events can appeal to a
wide spectrum of publics and will encourage community involvement. Examples
of special events would be bazaars, flea markets, auctions, fashion shows,
garden/home tours, art exhibitions, gala balls, variety shows, sporting
events, cookbooks, and community clean-up projects. It is reasonable to
plan at least a primary special event once a year and, if time and finances
allow, a secondary event.

Major campaigns usually cover funding over a period of three to
five years and promote expansion of the organization and its activities.
They are most effectively handled by direct one-to-one contact with leave-
behind materials such as a brochure, case statement, annual report, poster
and/or press kit. Certainly, mass media will be tools of a major campaign
as well as of annual appeals. Increased visibility with the public-at-
large will increase visibility within the specific audiences who make major
funding decisions. (See Chapter 12 for more information on fund raising.)

Program Measurement

The final component of a comprehensive public relations program is
the qualitative and quantitative review of the progress of the organiza-

tion's communications efforts. Surveys, generic or specific, should be conducted and studied to determine whether the program is accomplishing public awareness goals, and what, if any, changes are needed.

These surveys do not have to be major undertakings, but can be "soft soundings". Soft soundings are usually made by **telephone and** involve three to five questions designed to ascertain general trends rather than specific data. Every six months, call two or three members from within each of the organization's identified audiences (including the general public). Responses to these questions should provide the organization with an overview of specific audience/community awareness of the organization. Reports should be compiled and presented to the board of directors for a thorough oversight of the public relations effort.

Other methods for measurement of effectiveness can be designed for the comprehensive program or for specific components. (i.e., a particular special event or new program). Designate start and finish dates of the program and monitor increases in membership, funds, interested phone calls, minutes of air time and column inches of print generated as well as circulation and viewership figures of any media coverage.

Continuing analysis of the organization's public relations program will allow the organization to make adjustments or to focus efforts on specific audiences. However, if analysis indicates there is still a problem without an obvious solution, it is not out of the questions for the organization to consider approaching a public relations, marketing and advertising agency and requesting professional guidance for the development of the organization's public relations program.

More and more agencies and businesses are realizing the value and importance of nonprofit organizations and are willing to offer their expertise as a public service. There are, however, several considerations which should be discussed and resolved before entering such a relationship.

1. What services are needed by the organization and what services can the agency **provide?**

2. Are both parties willing to commit time and services?

3. Will there be a consistent contact person for both the agency and the organization?

4. Is the nonprofit organization willing to provide recognition to the agency? (This can be as simple as a credit line in the organization's printed pieces or can include offering a seat on the board to the agency).

5. Does the organization have the necessary funding to implement agency ideas and cover out-of-pocket expenses such as printing, typesetting, photography if and when necessary?

A professional relationship between an agency and a nonprofit organization can be short or long term depending on the particular needs of the organization and of the agency making the donation.

As mentioned earlier in this chapter, effective public relations takes work and planning to occur. A well designed public relations program can provide the momentum and awareness necessary for the viability of the organization. But no matter how well planned or implemented, the board of directors -- through its leadership, support and a strong belief in the organization-- provides the true public relations program of a nonprofit corporation.

Further Readings

N. Brigham, HOW TO DO LEAFLETS, NEWSLETTERS AND NEWSPAPERS. Boston: The Boston Community School, 1976

Foundation for American Communications, MEDIA RESOURCE GUIDE. Los Angeles: Foundation for American Communications, 1983

R. Gordon, WE INTERRUPT THIS PROGRAM: A CITIZEN'S GUIDE TO USING THE MEDIA FOR SOCIAL CHANGE. Amherst, MA: Citizen Involvement Training Project, 1978

T. Klein and F. Danzig, HOW TO BE HEARD: MAKING THE MEDIA WORK FOR YOU. New York: Macmillan, 1974

Phillip Kottler, MARKETING FOR NONPROFIT ORGANIZATIONS. Englewood Cliffs, NJ: Prentice-Hall, 1982

L.A. Maddelena, A COMMUNICATIONS MANUAL FOR NON-PROFIT ORGANIZATIONS. New York: American Management Association, 1981

P.J. Montana (ed), MARKETING IN NONPROFIT ORGANIZATIONS. New York: American Management Association, 1978

A. Richards (ed), SUCCESSFUL PUBLIC RELATIONS TECHNIQUES. San Francisco: Public Management Institute, 1980

Index

Organizational planning 109, 148
Organizational structure 91, 160
Orientation 7, 13, 63, 77

Performance appraisals/reviews 6, 103,
  105, 112, 115
Personnel 13, 20, 110, 130
Policy determination/setting 72, 90,
  105, 202
Powers of the corporation 19
Press kit 226
Press release 226
Professional advice 16, 185
Program monitoring 103
Program services 130, 165
Project planning 129, 148
Prudent person rule
  (see Reasonable care)
Public relations 97, 110, 130, 221
Public service announcement (PSA) 232
Publicity tools 225

Reasonable care 9, 10, 12, 16
Resource allocation 158
Resource development 3, 96, 110,
  157, 159, 163, 165
Restricted funds 158, 184
Robert's Rules of Order 60

Solicitation of contributions 206, 209
Staff accountant 162
Staff relations 87
Staff support 96
Stewardship 1
Strategic plan 126, 129, 157, 160, 201

Tax exempt 17, 188
Treasurer 162, 165, 188

Ultra vires 19
Unrestricted funds 158, 184

Variance analysis 173